EXTREME DOMESTICITY

GENDER AND CULTURE

A SERIES OF COLUMBIA UNIVERSITY PRESS

Nancy K. Miller and Victoria Rosner, Series Editors
Carolyn G. Heilbrun (1926–2003) and Nancy K. Miller, Founding Editors

For a complete list of titles see page 261

EXTREME
DOMESTICITY

A VIEW
from the
MARGINS

———

SUSAN FRAIMAN

Columbia University Press
New York

Columbia University Press
Publishers Since 1893
New York   Chichester, West Sussex
cup.columbia.edu

Library of Congress Cataloging-in-Publication Data
Names: Fraiman, Susan, author.
Title: Extreme domesticity : a view from the margins / Susan Fraiman.
Description: New York : Columbia University Press, 2016. |
    Series: Gender and culture | Includes bibliographical references and index.
Identifiers: LCCN 2016022755 (print) | LCCN 2016040222 (e-book) |
    ISBN 9780231166348 (cloth : acid-free paper) | ISBN 9780231543750 (e-book)
Subjects: LCSH: American literature—20th century—History and criticism. |
    English literature—20th century—History and criticism. | Women and
    literature. | Domestic relations in literature. | American literature—Women
    authors—History and criticism. | English literature—Women authors—
    History and criticism. | Home in literature.
Classification: LCC PS228.W65 F73 2016 (print) | LCC PS228.W65 (e-book) |
    DDC 810.9/9287—dc23
LC record available at https://lccn.loc.gov/2016022755

Columbia University Press books are printed on permanent
and durable acid-free paper.
Printed in the United States of America

COVER IMAGE: Curro Ulzurrun, *Paisaje con Niebla* (2007)
PHOTOGRAPHER: Manuel Blanco
COVER DESIGN: Rebecca Lown
BOOK DESIGN: Lisa Hamm

FOR JEFF

CONTENTS

ACKNOWLEDGMENTS

This book has been a while in the making and has, along the way, benefited from the support and input of many. The University of Virginia gave me time to write by granting me several Faculty Research Fellowships. I am hugely indebted to my generous colleagues in the English Department for their advice and friendship. Cindy Wall shared bibliographical references along with the wisdom of her own work on domestic description in early novels. Sandhya Shukla's astute reading of chapter 6 helped me clarify my use of ethnographic materials. Anna Brickhouse offered not only valuable feedback on chapter 5 but also, over the course of countless walks, a sounding board for developing ideas—and always with characteristic discernment and kindness. Rita Felski has been a source of inspiration and support throughout this project. My own thoughts on everyday life are crucially informed by her important contributions to this area. She read the first installment of this book and the last. There's no one whose professional and editorial judgment I trust more. For many fortunate years now, I have been buoyed up personally and professionally by Debbie McDowell, Vicki Olwell, Jahan Ramazani, Caroline Rody, and Chip Tucker. Over at the School of Architecture, Richard Guy Wilson saved me from an error in my discussion of Edith Wharton's *The Decoration of Houses*. To all of these wonderful UVA scholars, my heartfelt thanks.

I would also like to thank Anita Rose and Paul Fyfe for inviting me to speak at the 2015 Victorians Institute Conference; as it turned out, my remarks on *Mary Barton* for that occasion became the basis for a previously unplanned chapter of the book. Several other chapters appeared previously elsewhere. "Shelter Writing: Desperate Housekeeping from *Crusoe* to *Queer Eye*" first appeared in *New Literary History* 37, no. 2, 341–59. Copyright © 2006 Johns Hopkins University Press. "Domesticity Beyond Sentiment: Edith Wharton, Decoration, and Divorce" was originally published in *American Literature* 83, no. 3, 479–507. Copyright 2011, Duke University Press. It is republished by permission. "Bad Girls of Good Housekeeping: Dominique Browning and Martha Stewart" first appeared in *American Literary History* 23, no. 2 (2011): 260–82, and is reprinted by permission of Oxford University Press. I wish to thank the readers and editors of these journals for their many good suggestions. I am equally grateful to Jennifer Crewe, the director of Columbia University Press, Gender and Culture series editors Nancy Miller and Victoria Rosner, and the readers who reviewed my manuscript. Their incisive comments and queries at various stages were tremendously helpful in pushing me to clarify and unify my claims. Grace Vasington was the best possible research assistant; her hypercompetence and good cheer were a godsend in the last phase of readying the manuscript for production.

Being involved with two, incredible Charlottesville organizations— The Haven Day Shelter and Building Goodness Foundation—has deepened my appreciation for shelter. Thanks to them, I am slightly less ignorant of the difficulty faced by those who are precariously housed and more aware of concrete measures that can help alleviate this difficulty. I myself have been extremely lucky in matters of psychic as well as physical shelter. Tania Modleski has long been a mentor and collaborator in the project of keeping women and gender central to left intellectual work. Her unstinting support has sustained me throughout my career, and I will never be able to thank her enough. My dear friend Helen helped me with edits, fed me with kale, and let me organize her closets. For her wisdom, kindness, and loyalty, I offer my deepest thanks. Rachel is not only my exercise wife but also my interlocutor and confidante in all things. Her encouragement was as integral to the completion of this project as her friendship is to the richness of my everyday life. My mother's feminist example, unqualified support, and wonderful closeness are a continuing source of gratitude. Cory, by growing up and moving out, managed to nail my point that home life is never still. Much as I miss him, I admire how ably he is shaping a domesticity of his own. This book is lovingly dedicated to Jeff, partner in dwelling and traveling, whose insight guides my writing and my life and who shows me many times a day the preciousness of home.

EXTREME DOMESTICITY

INTRODUCTION

Doing Domesticity

S he does not make a grand entrance. For one thing, she is already there, inside the house. For another, it is part of the job description to be unassuming. Modest to a fault, she fans attention away from herself the better to care for others. As compliant wife and devoted mother, she has no equal. If she ventures outside, it is only to aid and enlighten the poor. She herself is not poor. Her appearance is neat and refined, her complexion fair. With a light step, she moves from room to room, ensuring that everything is in its place: children in bed, servants in the kitchen, linens properly starched and stowed. This space is her domain; we might almost say that home and mistress are consubstantial. Both are stable and contained, untouched by worldly flux, bustle, and mess. (Sex, which can be messy, is reserved for procreation.)

Synonymous with the home, this feminine creature is evidently more than that. She evokes not only a domestic space but also a set of domestic values: selflessness, constancy, piety, and purity. Through her, the house itself is imbued with moral significance; its propriety and hers are one and the same. Illustrating the natural deference of females, she attests as well to the solidity and rectitude of middle-class character. We are speaking, of course, of the Victorian Angel in the House (close cousin to the American True Woman), christened in 1854 by Coventry Patmore, touted by many a nineteenth-century moralist, and invoked if not always revered by novelists from Charles Dickens to George Eliot. Though physically delicate, the Angel is a formidable figure in the Anglo-American cultural imagination. She is not the subject of this book.

Repudiating this iconic figure, I join scores of feminists who have challenged her over the years. Virginia Woolf claimed to have strangled the Angel in the House sometime around 1931: "She died hard. Her fictitious nature was of great assistance to her. It is far harder to kill a phantom than a reality. She was always creeping back when I thought I had despatched her."[1] The domestic angel would, indeed, continue to return in only slightly varied guises. In the 1950s and 1960s, she reappeared as a staple of American sitcoms and television commercials, still focused on kids, kitchenware, and pleasing others, though wielding considerably less moral authority than her Victorian precursor. Never an intellectual, in this version she was ditzy, easily mesmerized by her reflection in sparkling plates and glasses. Despite her lack of gravitas, the postwar Angel managed as efficiently as ever to symbolize the well-run home and to conjoin all things domestic with conservative ideas about family, class status, and gender roles.

An auspicious sign of resistance came in 1963 with Betty Friedan's forceful attack on the "feminine mystique," the hype luring middle-class women into the confines of suburban housewifery and throwing away the key. The women's liberation movement would follow in the 1970s, launching a new campaign to debunk the Angel as an oppressive patriarchal fiction. Throughout the 1980s and 1990s, scholars shaped by this movement continued to counter the ideology of domesticity by providing more complex accounts of female lives and domestic realities across the centuries, including those of women defined in the first place as less than angelic and lacking in mystique by virtue of their race, class, and/or sexuality. Some of this work documented women's experiences beyond the domestic sphere as well as the overlap between public and private life. Other studies stressed the onerous, unpaid, or low-paid nature of much domestic labor. And still others formulated, from a feminist perspective, an appreciative understanding of domestic knowledge, rituals, and relationships. As we will see, my own project is especially indebted to this latter work for its de-trivializing, recuperative focus on "women's culture."

As Woolf warned us, however, the Angel in the House is nothing if not resilient. The Angel's bundling of woman, house, and a reactionary belief system is, in fact, readily available in the current century. Predictably, the "happy housewife" these days is most explicitly and fervently invoked by those on the religious Right, who cleave to her as an emblem of traditional "family values."[2] Here she serves a discourse naturalizing female subordination, denouncing homosexuality, and vilifying racial/national "aliens" along with the urban "liberal elite." More subtly and surprisingly, however, the figure of the housewife—along with "domesticity" as a general category—is also invoked by many on the academic Left as shorthand for essentially the same traditional views. As in conservative circles, in left formulations the house is similarly moralized and conventionalized, the domestic woman likewise taken to personify conformity, the difference being that now she is decried rather than celebrated.

My goal in the following pages is to sever domesticity from the usual right-wing pieties and the usual left derision. I am out to kill the Angel in the House once and for all—but not by shunning houses and housekeepers altogether. My strategy instead is to decouple domestic spaces, figures, and duties from a necessary identification with conservative "family values." While unbundling "house" and "women" from "conformity," I remain interested in the first pairing: the tie between domesticity and women. On the one hand, I deny the naturalness or inevitability of this tie, and my study includes a number of male and masculine homemakers. On the other hand, a key aspect of my project is to value domestic practices that are not only culturally coded as "feminine" but also, even today, largely shouldered and shaped by women. It is clear to me that contempt for domesticity is in part an effect of bias against spaces and practices strongly associated with women. By recuperating domestic life and those of all genders who create and sustain it, I hope to strike back against that bias.

In challenging the habitual binding of women and home to conservatism, I take particular issue with the same old linkage replicated under the banner of left politics. Needless to say, I share the left critique of domestic ideology as it has functioned in England and the United States since its emergence at the end of the eighteenth century; the preceding paragraphs are, indeed, the rudiments of such a critique. There is no question that the ideology of domesticity has been and continues to be mobilized for an ugly assortment of reactionary political ends. Certainly there are also actual domestic situations embodying this ideology. At the same time, however, there are countless numbers of women and households utterly incapable of approaching the affluent Angelic ideal, and many others who either ignore or actively reject it. All too often, important left critiques overlook these nonconforming versions of home, allowing the ideology of domesticity to color their views of domesticity *tout court.*

I will be fleshing out this claim shortly, citing specific examples of recent work in the humanities. For now, suffice it to say that collapsing the lived experience of domesticity into the ideological construct both homogenizes and demonizes the astounding diversity of actual home-making efforts and arrangements. Conflated with the bourgeois ideal, domesticity in all its iterations and ramifications is disparaged first of all as smugly traditional in its expression of gender, sexuality, and family. Moreover, insofar as the ideal is quite rightly implicated in shoring up capitalism, colonialism, and other structures of domination, in some accounts the whole of domestic life is thus tainted. As a result, houses and housewives, assumed to be backward in their own right, are also automatically held accountable for the policing of other groups.

How exactly does my book propose to claim domesticity while wrenching it away from such things as compulsory heterosexuality, selfless maternity, class snobbery, racial purity, the wanton display of stuff, and the illusion of a safely barricaded life? Mobilizing texts across periods and genres—from novels and memoirs to ethnographies and decorating manuals—my strategy is to replace these presumptive associations with other, more jarring juxtapositions: domesticity coinciding with female masculinity, feminism, queerness, and divorce; domesticity in the context of Victorian poverty, twentieth-century immigration, and new millennial homelessness. In lieu of the Angel, these works of fiction and nonfiction offer up a host of alternative homemakers. Some are gender rebels, others precariously housed; together they represent the deviant flip side of the domestic ideal. Though widely various, even apparently incongruous, all fall somewhere on a continuum of figures whose domestic imaginations and experiences exceed traditional boundaries—whether socially, psychologically, politically, or, in some cases, literally. Diverse as they are, all the characters assembled in the following chapters are outsiders to normative domesticity.

Mapping domesticity from the margins, I am hoping that *Extreme Domesticity* will contest received ideas about where and with whom domesticity lies, expanding our sense of its many possible forms and implications. To begin with, my title seeks to trigger and negate the assumption that "extreme domesticity" is, by definition, an oxymoron. I take "extreme" to suggest a number of meanings normally seen as antithetical to domesticity but that are offered here as perfectly plausible descriptions of home for the subjects of this study. Among these meanings are the following: extreme as a reference to dire circumstances due to such things as economic insecurity, physical vulnerability, and/or stigmatized identity; extreme in the sense of balancing on a knife-edge, as in X-treme sports; extreme in the sense of being seen as immoderate or outlandish; extreme in the sense of gender/sexuality that is shunned as X-rated, offensive to "family values" and off-limits to children; and extreme in the sense of occupying an eccentric position vis-à-vis the center, being on the outskirts of belonging, including the exilic state of being without national, marital, or other social standing. Finally, as we will see, while the versions of home in the pages to come are extreme in the sense of being "extra" to conventional domesticity, they are also extreme in the opposite sense—as images serving to distill key aspects of domestic life.[3]

DOMESTICITY AS CONFORMITY

Despite what might seem like a rough chronology—nineteenth-century materials predominant in the book's first half, yielding to late-twentieth-century texts—this is, at most, the loosest of genealogies, with no pretense to offering a historical narrative. My study is intended, rather, as a theoretical intervention into thinking about domesticity in the areas of literary and cultural studies. Certainly I am grateful to the last three decades of humanities scholarship for teaching us to recognize the far-reaching, hegemonic effects of domestic ideology. As I have mentioned, however, some accounts have allowed the actual panoply of domestic figures and practices to be subsumed by these ideological effects and to be, as a result, vastly oversimplified. You will recall that second-wave repudiations of domesticity were accompanied by feminist research into the history of women's domestic practices, placing value on subcultures characterized by child rearing, housekeeping, and homosocial ties. Some of the earliest, most compelling work along these lines was in the area of nineteenth-century American studies. Yet by the 1990s, Americanists not only questioned the separateness of the domestic sphere but also accused it of complicity with American individualism;[4] sugarcoated social control;[5] nationalist suspicion of the "foreign";[6] rampant consumerism;[7] and a quiescent culture of sentiment.[8] The recent tendency in American studies to demonize the domestic from a left perspective is tied, I suggest, to the axiomatic equation of domesticity with sentimentality, a structure of feeling understood to mask conservative views of gender, family, and nation. Chapter 3 questions this equation and turns to Edith Wharton's *The Decoration of Houses* (1897) for an antisentimental, feminist affirmation of the domestic.

Americanists are not alone in formulating progressive arguments over against conservative elements implicitly or explicitly marked as "feminine" and "domestic." Nancy Armstrong's influential *Desire and Domestic Fiction: A Political History of the Novel* (1987) sees nineteenth-century British fiction by and for women as a discursive machine turning "political information" into "psychological information" at the site of the domestic.[9] In Armstrong's Foucauldian account, the ostensibly apolitical, feminine realm of the home oversaw the achievement of middle-class hegemony, effected by both an abstract, feminine ideal and the domestic women who represented it. I have a number of problems with this argument, beginning with its claim that married, middle-class women in the early Victorian period—women without property rights,

divorce or custody rights, the vote, or even a separate legal identity—
were nevertheless the embodiments of hegemonic power, making them
(and not men) the very type of the "modern individual."[10] In more
general terms, Armstrong's case strikes me as overstated and one-sided,
adducing discursive patterns at the expense of material conditions,
domination at the expense of resistance, and class politics at the expense
of gender politics. As for domesticity, in this rendering (as in the formation Armstrong would critique), it is simply and completely coextensive
with middle-class supremacy. Moreover, if the entirety of middle-class
domestic life and middle-class womanhood is reduced to and blamed
for class domination, the existence of non-middle-class ideas and incar-
nations of home, gender, and family is erased entirely. Without being
an apologist for all aspects of domesticity, much less for the machina-
tions of domestic ideology, I propose to counter this reduction and era-
sure with images of home lives far more heterogeneous, unstable, and
politically contradictory than Armstrong would allow.[11]

In stark contrast to *Desire and Domestic Fiction*'s exclusive focus on
language, Elaine Freedgood's *The Ideas in Things: Fugitive Meaning in the
Victorian Novel* (2006) takes literally the mahogany furniture in *Jane
Eyre* and the checked curtains in *Mary Barton*, treating them less as
literary tropes than as domestic objects with a life of their own in the
late 1840s. Yet Freedgood's reading of Gaskell finally echoes Armstrong
in seeing the Bartons' cozy furnishings as no more than cover for a prehistory of exploitative labor practices. The retrieval of this prehistory is,
to be sure, an important contribution. At the same time, by ignoring the
daily labor, uses, and meanings that might further inform these objects
once inside a working-class home, such a reading reduces even the Bartons' humble domesticity to a careless consumerism, serving only to
obscure the misery of English, Indian, and West African producers. In
chapter 2, my own reading of *Mary Barton* points instead to Gaskell's
emphasis on domestic labor and domestic vulnerability in a working-
class context.

While the aforementioned studies take domesticity or domestic
things as their explicit target, other critical and theoretical paradigms
invoke the category of home more subtly and less self-consciously as

code for a variety of tyrannies and/or trivialities. I will mention just four examples, all of them notable for influencing (without fully defining) their respective areas, and all of which I have discussed at greater length elsewhere.[12] In postcolonial studies, Jane Austen's domestic fiction has been cited as exhibit A in the case against European imperial culture.[13] In cultural studies, women/mothers have been aligned with domestication, gentrification, and repression, disciplining the rebellious energies of working-class male youth.[14] In queer theory, the domestic realm identified with children has been taken to stand for the oppressively heteronormative.[15] And in contemporary animal studies, theorists have looked to Gilles Deleuze and Félix Guattari's *A Thousand Plateaus* (1987) for its summoning of wild animals defined in contrast to pathetic domestic ones. Across all four examples, as in American and Victorian studies, a gendered notion of domesticity is discredited by damning association with one or more of the following: a sentimental investment in the straitlaced, bourgeois family; individualism and consumerism as values and ways of life; the enforcement of class, race, and national domination; an oblivious, "apolitical" relation to social injustice; and the qualities of constraint, stasis, banality, and ontological "tameness."

Dusting and polishing a table, arranging objects on a shelf, putting a child to bed, buying groceries for guests, baking a cake, caring for pets, hanging checked curtains, nursing the sick, stashing things where they belong, dreaming of a beautiful space. These are just some of the actions performed by the odd mix of figures—from Robinson Crusoe and Mary Barton to Martha Stewart and Natalie on the Street—brought together by the following chapters. All are actions of a kind that we ourselves are likely to perform or benefit from. Indeed, all belong to the family of gestures indispensable to survival and fundamental to culture. Taking different, fluid forms in an infinite number of settings, none is intrinsically either positive or negative in its political implications. None, for that matter—even in the context of a conventional, middle-class household—means only one thing.[16] Yet the ignobility of domesticity, reiterated by the mutually reinforcing work of scholars across multiple subfields, is tantamount to the political common sense of progressive work in contemporary literary and cultural studies. *Extreme Domesticity* aims to show that such a characterization, however necessary, is far from sufficient. Selecting and reading my texts for their granular depictions of domesticity, their largely appreciative tones, and their examples of oppositional and/or marginal housekeeping, I hope to counter what has become the prevalent framing of a particularly loaded category.

Notwithstanding the consensus I've described, my study has benefited from important work in several areas attuned to the meaningfulness of domestic interiors, domestic details in fiction, and everyday domestic practices.[17] A number of progressive scholars have written enthusiastically about domestic spaces and concerns in relation to modernist ideas about gender, architecture, literature, and aesthetics. Judy Giles, Victoria Rosner, and Douglas Mao all have tied early-twentieth-century experiments in domestic living to new kinds of texts, social relations, and selves.[18] My own project, though not focused on a particular era, shares their conviction that the home may be a key site of aesthetic, political, and psychological innovation. Where I differ is in dealing less with explicit political aims and movements than with implicit emotional agendas and formal strategies. My discussion of Wharton, for example, finds a contrarian impulse not in her relation to late-century campaigns for domestic reform but in the photographs she chose to illustrate her celebrated design manual. As we will see, I read these stark images for their critique of the Whartons' troubled marriage. Exploring the psychological resonances of these and other interiors, I am further indebted throughout to that magical work by Gaston Bachelard, *The Poetics of Space* (1958).

I will shortly be introducing a mode of slow domestic description I call "shelter writing," and additional examples are threaded throughout the book. But while shelter writing appears in a number of different genres, its attention to the minutiae of domestic interiors and behaviors affiliates it closely with the realist novel. My project is therefore in dialogue as well with works analyzing the novel's historical infatuation with domestic detail, notably Michal Ginsburg and Lorri Nandrea's "The Prose of the World" (2006) and Cynthia Wall's *The Prose of Things: Transformations of Description in the Eighteenth Century* (2006). Along these lines, I should also mention David Trotter, whose topic in *Cooking with*

Mud: The Idea of Mess in Nineteenth-Century Art and Fiction (2000) is in some sense the inverse of mine. Both of us link the novel's concern with a highly particularized domesticity to broader anxieties about gender and class. But whereas Trotter's "mess theory" dwells on spills and clutter, I explore the more unexpected notes of dissent in some (though not all) depictions of cleanliness and order.

In its concern with the small, ordinary, and concrete, *Extreme Domesticity* is perhaps most closely allied to theories and studies of the everyday. Building on recuperations of *la vie quotidienne* in the tradition of Henri Lefebvre's *The Critique of Everyday Life* (1947) and Michel de Certeau's *The Practice of Everyday Life* (1974), it takes from these works an interest in the micropolitics of daily life, with an emphasis on subtle modes of resistance to the dominant order. As Certeau explains, his book illuminates "the clandestine forms taken by the dispersed, tactical, and make-shift creativity of groups or individuals already caught in the nets of 'discipline.' Pushed to their ideal limits, these procedures and ruses of consumers compose the network of an antidiscipline."[19] In one of the best-known examples of such ruses, or what Certeau also calls "tactics,"[20] a pedestrian appropriates the topography of a city through a series of choices and improvisations. Obeying some but not all the indicated pathways, he also "increases the number of possibilities (for example, by creating shortcuts and detours) and prohibitions (for example, he forbids himself to take paths generally considered accessible or even obligatory)."[21] Inspired by Certeau, my own focus is on domestic rather than urban topographies and improvisations: on detours around gender and marital norms; on makeshift shelters, some so "improper" they fail to register as homes. Like Certeau's collaborator Luce Giard, I explore tactical maneuvers in settings coded as feminine and apt to be the purview of women rather than men, private rather than public spaces, kitchens rather than streets or factory floors. I also follow in the footsteps of such subsequent feminist/queer theorists of the everyday as Laurie Langbauer, Rita Felski, and Sara Ahmed, who indicate the gender limitations of earlier work.[22] Felski, in particular, has criticized those who redeem the everyday, yet do so by touting rupture over routine.[23] Agreeing with Felski, my book does not condescend to domestic lives

anchored in repetition. Indeed, it defends the desire for domestic continuity and security, all the more so when it arises, as in many of my texts,
within histories of danger and dislocation.

KITCHEN WOMEN NATION

Having outlined the general historical and theoretical context for my
approach to domesticity, the scholarly debates and debts that inform it,
I want to stay for the next few pages with the figure of Giard. I offer this
brief discussion of her work as prelude to and foundation for continuing
to specify what I hope to accomplish in *Extreme Domesticity*. Coauthor
with Certeau and Pierre Mayol of *The Practice of Everyday Life*, volume 2,
Living and Cooking, Giard contributed the section on "Doing-Cooking,"
a study of the culinary practices of French homemakers. Certeau's
celebrated volume 1, first published in 1974, was translated into English
in 1984. Volume 2, by contrast, originally published in 1980, remained
unavailable in English until as late as 1998, a delay reflecting and contributing to its relative obscurity.[24] According to Giard, the U.S. publisher
of volume 1 rejected the second as too narrowly "French."[25] Yet it's
hardly a stretch to suggest that doubts about the work's "universality"
may have had as much to do with gender as nationality. It was, indeed,
precisely the neglect of women's everyday lives that drove Giard to produce "Doing-Cooking" in the first place. As she recalls, "I made a remark
that women were strangely absent. . . . I protested, I argued (it was the
time of feminist awareness), and I did so well that we decided to remedy this serious gap" (xxviii).

   The work that resulted, comprising the latter half of volume 2, sets
out to refute the common view of women's daily kitchen labor as intrinsically boring and conservative. It is, Giard admits, a view that she herself
once held: "For a long time, I still regarded as elementary, conventional,
and pedestrian (and therefore a bit stupid) the feminine savoir faire that
presided over buying food, preparing it, and organizing meals" (152). Her
study, drawing on in-depth interviews as well as her own experience,

redressed the general tendency to demean, along with these practices, the generations of French women who honed and transmitted them. In a lyrical passage, Giard expresses her desire to replicate and preserve in words the intricate gestural language of her illiterate female forebears (153). Through a self-effacing writing dedicated to "these non-illustrious women (no one knows their names, strength, or courage anymore)," she seeks to document their "basic gestures always strung together and necessitated by the interminable repetition of household tasks performed in the succession of meals and days, with attention given to the body of others" (154). The goal of her research, in short, was to recover and pay homage to the rich subculture she titles the Kitchen Women Nation (*le peuple féminin des cuisines*) (155). By hinging my project on the underacknowledged contribution made by hers, I am hoping, in some small fashion, to do the same for Giard.

There is, Giard observes, a contradiction in France between respect for food and disrespect for domestic food preparation, a female occupation judged to be "repetitive and monotonous, devoid of intelligence and imagination" (156). "Doing-Cooking" endeavors to show the time-consuming labor as well as the modes of intelligence and creativity needed to conjure a series of dishes for multiple palates three times a day every day of the year. Cooking, Giard argues, "is just as mental as it is manual; all the resources of intelligence and memory are thus mobilized. One has to organize, decide, and anticipate . . . take into consideration Aunt Germaine's likes and little François's dislikes" (200). "One has to calculate," she continues, "both time and money, not go beyond the budget, not overestimate one's own work speed, not make the schoolboy late. One has to evaluate in the twinkling of an eye what will be the most cost-effective in terms of price, preparation, and flavor" (200). Where many see mindless repetition, Giard sees women with the stamina and know-how to execute a precisely choreographed sequence of steps— women, we might say, who have mastered a specific set of techniques. (And is it really necessary to add that daily life itself hangs on the "monotonous" deployment of these techniques?)

It is also the case, as Giard explains, that while recipes may be repeated, the outcome is never exactly the same. Cooks must continually adapt to a changing set of circumstances. Leftovers must be incorporated, a stew stretched to accommodate one more, substitutions made for ingredients that have spoiled (200). The daughter updates her mother's recipe to suit prepackaged foods and modern appliances (208–11). As a result, Giard asserts, "one has to know how to improvise with panache" (200). Revised for practical reasons, recipes are further individualized as a matter of personal style and taste, so that cooking is revealed to be a space not only of repetition but also of creative deviation and reconfiguration: "Style affirms itself, taste distinguishes itself, imagination frees itself, and the recipe itself loses significance, becoming little more than an occasion for a free invention . . . a subtle game of substitutions, abandonments, additions, and borrowings" (201). Recalling Certeau's pedestrian, Giard's cook finds tactical opportunities to heed some directions while ignoring others, to invent shortcuts and veer from customary paths.

In another memorable passage, Giard lays out the micropolitics of buying food at a traditional market. No passive act of consumption, marketing emerges here in more than one respect as a sophisticated art. Multiple senses are brought into play: the discerning touch, practiced eye, and discriminating nose: "The outstretched index finger lightly touched the flesh of fruits to determine their degree of ripeness . . . a circumspect glance detected the presence of bruises on the apples, one smelled the scent of melons at length as well as the odor of chèvre cheeses, one muttered comments about the relationship between quality and price. All of this involved actualizing a certain competence" (205). If there is an art to picking melons, there is also an under-the-breath artfulness to getting them at a good price. "Each purchase," Giard points out, "was a chance for the buyer to use trickery with the vendor's trickery" (205). As Certeau might put it, each trip to the market is a chance for the "procedures and ruses" of the consumer to win back just a little bit of agency.[26] Thanks to her cunning, an experienced shopper may gain the subtlest of victories. She may enjoy a brief triumph not over the vendor—herself a mere coactor in what Giard calls the "innocent theater of the poor" (205)—but over the larger workings of power.

The whole back-and-forth of choosing and bargaining amounts, Giard says admiringly, to a "marvelous gestural ballet" (205). It is one of several places she compares the ordinary art of cooking with one that is nominally "higher." Take, for example, her lovely description of sifting flour in the old-fashioned way: "Wide-open hands held the fragile wooden circle of the sifter at two diametrically opposite points and shook it with a light tapping of the fingers applied alternately on each side. A tender complicity was established with this volatile and precious flour. . . . This gesture was done gently and in a measured fashion, restrained and silky like the touch of certain pianists" (204–5). Cook as dancer, cook as musician: adding to the mental and "tactical" aspects of putting meals on the table, here Giard points to the aesthetic dimension, one invoked as well by her choice to render this gestural idiom in highly poetic prose. Elsewhere, she more explicitly likens the culinary art she has lately come to value to the embodied process of composing in other media: "I learned the tranquil joy of anticipated hospitality, when one prepares a meal to share with friends in the same way in which one composes a party tune or draws: with moving hands, careful fingers, the whole body inhabited with the rhythm of working, and the mind awakening" (153).

This last passage hints at three more features of Giard's paradigm relevant to my own project. The first is her sense of domestic labor as emotional drama, saturated with positive as well as negative feelings—a cook's experience, here, of tranquil joy in lieu of weary resentment. As we will see, this drama is especially charged for the characters I consider, each of whom is either unable or unwilling to take "home" as a given; for them, contriving a livable space is all the more urgent, fraught, and potentially gratifying. The second feature I would highlight is her sense of domestic life as expressing and producing sociality. In Giard's scenario, a meal is prepared and shared as a fundamental rite of friendship. Likewise for my characters, domestic objects may serve to mediate desire, domestic activities to consolidate ties to family and community. But while some pursue domesticity as a mechanism of affiliation, others do the opposite. Needing to sever connections, they do so not by escaping the domestic altogether but by relocating/recreating it as a space of their own, removed from other people and conventional expectations. In either case, the act of homemaking is an act of situating oneself, physically and psychologically, in a measured relationship to others and society.

The third thing I'd like to pull from this passage is perhaps the most important. I take from this scene of *learning* to cook for *friends* an implied alternative to notions of women laboring in obedience to "natural" marital and maternal imperatives. As Giard explains in her opening paragraph, "What follows very much involves the (privileged?) role of women in the preparation of meals eaten at home. But this is not to say that I believe in an immanent and stable feminine nature that dooms women to housework and gives them a monopoly over both the kitchen and the tasks of interior organization" (151). The allocation of housework to women in modern France reflects, she continues, a particular cultural order, contingent on a set of political and material conditions that are by no means fixed and universal. Accordingly, she repeats: "I do not see the manifestation of a feminine essence here" (151). Later, Giard illustrates the role of such variables as poverty (173–77), regional agricultures (177–79), mechanization/commercialization (208–11), and a host of other geographical and historical factors, all combining to form and transform local culinary practices. In the de-naturalizing view I share with Giard, the gendered division of domestic labor, like every other aspect of domesticity, answers to a shifting context of layered climatic, material, technical, social, and economic forces (171–73).

This brings me to the last point I want to glean from Giard: that domestic cultures, in addition to varying by place and time, are uneven in their content and their gender politics. A good example of the former is Giard's discussion of the mixed effects of industrialization on the Kitchen Women Nation (208–13). For the most part, Giard mourns the loss of hands-on skill and satisfaction (in the kitchen as on the factory floor) for the contemporary cook who presses a button to shred, mix, or beat, no longer required to display her "ingenuity" and "empirical savoir faire" (212). Valuing the old "gesture sequences," Giard refuses to mock the do-it-yourselfers who now spend weekends trying to relearn them (213). In chapter 4, I follow her lead when I claim the artisanal expertise of Martha Stewart and her fans. At the same time, Giard is grateful for less drudgery in the kitchen (212) and opines that a culture frozen in time "decrees its own death" (213). The subsection "The Past-Present" ultimately embraces a hybrid kitchen in which tactical leverage is gained by claiming some things while refusing others, steering one's own path between old and new: "Between the symmetrical errors of archaistic nostalgia and frenetic overmodernization, room remains for microinventions . . . to resist with a sweet obstinance [*sic*] the contagion of conformism . . . to learn how to make one's own choices among the tools and commodities produced by the industrial era" (213).

As I say, the gender politics raised by domestic life are also capable of cutting both ways. Feminists must grapple with two interrelated tensions. The first involves stressing women's deeply ingrained tie to domesticity at the risk of seeming to derive this tie from some kind of feminine "essence." We have already seen Giard's efficient handling of this as a noncontradiction, recognizing cooking as a strongly gendered practice while also insisting on its status as a cultural artifact. A focus on cooking as a feminized realm gives rise, however, to a more persistent tension, one referenced only obliquely by Giard's text. This is the tension between, on the one hand, asserting the value of domestic cultures and women's creative shaping of them and, on the other, acknowledging the evils of domestic ideology as well as the unredeemable aspects of domestic labor, especially when imposed on women to the virtual exclusion of all else.[27] Giard's emphasis, to be sure, is on the positive aspects of domesticity. Her signal though largely unsung contribution to everyday studies is, indeed, a passionate elaboration of this position. As her introduction declares, "With their high degree of ritualization and their strong affective investment, culinary activities are for many women of all ages a place of happiness, pleasure, and discovery" (151). At the same time, by referencing *many* rather than *all* women, Giard leaves room, at least, for those who may feel stifled rather than inspired by cooking. Recall, moreover, that her study was motivated in the first place because the Kitchen Women Nation is an illiterate one, its mores unrecorded by generations of women "ceaselessly doomed to both housework and the creation of life, women excluded from public life and the communication of knowledge" (153). We may, finally, discern another nod to domesticity's dark side when Giard, describing women's culinary role in the passage just cited, inserts the word *privileged* followed by a question mark. Returning now to the intentions of my own project, I draw on Giard for her recuperative enthusiasm while keeping a question mark alongside my own claim that women (and men) can mobilize domesticity as a mode of self-assertion and language of defiance.

REINVENTING HOME

What I share with Giard above all is the desire to validate those sequences of gestures, typically though not always performed by women, without which there would be no domestic (or any) life. My own focus is less on cooking than on the furnishing of interiors, but I am driven by a similar concern to rescue domestic figures and practices from trivialization and neglect, whether in the popular or the scholarly imagination. Like Giard, I recognize both the mental and the manual agility required by these practices; the opportunities they offer for improvisation, artistry, and dissent; the grounding, ritualistic aspect of their daily occurrence; their ability to enact a complex range of feelings; and their organization of social relations. Beyond this, I see my book as frequently siding with a cluster of inferiorized categories associated with domesticity, all of them coded as "feminine" and subordinated to their opposing "masculine" terms. These include the ordinary, familiar, and quotidian; the detailed, insignificant, and small in scale; the bodily and especially tactile; the emotional, subjective, and personal; the enclosed, introverted, and local; the dependent, relational, and maternal. Needless to repeat, I do not regard any of these feminized qualities (or domesticity itself) as having a natural, necessary connection to women or, for that matter, as being positive in every instance. Some of my female characters actively reject them, whereas some of my male characters come to embrace them. I do, however, wish to situate the low status of domesticity within a larger discursive field and to recognize the role of gender codes in upholding hierarchies of value.

Giard's work also prompts me to say a word about methodology, since in this respect our projects are significantly different. Taking an ethnographic approach, "Doing-Cooking" draws on in-person interviews supplemented by Giard's personal experiences. As a literary critic, my objects of study are, by contrast, images of domesticity. Whether fictional or nonfictional, verbal or visual, canonical or popular, all are textual representations of one kind or another. In chapter 6, for example, my discussion of domesticity and homelessness makes use of several participant-observer ethnographies, but my analysis is obviously based on reading rather than doing ethnography. The same could be said of my relation to Giard's ethnography, which pertains to my project not only because it references and theorizes domestic behaviors but also because it so vividly illustrates their *textualization*. In this sense, Giard's relevance lies as much in her literary rendering of domesticity as in her primary research. "Doing-Cooking" is, indeed, of particular interest for its resemblance to "shelter writing"—the mode of concrete, step-by-step, carefully detailed description of domestic processes I explore in chapter 1. In short, while I see my inquiry as informed by and bearing on actual people and their homes, I approach them through a mediating web of depictions: the ideas, images, narratives, wordings, and visualizations that both reflect and construct our experiences of domestic life.

Before getting to an overview of my chapters, I want to mention two additional ways in which the tenor of my argument may be said to differ from Giard's. First, regarding the aforementioned feminist ambivalence toward domesticity, I would like from the outset to press more explicitly and emphatically than Giard does on what I think of as the "gothic" house: the house that imprisons rather than shelters women; that keeps them in thrall to norms of marital femininity; that hides domestic violence, exploits female labor, and thwarts female ambition; that binds some women in domestic service to others at the expense of their own households. I am grateful for the robust feminist tradition of fictional and nonfictional works critical of this debilitating house, and my idea is not to oppose but to support and supplement this tradition. To be sure, the gothic house is not my central concern, primarily because it has already been so thoroughly vetted by scores of writers from Harriet Jacobs and Charlotte Perkins Gilman to Arlie Russell Hochschild and Barbara Ehrenreich.[28] But it lurks in the background of my book as a whole and comes into greater visibility in chapter 5 when I take up immigrant figures and in chapter 6 when I consider homeless ones. So while it's certainly true that I second Giard's wish to value women's everyday labor and share her focus on the "felicitous" house,[29] my intention is by no means simply to romanticize domestic life. If my project is first and foremost a vindication, my challenge to habits of vilification is premised on the *ambiguity* of domesticity and the contradictions it poses, in particular, for women.

In keeping with my awareness of domesticity's doubleness, I am also less optimistic than Giard concerning the political leverage to be gained through culinary "microinventions" in and of themselves. The gothic house, it seems to me, is not so easily eluded, and the alternative modes of domesticity I adduce are accordingly more sustained, more fully imagined, and more sharply at odds with convention than the "tactical" moves described by Giard and Certeau. As I have said, my own account calls attention to unorthodox (though not unusual) homemakers who, whether by choice or circumstance, fall outside the domestic ideal. Some rebut traditional "family values" by reinventing home in ways that are feminist, queer, or otherwise "improper"; some rebut stereotypes of complacency by battling conditions of domestic insecurity; and some do both at once. Generally speaking, we may think of them as belonging to one of two categories. There are those I call the "bad girls of good house-keeping": domestic professionals who set rules of home maintenance while flouting (among other things) the cardinal rule of marital main-tenance. Others are Crusoe-like castaways or outcasts, scarred by domes-tic trauma, shunned by the mainstream as queer/poor/alien, in some cases lacking even enough to eat or a regular place to sleep. For exiles in this second category, piecing together a home is a play for self-preservation, self-expression, and belonging. Though distinct in obvious ways, the two groups overlap insofar as even privileged women may be abruptly dis-located (if not actually dispossessed) by divorce, scandal, queerness, or other such irregularity. For those well off to begin with, domestic loss and insecurity are more often a function of sex/gender than of class stigma; they are consequential nonetheless and, for some, may coincide with economic vulnerability. What they all, this motley crew of outsiders, have in common is a clash—whether flagrant or veiled, psychological or material—with domestic protocols. Flouting notions of proper domesticity, all represent a relation to shelter that is risky, embattled, and experimental.

PRECARIOUS SHELTERS

Chapter 1 sets the theoretical stage by defining and illustrating the concept of "shelter writing." Reaching back to *Robinson Crusoe* and forward to the reality TV show *Queer Eye for the Straight Guy*, my opening chapter focuses on the transgendered hero of Leslie Feinberg's *Stone Butch Blues* (1993). As mentioned earlier, shelter writing is a mode of slow description offering a precise, even tender, account of domestic actions. More than this, it is a descriptive mode occurring in the narrative context of domestic dislocation. Like Crusoe, its protagonists are the survivors of a wrecked domesticity, and their extramethodical homemaking bespeaks the magnitude of their loss. Shelter writing as I define it is thus a posttraumatic mode of realism that lingers over home renovation as an antidote to deprivation. Though not all my subsequent chapters include examples of shelter writing per se, most involve a similar emotional logic: hyperinvestment in homemaking as compensation for domestic deprivation or difficulty. Needless to say, in some contexts, obsessive home improvement may be simply an assertion of elite status by means of enlarged rooms and accumulated trophy objects. But for those battling the gothic house or a crisis in housing, the political meaning of fixating on domestic arrangements is more complex, if not antithetical. For the poor or transgendered person, the placeless immigrant or the woman on her own, aspiring to a safe, stable, affirming home doesn't reinforce hierarchical social relations but is pitched, precisely, against them. Still musing on the politics of hyperinvestment, the thoughtful reader might then be moved to ask, So which are you doing—stressing domestic precariousness or defending domestic stability? Because a sense of precariousness often (and logically enough) goes hand in hand with a longing for stability, my answer to this question is, both.[30] While underlining the first, I am therefore equally committed to exploring and honoring the second.

Chapter 2 turns to Elizabeth Gaskell's *Mary Barton* (1848) for its warmly detailed portrayal of domestic labor in a Victorian working-class community, from preparing food and sewing curtains to caring for children, the sick, and the dying. Taking up as well the novel's many amateurs—scientists, sleuths, and more—I shift the discussion of this industrial novel from waged to unwaged industry, from the masculinized factory floor to the feminized workplace of the home. As I show, Gaskell underlines the productivity of a sphere more often identified with simple consumption. Like Giard, she makes a point of itemizing the calculations and competencies required to shop, cook, serve guests, and wash up afterward, all in the narrative context here of past starvation, present poverty, and a highly uncertain future. With its step-by-step accounts of culinary and kin work, *Mary Barton* clearly includes a number of passages approximating my definition of shelter writing, the difference being in its handling of chronology. Whereas my ur-example of *Robinson Crusoe* depicts homemaking after trauma, *Mary Barton*'s thickest description of homemaking immediately precedes the trauma of Mrs. Barton's death, the first of many catastrophes stemming from industrial conditions. The underlying "shelter" logic of these two British novels is nevertheless similar: in both cases the specific materiality and value of homemaking is made more sharply visible in the context of dire circumstances. (This might, indeed, be seen as a logic at work in the realist novel broadly speaking, but that's a notion better elaborated elsewhere.)

If domesticity in *Mary Barton* functions as a means of affiliation with both family and community, the opposite is true of the text taken up by chapter 3: Edith Wharton's late-century guide to interior design, *The Decoration of Houses* (1897). Much as I appreciate Gaskell's Giardian caress of everyday domestic life, it is unfortunately true that her ending permits romantic consummation and cozy family life to compensate and, effectively, to apologize for industrial ills. By way of contrast (on this point among others), my third chapter turns to Wharton as a woman whose love of houses and interior design was extricated from—indeed, in my view, directly opposed to—sentimental conceptions of marriage and family. My analysis of *The Decoration of Houses* sees its photographs of tranquil and depopulated rooms as antidotes not to economic turmoil but to the emotional turmoil of her doomed cohabitation with Teddy Wharton. Wharton's cold images of domestic interiors contradict the warm and fuzzy ones featured in Clarence Cook's rival design manual, *The House Beautiful* (1877), while also serving to contest the tendency in American studies today to treat domesticity and sentimentality as interchangeable terms. Although *The Decoration of Houses*, with its highly attenuated narrative, doesn't meet the criteria for "shelter writing," it functions for Wharton in a similarly therapeutic manner, as a reinvention of home shored against a miserable, ill-fated marriage.

Chapter 4, focusing on Dominique Browning and Martha Stewart—celebrity domestic pundits who are also conspicuously divorced—continues the project of claiming a domestic culture at odds with the ideals of marriage and maternity. Beginning with some nineteenth-century precursors, I propose a tradition in which domestic zeal and expertise are linked to women who resist compulsory heterosexuality; who are childless, child averse, or single mothers; whose domesticity does not preclude and may actually foster professionalism; whose sexuality veers toward the autoerotic if not fetishistic. In this "bad girl" tradition, domesticity is reconfigured as a language of female self-sufficiency, ambition, and pleasure. My survey of nineteenth-century figures is followed by comments on Stewart's greedy and grandiose domesticity, along with a reading of Browning's *Around the House and in the Garden: A Memoir of Heartbreak, Healing, and Home Improvement* (2003). Turning to Browning's memoir for its celebration of postmarital nesting, this chapter also offers it as a textbook example of shelter writing: the how-to idiom of home renovation appearing "in answer" to a backstory of domestic upheaval.

My last two chapters close the frame by returning to depictions of domesticity sharpened by ever more extreme threats to safety and stability. Chapter 5 discusses three novels written by women who share the immigrant backgrounds of their characters: *The House on Mango Street* (1984) by Sandra Cisneros; *Lucy* (1990) by Jamaica Kincaid; and *Blu's Hanging* (1997) by Lois-Ann Yamanaka. In each of these texts, a figure comes of age in a problematic house and responds not by fleeing domesticity but by struggling to remake it on her or his own terms. As works of immigrant fiction, they are of particular interest to my larger argument, for several reasons. First, they dramatize linguistic as well as other forms of domestic hybridity: Spanish or Hawaiian pidgin interwoven with "standard" English; meals consisting of white bread served alongside Japanese *nishime*. They also happen to offer striking examples of heterogeneity within a single household: differences and inequalities between males and females, adults and children, employers and employees. Above all, by hinting at histories of conquest, slavery, and internment, they give us instances of domestic dislocation not only in space but also over time; not only of individuals but also of groups; removal from one's home or homeland not only by choice but also by force.

If the initial aim of chapter 5 is to specify the miscegenated cultures and instabilities of immigrant homes, its ultimate aim is to suggest the complexity and underlying fragility of all homes. Something similar may be said of my final chapter and conclusion, in which I call on non-fictional works across several genres—journalistic accounts, ethnographies, memoirs, and a documentary film—to explore domesticity in the context of homelessness. My readings of these late-twentieth-century texts are posed against two common ideas about the so-called homeless: either that they are utterly, tragically deprived of domesticity or that they have willingly abandoned it for the romance of the road. Chapter 6 argues instead that domesticity is not absent for this population so much as it is broken and embattled. The various figures I consider do not entirely (much less willingly) forfeit such things as privacy, routine, kinship, and a place to keep stuff. They do, however, struggle on a daily basis to approximate these and other components of domestic life. My closing chapter takes a look at how the forms and meanings of domesticity are influenced and highlighted by this struggle. What many of my texts further explore is the rift between sheltered observers and the unsheltered people they depict. Yet the homeless and housed subject may not, I suggest, be opposed so much as imaginatively enmeshed: while the first is anxious to reassemble the pieces of "home," the second is anxious, at a barely conscious level, to stave off exposure and exile. Neither can avoid the signs of instability (fluid circumstances, fallible residences, shifting affiliations, transient bodies), and both are driven thereby to pursue some version of domestic comfort and continuity. I close this chapter and the book as a whole on a hopeful note, with several accounts that succeed in recognizing our common investment in domestic life.

I take the title of this introduction, "Doing Domesticity," from Giard's "Doing-Cooking." The point, of course, is to stress that domesticity doesn't just lie there, isn't a given, can't be taken for granted. Someone (probably female) *does* it. Someone (feminized if not female) produces several meals a day, a place to sleep, a degree of cleanliness and order, and perhaps a touch of beauty. The effect of my outré homemakers is to defamiliarize these practices and thus to bring them into higher relief. Schooled by their extreme and eccentric efforts to redo home, we may, I am hoping, more clearly recognize the hard work and creativity responsible for domesticity everywhere. As I have stressed, my cast of incongruous characters also goes to show the differences within as well as between domestic arrangements even while suggesting a common crusade against the forces of entropy. Domesticity is, to be sure, a discursive as well as a material construction, and I have emphasized my wish to trouble the conventional—and conventionalizing—formulation. But if domesticity is not always simply reactionary, neither is it always simply progressive. The element of privacy, for example, may mean, for women, a secluded study; for the poor, relief from surveillance; for those who are vulnerable in the street, physical safety. Then again, it may mean locking "undesirables" out while locking women in; it may offer cover for domestic violence. In my understanding, if domesticity is something *we do*, its variable political implications are a function of what *it does*—the subsequent effects it has, for better or worse, in a particular instance. I hope the pages to come will therefore be seen as both a vindication and an inquiry: a vindication of domestic practices and an inquiry into the multiplicity of domestic meanings.

1

SHELTER WRITING

Desperate Housekeeping from *Crusoe* to *Queer Eye*

The history of the novel is full of women burdened by a stifling or terrifying domesticity. From the bored Emmas (Woodhouse and Bovary) to the incarcerated Bertha Mason, they are driven to various extremes by too much house, by interior spaces too cushioned or confining. In contrast to those made desperate by an excess of domesticity, the figures that concern me in this chapter embody an opposite logic: they are driven to domesticity—the refuge of four walls, the consolation of a table—by desperate circumstances. Taking up a range of texts (many of them novels), I focus on protagonists who, far from being trapped inside, are outcasts or castaways of some kind. For these characters, who are outsiders to polite society and at times literally out of doors, domestic spaces and domestic labor mean neither propriety and status nor captivity and drudgery but safety, sanity, and self-expression: survival in the most basic sense. The blow-by-blow accounts of their efforts to make and keep house exemplify the mode I call "shelter writing." It is a mode that may center on anyone whose smallest domestic endeavors have become urgent and precious in the wake of dislocation, whether as the result of migration, divorce, poverty, or a stigmatized sexuality. This chapter theorizes forms of shelter writing and analyzes, by way of illustration, a text in which domestic shelter is lost, longed for, and finally recreated by a narrator who is transgendered.

My exemplary text is *Stone Butch Blues* (1993) by Leslie Feinberg, a writer known for her essays and activism on transgender issues as well as for this self-evidently autobiographical novel. The book is narrated in the first person by Jess Goldberg, a masculine woman from a working-class family in Buffalo, New York, who comes of age in the 1950s. Strongly male-identified, Jess briefly considers transitioning to male, and during this time she passes as a man. Throughout the novel, we see her working alongside men and other butches on the factory floor, riding her motorcycle, and drawn to feminine women. We also see her rejected and brutalized from an early age for so radically controverting gender norms. No wonder Judith Halberstam devotes a central chapter of *Female Masculinity* to Feinberg's title character, stressing Jess's working-class masculinity and defending her "stone" sexuality. My own reading builds on and supplements this emphasis by bringing out other, complicating aspects of Jess: what I elsewhere identify as her "butch maternity" and also, of particular interest here, her butch domesticity.[1]

The relevant passage occurs toward the end of *Stone Butch Blues*, shortly after Jess has set out from Buffalo and washed up on the shores of Manhattan. For a month she's been crashing in makeshift, semipublic quarters and bathing in Grand Central Station, until at last she has the money for a real apartment. Handing over her cash to an indifferent super, she is free to take the measure of her new place:

> I locked the door of my apartment and turned to look around. It needed paint: yellow for the kitchen, sky blue for the bedroom, creamy ivory for the living room. I needed rugs. And dishes, silverware, pots and pans. Cleanser for the sink.
>
> I opened my duffel bag to look for a pad and pen to make a list. There was the china kitten that Milli had left me. I placed it gingerly on the mantle in the living room. . . .
>
> I decided to buy some yellow calico curtains for the living room windows, like the kind Betty had made for my garage apartment. I glanced at the door once more to make sure it was locked.[2]

A few pages later, the day-by-day account of intensive nesting continues:

> Every time I got a paycheck I used part of it on my apartment. I spent one whole weekend spackling the cracks in my walls and ceilings. As I applied paint to each room with broad strokes my spirits lifted.
>
> On my most ambitious weekend I sanded all the wood floors. Then I started from the furthest corner of the apartment and polyurethaned myself out of the door. That night I slept at a 42nd Street theater again—just for one more night!
>
> The floors were dazzling. It added a new dimension underfoot, as though the ceilings were raised, or the apartment had grown in size.
>
> I found a black Guatemalan rug at a flea market. It had tiny flecks of white in it. I unrolled it in my living room and stood back to look. It reminded me of the night sky filled with stars.
>
> Gradually I bought furniture—a sturdy couch and reading chair, a mahogany kitchen table and chairs. At the Salvation Army I found a bed—the head and footboards were ovals carved out of cherry. I went crazy buying sheets at Macy's. . . .
>
> I bought thick, soft towels and fragrances for my bath that pleased me.
>
> And then one day I looked around at my apartment and realized I'd made a home.[3]

I offer these paragraphs by way of general introduction to the meanings, satisfactions, embarrassments, and divergent uses of shelter writing. Often, as here, it is embedded in a longer text: a few pages lingering over the shaping of a domestic space; part of a chapter detailing the pleasures of securing and supplying, ordering and adorning, taking a room from mess to thoughtful arrangement. Someone rigs up a shelter, hauls in scraps, and refurbishes them for household use; now he piles pillows on a mattress, pulls a blanket straight; next she arranges crockery in a cupboard, each piece a smooth weight in her hand; later she cleans from top to bottom, restoring order and brightness; and every day there are soothing, sometimes wearying rounds of neatening and freshening. Practical, aesthetic, and perhaps metaphysical desires coalesce in these

FIGURE 1.1 Charles Copeland, "Robinson Makes Baskets." (From Daniel Defoe, *The Life and Strange Surprising Adventures of Robinson Crusoe*, ed. W. P. Trent [Boston: Athenaeum, 1916]. Courtesy of the University of Illinois at Urbana-Champaign)

passages. Memory comes into play (Milli, Betty, star-filled nights) along with desire. Ideological as well as emotional agendas are advanced. Small, specific, oft-repeated actions, meaningful in themselves, indicate larger and more profound ones—Mrs. McNab and Mrs. Bast, for example, scrubbing against death and decay at the heart of *To the Lighthouse*.

Of course, the ur-shelter text is *Robinson Crusoe*, in which Crusoe structures time as well as space, saving his skin while preserving his reason, by methodically devising a domesticity of his own (figure 1.1).

For while Crusoe has often been taken as a prototype of the explorer or entrepreneur, I agree with Pat Rogers in "Crusoe's Home" (1974) that Daniel Defoe's hero is, above all, a homemaker, busying himself with an array of domestic arts from building and furnishing a shelter to making pots and baking bread.[4] What we are most fascinated and moved by, what we recall if we recall anything about this novel, are the almost technical descriptions, many of them in journal form, of the household tasks Crusoe undertakes not simply to survive but also to create, as he puts it, "some order within doors":

Dec. 11. This day I went to work . . . and got two shores or posts pitched upright to the top, with two pieces of boards a-cross over each post; this I finished the next day; and setting more posts up with boards, in about a week more I had the roof secured, and the posts, standing in rows, served me for partitions to part of my house.

Dec. 17. From this day to the twentieth I placed shelves, and knocked up nails on the posts to hang every thing up that could be hung up, and now I began to be in some order within doors.

Dec. 20. Now I carry'd every thing into the cave, and began to furnish my house, and set up some pieces of boards, like a dresser, to order my victuals upon, but boards began to be very scarce with me; also I made me another table.[5]

In this discourse, characters use broom and hammer, muscle and imagination to stay death, cling to life, or simply keep house. Sentences devoted to homemaking and housekeeping occur, though largely unremarked, throughout the history of the novel from Defoe to writers like Charlotte Brontë, Elizabeth Gaskell, Virginia Woolf, Radclyffe Hall, and on up through Feinberg. It should not surprise us, then, to be told that Woolf's Mrs. McNab and Mrs. Bast salvage a basin, a tea set, and . . . the works of Sir Walter Scott. A central project of the realist novel—its production of interiority—is effected in part through the concrete, systematically detailed domestic gestures of a Robinson Crusoe or a Jess Goldberg. Descriptions like Defoe's and Feinberg's are intrinsic to the meaning and inextricable from the grain of the genre.[6] They are not, however, confined to it. In contemporary culture we find instances of shelter writing, broadly speaking, in media such as house magazines and reality television. *House Beautiful* (1896–present), *Martha Stewart Living* (1990–present), *Queer Eye for the Straight Guy* (2003–2007), and *Love It or List It* (2008–present) all offer versions of this domestic microdrama: the step-by-step creation, restoration, or transformation of one's living space. Nor is it surprising that we find such a scenario more often on the small than on the large screen. Television's cheerful traffic in the seemingly insignificant, its penchant for the domestic, and its commitment to repetition conduce quite naturally to scenes of self-discovery in a newly Windexed mirror. Before returning to the passage from *Stone Butch Blues*, I want to consider at some length the theoretical parameters and political implications of this discourse about dwelling.[7]

TOPOGRAPHY

Of interest here are both content and form. While attending to shelter and shelter making as things and actions referenced, I would also identify the generic attributes of shelter *writing*. Since most of my examples are literary, they might seem to fall under the rubric of description (*ekphrasis* in classical terms) and, more specifically, *topography*, or the description of landscapes and places. Translating the visual into the verbal, concerned with space rather than time, representing objects that exist simultaneously rather than events that occur sequentially, description is often posed against narration.[8] Yet theorists of this mode, like Michel Beaujour, note that descriptions of what appear to be static, ornamental scenes shade easily into those of movement and function. Descriptions of gardens, for example, captured as if on canvas, dissolve into descriptions of flowers swaying and gardeners watering, a different kind of description, if not a different register altogether.[9] Certainly this is true of my homemaking examples, in which interior description functions not apart from but *as* narrative, depicting interiors as they are actively envisioned, handled, and renewed. More important, such descriptive passages qualify as shelter writing only in a particular narrative context—one involving a history of deprivation or difficulty regarding shelter.[10]

Descriptions are suspected, too, of fetishizing the detail, thereby not only losing the narrative thread but also causing characters to recede, eclipsed by unimportant particulars, in effect reversing the proper relation between figure and ground.[11] But the kind of description I am specifying here, however in love with itemizing particulars, does not actually stray from so much as stage the protagonist in her or his relationship to domesticity. Passages devoted to walls and ceilings, pots and pans, seemingly digressive and even "skippable,"[12] contribute crucially to the establishment and development of characters. Indeed, as I began by saying, the mode I am defining turns on a protagonist whose abjection gives peculiar significance to her or his interaction with domestic objects and occupation of domestic spaces. There is one last point to make about shelter writing as descriptive writing, in the impurest sense. According to Beaujour, description is best understood, despite its seeming empiricism, as a register of *fantasy*, the rendering of a dreamscape. "As the multifaceted mirror of Desire, description bears only an oblique and tangential relationship to real things, bodies and spaces. This is the reason why description is so intrinsically bound up with Utopia, and with pornography."[13] My subset of shelter writing does, it is true, involve both dreaming and desire, and these may have an erotic as well as a political cast. At the same time, I want to insist equally on its status as a materialism or, more accurately, a realism—a mode very much invested in highly specified, physical depictions of things/bodies/spaces and their function in a given text on a literal as well as a figurative level. This is especially true insofar as the descriptions show daily, repetitive, and, in the case of housekeeping, ostensibly nonproductive physical labor as valuable in and of itself.

TOPOANALYSIS

As I have mentioned, one of the most helpful intertexts for my notion of shelter writing is *The Poetics of Space* (1958), a meditation on the emotional meanings of interiors by Gaston Bachelard. Like Bachelard, I attend primarily to the house imagined as a "felicitous space,"[14] a space that protects and consoles. "Hostile space is hardly mentioned in these pages" (xxxvi), he tells us in his introduction. Instead, his is a poetics of the safe, snug interior; the house evoking a nest, cradle, or shell; the house whose predominant affect is maternal. According to Bachelard, this sense of the house as refuge is only heightened when tested by the elements—by snow, for example, or by storm. When the house is besieged, it becomes, in our imaginations, more intimate, more fiercely protective (38–47). His work encourages us, moreover, to see the domestic space as "the topography of our intimate being" (xxxvi). Engaging in "topoanalysis," he takes us on an affectionate tour of its most hidden recesses: its cellars and garrets, its nooks and crannies, and the smaller containers contained therein—drawers, chests, and wardrobes, or what he charmingly calls "the houses of things" (xxxvii). The house for Bachelard is therefore at once what encloses us and what we enclose, a figure for the womb and a figure for the psyche, the place in which we dream and a set of images for what is dreamed. In either case, the house in *The Poetics of Space* is never an impersonal monument or sterile showcase but is always inhabited, touching us and responsive to our touch.

For me, too, as I have said, descriptions of interior spaces do not, as early critics of description feared, overshadow the people who live there. On the contrary, in my account they serve to produce and determine character as well as to enact and reveal it. Shelter writing is further compatible with Bachelard's paradigm of the house as cherished and cherishing. My view of Charlotte Brontë, in particular, resonates with his discussion of smallness and snugness, the cozy rather than palatial. At the same time, taking off from Bachelard's brief remarks about the house under storm, my own readings develop and insist more strongly on the house as *refuge*, on renderings of enclosure in continual tension with exposure, a sense of safety coinciding with intimations of danger. While my emphasis is on a similarly positive domesticity, one can hardly approach someone like Brontë without, at the same time, taking full account of a domesticity that can kill. Reading Brontë means reckoning with dwellings that sicken and rooms that madden, interiors that are haunted, claustrophobic, and predatory. As I have stressed, a major challenge of my project is to claim shelter writing without reinstating a romance of the house oblivious to its gothic aspects, especially where women, both middle and working class, are concerned. As Ben Highmore has argued in a piece appreciative of domestic routines from chopping vegetables to bathing children, work in the home is always profoundly ambiguous, involving frustration as well as reverie, oppression as well as artistry, resentment as well as love.[15] So while my subject is not the gothic interior (Brontë's attic, Jacobs's garret, Gilman's yellow room), I take for granted and would keep continuously in mind the coexistence of this evil twin: the dark side of the felicitous house.[16]

My good house image is thus significantly more qualified and contingent than Bachelard's. I differ, too, from Bachelard by emphasizing domestic *labor*—in pursuing not a poetics of houses so much as a poetics of housework. For the most part, the French philosopher's house is a serenely dustless place in which we have little to do but give ourselves over to dreaming and repose. And when housekeeping does make a fleeting appearance in *The Poetics of Space*, it is valued as a mental rather than merely physical exercise. "But how can housework be made into a creative activity?" Bachelard asks. The answer is *consciousness*, "for consciousness rejuvenates everything, giving a quality of beginning to the most everyday actions" (67). In Bachelard's rather rapturous description, wiping a table is no longer a routine act of maintenance but a singular act of creation, quite akin to God's breathing life into Adam: "When a poet rubs a piece of furniture—even vicariously—when he puts a little fragrant wax on his table with the woolen cloth that lends warmth to everything it touches, he creates a new object; he increases the object's human dignity; he registers this object officially as a member of the human household" (67).

These are lovely lines to be sure, and it is part of my project as well to recognize consciousness and creativity as elements of the everyday world of waxing. I share, too, Bachelard's admiration for those who *write* about this world. "There is also," as he puts it, "the courage of the writer who braves the kind of censorship that forbids 'insignificant' confidences" (71). One of my goals is likewise to celebrate the courage of writing that declines more obviously heroic and dramatic subjects for sentences given over to the most minor gestures, the lowest forms of work, and those who perform them. I would call attention, however, to a phrase set off between dashes in the preceding passage: "even vicariously." When a poet waxes—even vicariously—he creates a new object. What does this mean? How exactly does one make an effort of fingers and forearm, squint at the scarred wood, smell the fragrant wax, feel the weariness in one's shoulder "vicariously"? Can you really agitate a can of Lemon Pledge, give it a brain-rattling shake, depress the nozzle, and avert your face *vicariously*?

What this phrase serves to indicate is the actual remoteness of the laboring body from Bachelard's vision. A few pages later, he cites Rainer Maria Rilke on the pleasures of dusting, which the poet discovers one day "in the absence of his cleaning woman" (70). Apparently Rilke was required as a child to help his mother with this chore, so he speaks of it with touching lyricism from the standpoint of a man (unlike his mother, his cleaning woman, or himself as a child) for whom dusting once was *but is no longer* a daily obligation. As Bachelard correctly observes, Rilke's rhapsody is animated by the *"nostalgia for work"* (71 [italics in original]). In other words, both men celebrate domestic chores only by locating them elsewhere, whether in space or time—projecting them onto another person or tying them to an earlier moment. The effect of doing so removes from housekeeping the taint of repetition and banality, not to mention obligation and exploitation, while also eliding the body whose relation to this work is neither vicarious nor nostalgic but intimate and immediate: the body of the child, the body of the mother, the body of the cleaning woman.[17] All these absented bodies are, of course, strongly marked as feminine. Bachelard himself recognizes that "the 'wax' civilization" (68), as he calls it, is gendered, and to his credit he documents and celebrates it anyway. But despite his wax envy, I would argue that Bachelard is finally unable to fully enter this culture. And perhaps the difficulty lies in his imaging of the house, as we have seen, in largely maternal terms. Defining the house *as* mother, caring for him and sheltering his dreams, Bachelard cannot sustain a sense of the house as the mother herself might inhabit it. Largely missing from his poetics is that less dreamy, less restful, and more demanding space—the house that cares for you only insofar as you perform the feminizing tasks of dutifully, tediously, and tenderly caring for it.

In sketching out a feminist poetics of interiors, I therefore draw on Bachelard but privilege the strongly gendered, frankly physical responsibilities of housekeeping as he does not. My house space, as I say, is material as well as metaphorical, and I not only pay more attention to the storm raging outside but also construe the storm as a confluence of social pressures and dangers. In my renderings of domesticity, interior is always pushing back against a threatening exterior; the "private sphere" is never sealed off from but is always produced and interpenetrated by the public. This is, indeed, definitional to shelter writing, which describes the effortful creation of a private space by and for those who have been battered by the outside world. For figures like Jess Goldberg, a room of one's own is hard to come by and impossible to count on.

THING THEORY

In regard to other adjacent theoretical discourses, my interest in tables and chairs calls to mind such works in object studies as Bill Brown's *A Sense of Things: The Object Matter of American Literature* (2003).[18] Of particular interest are Brown's comments on objects, people, and houses in paintings by John Singer Sargent as well as novels by Henry James. He observes, for example, that human figures in both James and Sargent tend to be deanimated. Turned into objects, they can then be acquired as collectibles or grouped into still lifes, like so many vases. He describes this phenomenon in memorable terms as the "ontological democratization of person and thing,"[19] and it strikes me that this alchemy, stiffening children into urns, reverses the ritual celebrated by Bachelard, in which furniture is enlivened through touch. Brown also addresses the way in which household objects (golden bowls and whatnot) function in James as placeholders for ideas and as go-betweens, formulating and mediating relations between characters.[20] I am concerned with the latter as well—objects as they serve to gauge the distance and code the intimacy between people. But generally speaking, I am closer to Bachelard in being drawn to descriptions of houses that breathe as opposed to people objectified.

Indeed, there are several other ways in which my interest in "things" might be distinguished from Brown's. First, whereas for him the primary register is visual, I am equally concerned with the tactile, with objects not only seen but also handled. Second, the discourse of shelter writing is one in which verbs take precedence over nouns, while I suspect that for Brown the opposite is true. Another way of saying this is that I focus on what Michel de Certeau calls "spaces," defined by operations and itineraries, whereas Brown is arguably more about "places," defined less by actions than by objects.[21] For Brown, James's well-appointed country houses and villas are understandably pivotal. For my purposes, however, the long-standing residential edifices in James are too much taken for granted. They serve in his novels typically as static backdrop or else as starting premise, as in his famous metaphor in which their windows are the lenses through which all else is seen. Paintings and pianos, curtains and crucifixes in James are always already in their places— as they are also, say, in Jane Austen—and we hardly expect Isabel Archer or Elizabeth Bennet to lift a finger in their care.

Houses in James and Austen are apt to be trophy houses, their owners smug and proprietary. Pemberley in *Pride and Prejudice* is a preeminent example, and we needn't look far in this novel for another. When Mr. Collins leads Elizabeth on a quantifying tour of his house and land, he might as well be counting out coins. Comfortable residences cared for by invisible hands, homes in Austen are also generally secure. Though Mr. Woodhouse frets about drafts, and his turkey coop is actually raided, their aura in *Emma* and elsewhere is one of inviolability. Even when daughters fail to inherit, aristocrats are forced to downsize, or the moral foundations of a Northanger Abbey or Mansfield Park prove shaky, the prospect in Austen is of a contracted space—a parsonage perhaps, or even a boat. What we do not find in Austen is someone sleeping in a tree, as Crusoe does, or wandering the moors, as Jane Eyre does: someone bereft of shelter altogether.[22]

By contrast, there is something dire about the house passages I am highlighting. Think of Brontë instead of Austen, *The Well of Loneliness* rather than *The Golden Bowl*. The dwellings involved, if old, are neglected or war torn; often they are small, rickety, rigged up. Despite the wealth of a character like Stephen Gordon, what my instances of shelter writing stage is not a complacent sense of class pride and entitlement so much as gratitude, relief, pride in ingenuity, and other feelings born of a sense of physical and social precariousness. They are, as we have seen, apt to occur in the context of a shipwreck or some other traumatic exile; their descriptions of towels and tea sets are frequently just pages away from homelessness, social unrest, personal and political violence; and the comfort they represent is usually all too temporary. Likewise, the characters therein are marginal in one way or another. They are all, in a manner of speaking, *survivors*, and their relationship to beautiful, functional, and safe interiors is underwritten by terror and longing. I term this mode "shelter writing," then, in part to stress its concern with our most primitive fears and desires, with our Crusoe-like need, first of all, for shelter. Dramatizing as well an attraction to order and ornament, it may (but does not necessarily) shade into a less defensible desire for goods, respectability, and status.

REDEEMING ROUTINE

In addition to theories of description, Bachelardian "topoanalysis," and object studies, clearly my discussion of homes and women, dishes and dusting, is engaged with that body of scholarship—stretching from Henri Lefebvre to Ben Highmore and feeding into cultural studies—

concerned with the texture of everyday life. Arguing that Luce Giard is underrecognized for her pioneering work on the daily lives of women, I have already elaborated on her probing and poetic study of the Kitchen Women Nation. I have also agreed with Rita Felski that the comforting aspect of routine is not to be slighted. As she puts it so concisely, "There is scant recognition that everyday life might include desire 'from below' for order, stability and the security of ritual."[23] Like Felski, I question the fetishizing of rupture, and like Giard, I offer in its place an appreciative exploration of domestic stability and ritual. What shelter writing helps us see—with its lingering descriptions, checklists of steps, and loving manipulation of objects—is the heightened value of domestic routine for figures "below" the threshold of a reliable and sufficient home life.[24]

Before returning to *Stone Butch Blues*, I want to briefly reiterate what I see as the theoretical and political stakes of looking at shelter writing and other depictions of outsider domesticity. I have said that a central goal of this book is to counter the assumption of many left critics that houses—people inside houses, practices sponsored by houses—are somehow inherently bourgeois and suspect. Domesticity, particularly from the eighteenth century onward, has been tainted by several associations. First, modern households are identified with consumerism. No longer sites of production, the argument goes, houses serve primarily as showcases for portable property, signs of genteel taste and wealth, consolidating middle-class status and shoring up class hierarchies. Second, domesticity is taken to be coextensive with propriety. The good nineteenth-century homemaker enforces familial and racial as well as class codes, not only buying the right stuff but controlling children, disciplining servants, and stamping out dirt. Her purifying regime may do the additional symbolic work of preserving the "domestic" from contamination by "foreignness," thereby furthering nationalist agendas. Finally, despite scholarship challenging the complete separateness of public and private spheres, domesticity remains tied to notions of privacy and individualism at odds with oppositional politics.[25]

As I have explained, while agreeing with the gist of these critiques, I am troubled by the slip that sometimes occurs from recognizing the conservative effects of domestic ideologies to repudiating domesticity altogether—a repudiation that effectively devalues real homemakers and discounts their labor *as labor*. It is important to remember that these workers are themselves more constrained than empowered by the domestic ideal. It is also the case (as Giard's study so powerfully shows) that their lived, material reality goes far beyond it. Above all, my argument throughout *Extreme Domesticity* is that desiring shelter—the impulse to make and maintain this, the finding of security and pleasure in domesticity—is not necessarily conservative, although it may be. As the example of *Stone Butch Blues* demonstrates, it may also be quite the opposite.

This brings me to a few additional remarks on my feminist investment in domestic description, bearing in mind the problems it poses for progressive scholars generally and feminists in particular. As I noted in the introduction, domesticity belongs to a set of categories generally coded as "feminine" and denigrated as such. To a long list including the trivial, the habitual, and the emotional, we may now add the mode of descriptive writing. Redeeming these categories is a long-standing feminist strategy for flipping the switch on normative hierarchies. My own recuperative project builds on a venerable body of scholarship going back to Tania Modleski on the popular romance, Naomi Schor on the detail, Bonnie Zimmerman on the lesbian novel, among a great many others.[26] My comments on shelter are also, of course, informed by more recent feminist thinking. To begin with, although domesticity is undoubtedly gendered—more likely to be the domain of women, the purview of women writers, and, in any case, marked as "feminine"—it is nevertheless available to men as well, a point underlined by the comments on *Crusoe* and *Queer Eye* bookending this chapter. Note, too, that while gender remains an important axis of analysis, an examination of labor, things, and taste means that class, in addition to sexuality and race, is at every turn an equally indispensable category. Finally, while wishing to vindicate homemaking, I see domesticity as both contested and impure—so that home and homelessness, security and insecurity, interior and exterior, feminine and masculine, manual and mental labor, queer and straight do not oppose so much as encounter and inform one another. Committed, then, to antiessentialist and intersectional readings, attuned to the instability as well as the utility of its binary terms, this project retains a certain affective and ideological affinity with earlier studies of "women's culture" yet also obviously benefits from the post-separate spheres and post-identitarian work of subsequent feminist and queer theorists.

QUEERING DOMESTICITY

In conclusion, let us return to Jess Goldberg, that emotionally guarded, motorcycle-riding, union-organizing, granite-hard stone butch who tells us, brimming with girlish enthusiasm, that she went crazy buying linens and bath products at Macy's. This passage is, first of all, a love letter to domesticity: to kitchenware and coordinated colors, to cleaning a sink, sanding a floor, unrolling a rug, and standing back to look. It is striking in this context not only for entering a narrative register easily scorned as trivial and sentimental—pages lifted from a women's magazine—but also for doing so in relation to a character so thoroughly at odds with the normative gender of this register. Like mannish lesbian writer Radclyffe Hall and her character Stephen Gordon, both of whom are fussy housekeepers; like Crusoe with his earthenware pots; like Brontë's Monsieur Paul, who displays a flair for decorating at the end of *Villette*; and like the straight and gay men who bond over end tables in *Queer Eye for the Straight Guy*, Jess, in this burst of butch domesticity, mixes and matches traditional gender traits.[27] Affirming domesticity, Feinberg's novel also clearly uncouples it from any simple, natural relation to womanhood.

"It needed paint," Jess says of her neglected interior. "I needed rugs," she continues. It needed paint; I needed rugs. From "its" needs to mine— what this subtle evolution maps for me is the way decorating imperatives coincide with psychological ones, so that homemaking, as Defoe certainly knew, can be a form of self-fashioning. "I made me another table," Crusoe recounts, and the effect of his vernacular is to embed a second claim: "I made me." Jess is more explicit, declaring that with each stroke of paint, her spirits lifted. The repetition of "need" further clarifies the urgency (really, the lifesaving necessity) of this practical as well as spiritual endeavor for Jess. For hers is no idle act of redecorating by a wealthy woman with too much time on her hands. It is, rather, an audacious effort to produce a basic sense of physical and psychic security by someone who has been repeatedly violated, who has never in her life felt truly safe. We see what is at stake for her in the passage's other repetition: Jess's locking of the door, and then, moments later, checking again, "to make sure it was locked."

Home, then, as safety from the storm outside, enclosure in whisperingly close dialogue with exposure. Interior is also more positively linked to exterior as Jess makes forays out into the world, like Crusoe swimming out to the wreck and returning with recycled riches. Notice as well the sky-blue paint Jess uses for her bedroom, the rug like a night sky, the ceiling raised up by dazzling floors—for isn't the vertiginous effect of these to produce an outdoors within an indoors, constellations glimmering underfoot? Here again I am reminded of *Villette*'s penultimate chapter, in which Monsieur Paul unlocks a door and we discover, along with Lucy, that her charming little house opens onto the school where she will teach, so that for her, too, private and public spaces intermingle.[28]

In addition to mixing up girl and boy, inside and outside, what else is happening here? This passage assembles and itemizes stuff (rugs, dishes, curtains, and couch) but is more significantly about actions: cleaning and placing, spackling and painting, sanding and polyurethaning. It is, in other words, about work—the degraded labor of cleaning and the strenuous labor of building that here fits with Jess's working-class status but that, in other contexts, may contradict and complicate the status of a monied character. Take the slave-owning Robinson Crusoe, for example, who spends entire days driving posts into the ground. One cannot deny the commodity fetishism of much homemaking, and certainly shelter writing often helps clinch middle-classness by narrating property accumulated, refined tastes implemented. Even for Martha Stewart, however, merchandising and consumerism go hand in hand with an oddly anachronistic craft ethic. Why *buy* a concrete planter if you can mix one up and pour it out yourself? Suffice it to say that shelter writing describes a kind of unpaid domestic labor, productive as well as consumptive, physical as well as managerial, repetitious but wrongly disparaged as unskilled, which has always confounded the neat class categories derived from masculine wage work outside the home.

Passages like this one thematize and valorize manual labor, but not to the exclusion of mental labor. I have already indicated my agreement with Bachelard that sweeping and polishing should not be dismissed as lacking in creativity and consciousness. Indeed, in the case of Jess Goldberg and especially Robinson Crusoe, physical tasks are accompanied by imagining, by planning, and also, surprisingly, by *writing*. In Defoe's novel, the blow-by-blow account of building and furnishing a shelter is interrupted by interpolated material from Crusoe's journal giving us (bizarrely enough) a second blow-by-blow account of building and furnishing his shelter, much of it repeating what has just come before. Once again, we hear how he enlarges his cave, secures it with a semicircle of posts, makes a table, and so on.[29] There are several points to be made about this. First, it resembles Jess's relocking her door, suggesting the vulnerability and fear underwriting these narratives. In fact, both homes will subsequently be damaged (Jess's by fire and Crusoe's by earthquake), requiring them to be relocated and rebuilt. In this sense homemaking, which appears teleological compared to housekeeping, may also actually be work that is never done, a kind of ritual necessarily repeated many times throughout a lifetime, especially for someone like Jess.

Second, notice that Crusoe's interpolated journal constitutes an inside story, a narrative inside the narrative. The result is that Defoe, at the level of form, appears to replicate and trope his character's construction of an interior. More broadly speaking, Crusoe's journalizing references Defoe's own act of narration, suggesting that shelter writing may often go hand in hand with novelistic self-referentiality. By launching *Stone Butch Blues* with Jess's letter to a long-lost love, Feinberg, too, stages Jess in the act of writing. Here in her New York apartment, Jess does no more than grope around for pad and pen; it is tempting nonetheless to take the paint as well as the pen in this scene as figures for Feinberg's own artistry. I want to propose, in short, that descriptions of characters making and keeping house may offer writers a store of images for their own barely waged work of conjuring and furnishing the spaces in which people dwell.

There remains the matter of the china kitten, which would surely be verboten in Martha Stewart's book.[30] For me, this tchotchke on the mantle reinforces the point that home decoration discourse may range widely among class idioms and serve diverse purposes when it comes to constructing identities. As we will see in the following chapter, Elizabeth Gaskell's *Mary Barton* describes a room resonant with the desire we have seen elsewhere for order, comfort, and beauty, but here the scene also functions to identify the Bartons as members of the Manchester proletariat at a time of intensifying class struggle.[31] Finally, if the kitten is a class marker, it is also a marker of desire: a memento of Jess's old love Milli, just as the yellow calico curtains are reminders of Betty.

It is revealing to juxtapose Jess's kitten with household objects lovingly detailed by an earlier lesbian novel in a different class key: the handsome furniture, old blue brocade bedspread, ivory hairbrushes, and other fine things in the Paris house belonging to Stephen Gordon in *The Well of Loneliness*. When Mary moves into this refurbished space on the rue Jacob, she immediately feels that "the bed could only have been Stephen's bed; it was heavy and rather austere in pattern. . . . The chairs could only have been Stephen's chairs. . . . The dressing table could only have been hers. . . . All these things had drawn into themselves a species of life derived from their owner."[32] Just as Jess realizes she has "made a home," Hall's narrator tells us that "now for the first time the old house was home. Mary went quickly from room to room humming a little tune as she did so, feeling that she saw with a new understanding the inanimate objects which filled those rooms—were they not Stephen's? Every now and again she must pause to touch them because they were Stephen's."[33] Touch, as I say, is a conspicuous sense in shelter writing, and this may be not only because floors require sanding and sideboards waxing but also because the things we brush up against in our homes may mediate—as they obviously do for Mary—our intimate, tactile relation to those we love. Apparently Hall herself took a rather erotic pleasure in domestic objects and spaces: caressing the worn wood of her antique furniture, sharing in what Una Troubridge described as an "orgy" of selecting the most beautiful items for their first home.[34] And of course, in a queer context there is especially good reason for beds and dressing tables to function as the sites of displaced erotic feelings, both claiming and coding illicit desires.

I want to conclude by briefly observing the way this works on the early reality-TV show *Queer Eye for the Straight Guy*.[35] In this upbeat makeover drama, five gay men storm and swish into the most intimate spaces of the life of a hapless straight man. Commandeering his house, they proceed to pull apart, as Bachelard might say, the houses of his things: his medicine cabinet, freezer, and sock drawer. Mocking the absence of skin-care products, holding their noses at moldy food, tossing mismatched clothing to the floor, they leave nothing untouched—including the man himself. For despite the relentless dropping of brand names, what is genuinely moving about this show is the way straight men who begin insecure and out of sync are renovated at a spiritual as well as cosmetic level. Somehow, over the bodies of textured sofas and vintage martini glasses, men are enabled to confess their profound sense of vulnerability. Schooled in the performance of mundane domestic tasks, they discover rituals expressive of their yearning for safety, order, beauty, and connection to other people, men as well as women. Outed as islanded Crusoes, survivors of the shipwreck that is conventional masculinity, they learn to redefine themselves not through daring exploits in the public sphere but through the smallest, most banal gestures in the private. If this happens under queer auspices, is that because, as everyone knows, gay men are the divas of good taste? Or does the expertise of the Fab Five lie elsewhere—in their heightened understanding of the need we all share for shelter, in their privileged relation to shelter writing as a discursive effect of the unsheltered life?

2

BEHIND THE CURTAIN

Domestic Industry in *Mary Barton*

In chapter 1, I undertook to connect the dots between stories of wrecked domestic life and the slow, anxiously detailed descriptions of Crusoe securing a roof, Jess sanding a floor—both characters reinventing home in the aftermath of dislocation. This chapter takes up another tale of desperate housekeeping: Elizabeth Gaskell's industrial novel, *Mary Barton: A Tale of Manchester Life* (1848). As noted earlier, however, Gaskell departs from my narrow sense of shelter writing as a posttraumatic mode by reversing the sequence of trauma and domestic description. In this case, the vividly rendered scene of tea at the Bartons immediately *precedes* Mrs. Barton's sudden death. Instead of a therapeutic logic operating at the level of a single character, Gaskell's is a broader, social logic serving to underline, for both readers and characters, that the security of "tea" is provisional at best. The emphasis implied by this chronology falls, we might say, less on the effort to rebuild a home than on the imminence of its collapse. Anticipating my turn to immigrant figures in chapter 5 and homeless ones in chapter 6, instability in *Mary Barton* is not backstory so much as ongoing reality woven into the very fabric of domestic life. Gaskell ties it, of course, to a very specific setting, historical moment, and class milieu: Manchester in the early 1840s, when squalid living conditions, high food prices, and intermittent factory work meant great hardship and uncertainty for working-class families. As

Friedrich Engels said of conditions in 1844, "Insecurity is even more demoralizing than poverty. English wage-earners live from hand to mouth, and this is the distinguishing mark of their proletarian status." The proletarian, he continues, "is at the mercy of chance. . . . Every commercial crisis, every whim of his master, can throw him out of work. He is placed in the most revolting and inhuman position imaginable."[1]

My reading of *Mary Barton* explores working-class domesticity in the face of this extreme insecurity, conditions at once threatening its existence and highlighting its importance. I suggest, moreover, that whereas Engels linked proletarian status to the cruelty of discontinuous wage earning, for Gaskell proletarian life is further marked by the needful *continuity*, through good times and bad, of *unwaged* labor, from cooking and sewing to other kinds of amateur employment. Raymond Williams famously chided *Mary Barton* for launching a bold class plot centered on the Chartist weaver John Barton, only to abandon it for "the familiar and orthodox plot of the Victorian novel of sentiment" centered on Mary Barton.[2] While agreeing with Williams on the novel's ultimately ambiguous politics, I see Mary's story, no less than her father's, as one of class struggle and labor—the difference being that her labor is often unrecognized as such. Williams himself commended the fidelity to working-class feelings evident in *Mary Barton*'s opening walk and subsequent tea, the visit to the starving Davenports, and Job Legh's study of insects (87–88). He likewise praised Gaskell's documentary method, citing as key examples "the carefully included details of food prices" and "the itemized description of the furniture" (87). My own reading, focused on the book's early chapters, singles out these very same scenes and details, not for their general contribution to verisimilitude, however, but for their specific recognition of unpaid labor, by Mary and many others, as it sustains the lives of poor families.

Even critics forcefully defending Mary's side of Williams's binary (downplaying the courtship plot by seeing Mary as an agent of domestic realism, by celebrating her sphere for its "maternal" ethic, or by stressing her public as well as her private acts) have tended to overlook that the world of everyday domesticity is one of *work*.[3] In a typical phrasing, Rosemarie Bodenheimer alerts us to Gaskell's skillfully drawn "scenes of familial or neighborly mutual help."[4] While admiring this essay overall, I would note that "help" in this sentence indicates kindliness while failing to capture the physical and emotional heavy lifting of what anthropologists more aptly refer to as "kin work." Likewise, when Catherine Gallagher describes the novel's domestic circle as one of "duty and affection,"[5] the word *duty* leavened by *affection* hardly does justice to the daily toil of feeding and clothing a struggling family. Domesticity in *Mary Barton* has, in short, generally been discussed in terms of its authenticating details and benevolent moral atmosphere. While it does function in these ways, the goal of this chapter is once again to bring out what I have called the *doing* of domesticity. Taking us inside a working-class home and lingering there, Gaskell invites us to acknowledge not only a space but also a set of practices. As we will see, her strategies for dramatizing the moment-to-moment rigors of domestic labor include denaturalizing it through depictions of male as well as female workers; accentuating it by comparison with the work of skilled amateurs; and breaking it down into a series of microactions, recounted in the step-by-step fashion we have already seen in Luce Giard's "Doing-Cooking" and in my previous discussion of shelter writing.[6]

BY THE POOR FOR THE POOR

Mary Barton's classification as an "industrial novel," grouped with *North and South, Hard Times, Sybil, Alton Locke,* and *Felix Holt,* dates back to Williams, who astutely gauged its mix of middle-class sympathy and fear regarding the effects of industrialism on the urban poor (87–91). Staging the suffering, anger, and activism of factory workers, probing the rift between what Gaskell's London Trade Unionist terms "the idle and the industrious classes" (236), the novel no doubt earns this denomination. Yet its opening chapter declines to introduce John Barton the weaver and George Wilson the spinner at their noisy machines or even in Manchester proper. We meet them, instead, strolling through the fields outside town along with throngs of other working-class families drawn to this rural setting on a beautiful May evening. Noting that the old black-and-white farmhouses speak "of other times and other occupations,"[7] Gaskell's narrator appears to be setting up a nostalgic opposition between an earlier, preindustrial mode in which the natural rhythms of labor are interwoven with domestic life and the reigning industrial mode in which labor is located outside the home and regulated by the factory bell. In E. P. Thompson's classic analysis, one effect of industrialization was to consolidate the shift from what he called "task-orientation" to "time-orientation": the shift to labor disciplined by the clock within a regime of market relations. It is the latter mode that John Barton so bitterly references in his opening tirade against the idle and oblivious rich: "We pile up their fortunes with the sweat of our brows; and yet we are to live as separate as if we were in two worlds" (45).

Barton makes this observation to Wilson as the men continue their walk through the countryside, each of them carrying one of Wilson's twin infants. As I am not the first to notice, these two factory workers walk onstage cradling babies, and subsequent pages provide additional images of men as well as women busy with the hands-on work of caring for children, in contexts both tragic and comic.[8] Chapter 1 closes with the burden of child care being passed along to the next generation. As Barton tells young Mary and Jem, "If Wilson's arms be like mine they are heartily tired" (47). While Mary reaches for one infant, and Jem coos to the other, the narrator's attention lingers on Wilson: "'Twins is a great trial to a poor man, bless 'em,' said the half-proud, half-weary father, as he bestowed a smacking kiss on the babe ere he parted with it" (47). I have several points to make about this opening attention to babes. They are at once a blessing and a trial, source of paternal pride and weariness. Moreover, Gaskell shows them weighing on a poor man in a sense that is physical as well as fiscal. If Wilson provides for the twins with his factory wages, here we see him performing the intimate labor of literally supporting their small bodies. There is a further, emotional aspect to this kind of support, involving such things as the bestowal of "smacking" kisses. Later, when these same two men step in to rescue the starving

Davenport family, their practical actions are accompanied by what the narrator describes as "heart-service" and "love-work" (9). As many of us well know, in contrast to factory work, arm-wearying love work of this kind is neither spatially nor temporally set apart; it follows you into the countryside on your holiday, mixes it up with your time off-the-clock. Finally, as I began by observing, despite its unrelenting and arduous character, this kind of care work on the part of family members is entirely unwaged.

I suggest that Gaskell's pastoral opening is not, therefore, a nostalgic lament for preindustrial task-oriented work but, on the contrary, a sequence stressing the continued relevance and necessity of task-oriented work such as child care alongside and on top of time-oriented work in the mills and elsewhere. When the London activist spoke of the wronged "industrious" class, as opposed to the "idle" class, he was presumably thinking only of industrial work. Gaskell, however, is clearly anxious to emphasize that working-class industriousness involves a great deal of unpaid as well as paid labor. As we will see, child care is just one of numerous domestic labor practices falling loosely under this rubric. I also consider the book's many examples of amateur achievements in other areas—scientific, artistic, civic, and medical—lauded by Gaskell as comparable if not superior to the work of professionals. While not directly tied to the home, in *Mary Barton* these amateur practices are effectively brought inside, their performance bound up with loyalty to family and friends. At the same time, by touting the achievements of working-class amateurs in an era of rampant professionalization, Gaskell separates merit from remuneration, to the credit of all those laboring on the fringes of the cash economy.

Following, then, what I take to be Gaskell's lead, my goal in this chapter is to explore and recuperate the evidence of industry shown by this industrial novel to occur outside the context of market relations.[9] My point, I should stress, is not to romanticize this labor but to recognize its significance and acknowledge those who tirelessly perform it. Nor do I mean to discount the critique of capitalism and industrial working conditions so strongly voiced by John Barton—a critique I see as only partly undercut by the narrator's nervous disclaimers, Barton's eventual discrediting, and the final, strained attempt at class reconciliation. It is notable, however, that Gaskell never actually ushers us inside a textile mill, never offers a perspective from the factory floor, never directly shows us the machinery that disabled Mrs. Wilson on the eve of her wedding (131). Her novel of working-class labor in the Victorian period is thus, in my reading, a commentary on not just factory but also house work; not just exchange but also use value; toil not just for the rich but also by the poor for the poor.[10]

RETHINKING THE DOMESTIC SPHERE

Before returning to Gaskell's opening chapters, I would offer a few observations about how this reading helps complicate current understandings of domesticity. With its emphasis on domestic vulnerability and domestic labor, *Mary Barton* offers several rejoinders to what I have described as axiomatic assumptions in contemporary left cultural criticism: that the home is invariably a site of indolent consumption, bourgeois individualism, private property, and conservative values. To begin with, like Giard in "Doing-Cooking," Gaskell points to the home as a place of production as well as consumption; or, to put it more precisely, both writers require us to see that consumption necessarily involves a good deal of production. Foodstuffs in *Mary Barton*, to take just one example, though not homegrown, must still be purchased, prepared, and served up. Textiles too, though factory made, must still be sewn into bedclothes, dresses, shirts, and the like, a topic on which I will have more to say later. Even today, despite the theoretical interventions of Marxist feminists, we are likely to overlook or belittle such activities, to forget that breadwinning is not the same as literally putting bread on the table.[11]

We might note, in addition, that domesticity in *Mary Barton* hardly functions to cordon off the nuclear family, much less to idealize the autonomous individual. On the contrary, domestic work takes women and men out of their own homes and into a neighbor's, whether to borrow a cup or dress a corpse. Such ties of practical interdependence are all the more important—fundamental to survival, in fact—given the fragility of domestic life for Gaskell's main characters. Just as collectivity trumps ownership for these figures, so community appears to trump privacy. A more accurate claim, however, might be that privacy operates and signifies differently for the Bartons, Wilsons, and Leghs than it does for the wealthy Carsons. Among family and friends, privacy in crowded quarters may be a matter of tact rather than separate rooms, thick walls, and closed doors.[12] A desire for privacy may also be a defensive response to middle-class intrusion, stemming in this context not from privilege but from its lack. Finally, if privacy has divergent meanings in Gaskell, so domesticity in general is shown to take multiple, shifting forms. In addition to the predictably stark contrast between the domiciles of rich and poor, we are given a spectrum of working-class interiors— from the Bartons' cozy room and the Leghs' eccentric "wizard's dwelling" (76) to Alice Wilson's "humble cellar" (53) and the Davenports' squalor. And if the Bartons' coziness proves fleeting, in Gaskell's reckoning even the Carsons' plush domesticity is not immune to the disruption of sudden death.

Qualifying the scholarly consensus I've described, I do want to acknowledge the significant body of work by feminist critics (not to mention historians) articulating more complex views of middle-class domestic life. Demonstrating the contradictions in Victorian ideologies of gender, the managerial role of middle-class women vis-à-vis servants, and the overlap between private and public spheres, Mary Poovey, Elizabeth Langland, and Cathy Davidson, among others, have demonstrated the disparity between actual middle-class womanhood and the reigning domestic ideal.[13] At the same time, they have noted the double function of this ideal to mark class as well as gender boundaries. Set off from and subordinate to her male counterpart, the proper lady was further defined by her superiority to lower-class women. Her home-centered femininity was framed in opposition to that of women who left their homes for low-wage work at any number of menial jobs, from domestic service in another household to dressmaking, factory work, street selling, mining, and prostitution.

Feminist scholars addressing, in turn, the lives of these working-class women have understandably considered them primarily in their capacity as paid laborers.[14] The very term *working-class*, with its reference to wage labor, serves to encourage such a focus. Notwithstanding the importance of this scholarship, a side effect has been a tendency to neglect the realm of work performed without wages. Ironically, if middle-class women's domestic activity has been underestimated, working-class women's more arduous domestic duties have often been overlooked entirely, precisely because many of these women engage, whether inside or outside the home, in various forms of remunerated labor. Yet unless they were in service, the Mary Bartons and Alice Wilsons would, as a matter of course, have topped off their wage work as dressmakers or laundresses with a second shift in the sphere of family relations.[15] It is this second shift, performed in the shadow of Manchester's mills by women and occasionally men, that Gaskell's novel urges us to appreciate.

RECOGNIZING UNPAID LABOR

As I have suggested, Gaskell deploys several strategies to lend phenomenological heft and ethical meaning to forms of unpaid labor more often feminized, trivialized, or simply ignored. To begin with, although Mrs. Barton is actually pregnant when we meet her in chapter 1, we have already seen the extent to which this opening section identifies babies and baby care more strongly with fathers than with mothers. Here and elsewhere, by showing us men nursing children with varying degrees of competence, Gaskell prevents us from taking this job for granted as an easy, instinctive expression of motherhood; she prevents us, that is, from overlooking its status as labor, no matter who does it. At the end of chapter 1, driving home the point that males can nurture as well as females, Gaskell's narrator begins by informing us that Mary reached for one of the twins "with a girl's fondness for infants" (47); yet this fondness is no sooner attributed to girls than we are told, in the very same sentence, that "young Wilson seemed to lose his rough, cubbish nature as he crowed and cooed to his little brother" (47).

Later episodes continue to decouple nurturing from females, relocating it in the broader, more visible category of care work. To her portrait of young Wilson crowing and old Wilson kissing, Gaskell adds the tale of the two grandfathers. In Job Legh's humorous telling, he and old Jennings slowly master the art of caring for their newborn and newly orphaned granddaughter Margaret. Initially at a loss, as they wend their way from London to Manchester, the two men become slightly less inept at caring for the tiny infant. As the grandfathers learn that "two jiggits and a shake" (152) is the trick to putting her down, readers are reminded that child care is a difficult and acquired skill, based on knowledge rather than nature. Also relevant here is Wilson's and Barton's love work on behalf of the Davenports (on which more later). And if the novel features scores of men as "rough, tender nurses" (99), it also gives us Mrs. Wilson, George's irritable wife, who describes herself as "a born goose at house-keeping." With factory work her only experience, as a young bride Jane Wilson couldn't so much as boil a potato (164–65). Throughout *Mary Barton*, the often unrecognized work of attending to the bodies of others is both carefully rendered and systematically de-gendered, encouraging us to see it anew.

A second strategy for shedding light on unpaid labor among the poor is to juxtapose amateur workers with professional ones and, with each example, to assert the superiority of the self-taught and unwaged. Embedded in personal relationships, amateur practices prove especially effective in large part because they are motivated and sustained by emotion. In Gaskell's narrative, they function to forge and consolidate kin ties, and this is a key factor tying them to practices more explicitly directed at caring for family. As I have suggested, they also invite us to recognize all unpaid laborers. At a moment when workers in factories are organizing while others (from doctors to firemen) are professionalizing, Gaskell's amateurs point to the spectrum of workers unaccounted for by either of these formations.

Old Job Legh is a factory worker; his granddaughter Margaret, a seamstress. But instead of identifying these two figures with their wage work, Gaskell's early chapters elaborate at length on their talents, training, and achievements in areas for which they receive neither money nor, outside their immediate circle, recognition. Chapter 5 opens by identifying Job with a "class of men" in Manchester and beyond who "throw the shuttle with unceasing sound, though Newton's 'Principia' lie open on the loom" (75). While to most, they are naught but anonymous factory hands, Gaskell would have them acknowledged as learned physicists, mathematicians, botanists, and entomologists. To make her case, we are told the story of distinguished botanist Sir J. E. Smith traveling to Liverpool to confer with one Mr. Roscoe about an exceptionally rare plant. Mr. Roscoe, however, is unable to help and refers his colleague to an unnamed weaver in Manchester. Arriving there, Sir J. E. Smith "inquired of the porter who was carrying his luggage if he could direct him to So and So" (76). As luck would have it, the porter is friends with the erudite weaver and is himself a skilled botanist. From these two, the titled professional gains the information he sought. This story is immediately followed by a lovingly detailed portrayal of Job, introducing him to young Mary and to us as a veritable wizard of entomology. Reiterating the prowess of amateurs, the sequel also functions, in the keen-eyed person of Job, to give "So and So" a name, a physiognomy, and a place.

The place, as Gaskell describes it, is an abode perfectly expressive of Job's specialized interests—the walls hung with "impaled insects" instead of pictures, the table piled with "cabalistic books." It is furnished as well with a granddaughter he caresses "as a mother caresses his first-born" (76). As we have heard, Margaret has made a mother of old Job since her infancy; now, for Mary's benefit, she domesticates his scientific jargon with the comic tale of a deadly scorpion on the loose inside their house (77–78). Domestic props featured in this drama include the chair Margaret jumps on, the iron she threatens to drop on the creature, the tongs Job finally uses to seize his specimen, and the tea kettle into which he drops it. The effect of this extended passage overall is twofold: it rescues Job's after-hours wizardry from obscurity while also locating his passion for entomology firmly in the bosom of home and family.

Margaret, too, works for wages, in her case at plain sewing that over time has strained her eyesight almost to the point of blindness. As with her grandfather, however, the seamstress's lowly employment and careworn appearance are belied by a hidden power—the power of her magnificent singing voice—and Gaskell praises the naturalist and musician in interestingly similar terms. For while Mary is enthralled by the pathos of Margaret performing "The Oldham Weaver," the narrator remarks that a more correct musician "might have paused with equal admiration of the *really scientific knowledge*, with which the poor depressed-looking young needle-woman used her superb and flexile voice. Deborah Travers herself (once an Oldham factory girl, and afterwards the darling of fashionable crowds . . .) might have owned a sister in her art" (74 [italics added]). As Gaskell insists, this amateur performance is not a naive, spontaneous outpouring but a technical feat based, like Job's study of insects, on "really scientific knowledge." Again as with Job, Margaret's skill is touted by means of favorable comparison with a professional, the significant difference being that she herself will soon become a professional singer and earn good money thereby.

But while Margaret's professional gigs are certainly significant, enabling her to support Job and aid the Bartons, the only scenes of singing we actually witness are those occurring informally at home for the pleasure of close friends and family. Of those detailed by the narrator, one scene takes place at Alice Wilson's (71–74), another at the Bartons' (138–39), and a third at her grandfather's (202). The first is notable for Gaskell's interpolation of "The Oldham Weaver": seven darkly comic verses about the plight of the poor.[16] It is, however, not only the song's content but also its occasion and setting—three women gathered in Alice's sparse but carefully arranged and tidied room to sip dearly purchased tea from mismatched cups (65–66)—that generates a sense of solidarity. Singing in this case is primarily an accompaniment to Alice's hospitality and the friendship initiated between two young seamstresses. In the third instance, Will the sailor first hears Margaret's siren song and is immediately smitten. In short, while Margaret the professional is beloved by a larger public, what Gaskell dramatizes is the way her musicianship, beguiling both Mary and Will, enlarges her domestic circle.

Before returning to domestic work in the narrower sense, I will touch on three additional examples of volunteers proving more adept than those paid to do the job. Each involves an area that was, in 1848, only recently professionalized. The first is firefighting, originally systematized at the instigation of insurance companies. An early example was the London Fire-Engine Establishment, formed in 1833 by ten companies collaborating to install engine stations and full-time, uniformed fire brigades throughout the city.[17] So it should not surprise us when, at the end of chapter 5, the fire in Carson's mill occasions both a comment about insurance coverage and a crowd anxious for the arrival of professionals and their engines. The brigade gets there, however, only to find that "the plugs were stiff, and water could not be got" (89). Moreover, while firemen help Jem Wilson rig up an "aerial bridge" to the burning building, it is Jem who goes back and forth, risking his life to save two men, one of whom is his father. When asked why Jem Wilson was permitted to go twice, a fireman replies that Jem "were off like a shot; only saying he knowed better nor us where to find t'other man. We'd all ha' gone, if he had na been in such a hurry, for no one can say as Manchester firemen is ever backward when there's danger" (93). The takeaway, I think, is not the firemen's lack of bravery but the contrast Gaskell sets up between professionals hired, in the first place, for the sake of business interests, and a daring amateur motivated by reasons that are deeply personal as well as ethical.

Staging Jem's valor and Mary's still unacknowledged feelings, the fire episode also, of course, serves the more obvious purpose of forwarding Gaskell's courtship plot. Yet this plot stalls until Mary takes her own turn at heroism by acting, this time, to save Jem's life. In keeping with our theme, she does so in like fashion—that is, by outperforming another band of professionals. The Metropolitan Police Act of 1829, spurred in part by growing fears of working-class unrest, first formalized policing in London. It was followed by the County Police Act of 1839, passed on the heels of the first People's Charter and, in 1842, by the addition of a detective department to the Metropolitan Police (figure 2.1).[18] Police appear frequently in Gaskell's novel—beat policemen, servers of subpoenas, a plainclothes detective, even the superintendent himself—and always in a manner bearing out working people's wariness of law enforcement. John Barton is struck by a policeman on his way to petition Parliament (144); another falsely imprisons Esther for drunkenness (170); and a third, witnessing Harry and Jem's altercation, automatically seizes the poor man while deferring to the rich (230). The superintendent is described as jaded. Although he was anxious to find Harry's

FIGURE 2.1 Manchester city police peelers parade in the yard of the city's Albert Street Police Station in the 1850s. (Courtesy of the Greater Manchester Police Museum and Archives, Manchester, United Kingdom)

murderer, "It was so common to him to be acquainted with crime, that he was far from feeling all his interest absorbed in the present case of violence" (265). Finally, the detective recruited by the senior Carson walks in on Mrs. Wilson and willfully exploits her naiveté; falling for his working-man's disguise, she readily identifies the murder weapon as belonging to her son (275).

Both the altercation and the weapon are, of course, false leads. Despite the police's supposed expertise, it is our gutsy heroine who actually unravels the mystery and, poaching on lawyerly turf as well, succeeds in proving Jem's innocence. Mary's unlikely sidekick in detection is Esther The Fallen Woman, who hunts for clues and spots the telltale piece of gun wadding, evidence that had gone unnoticed by the police. Acting on her sympathy for the people and suspicion of the authorities (289–90), Esther turns the paper over to Mary who, sharing this suspicion, immediately burns it. For the same reason, once Mary realizes that the paper exonerates Jem while implicating her father, she bypasses the police and takes things into her own hands. Determined to establish an alibi for Jem, she refuses to cede this task even to Job: "She durst not trust to any one the completion of her plan; they might not have energy, or perseverance, or desperation enough to follow out the slightest chance; and her love would endow her all these qualities" (340). "No one could have her motives," she reasons, "and consequently no one could have her sharpened brain, her despairing determination" (340–41). As with Jem's rescuing of his father, Mary's brilliance and bravery derive from a depth of personal, emotional engagement that professional status tends, precisely, to preclude.

Gaskell's lawyers—with their seen-it-all, blasé assumption of Jem's guilt—come off scarcely better than the police. Old Job, however, is an admirer of the legal profession; as the narrator puts it, his respect for lawyers was nearly equal to his contempt for medical men (338).[19] Returning now to the novel's early chapters and to scenes set at home, we meet a medical man whose all-too-fleeting appearance offers some justification for Job's contempt. Chapter 2 has shown us Mrs. Barton in high domestic mode, preparing a hearty tea for the Wilsons, a scene to which we will return in a moment. Just a few pages later, in the middle of that same night, Mrs. Barton goes into life-threatening labor with alarming suddenness. Her panicked husband flies to the doctor, who "was very long in hearing the repeated rings at his night-bell, and still longer in understanding who it was that made this sudden call upon his services" (55). Asking Barton to slow down and doubting that the patient is really so bad, the medical professional arrives too late. Unable to comfort the stunned family, our sleepy physician wastes no time in returning to his bed. Who, then, attended to the dying woman and who carries out the ritual of bathing and dressing her body after death? In striking contrast to the doctor, an unnamed neighbor, similarly roused from deep sleep, starts up and relieves Mary at her mother's bedside in, the narrator specifies, "less than five minutes" (55). After the doctor leaves, Barton appears frozen in place, so stupefied is he by grief. He does, however, manage to register the neighbor's motions and what they mean: "He heard the stiff, unseasoned drawer, in which his wife kept her clothes, pulled open. He saw the neighbor come down, and blunder about in search of soap and water. He knew well what she wanted, and *why* she wanted them, but he did not speak, nor offer to help. At last she went, with some kindly-meant words" (56 [italics in original]).

Once again, the upshot for me is less a repudiation of those who are paid for their services than an appreciation of those who are not. And while Jem's and Mary's heroic efforts to save lives are exceptional, the neighbor's ordinary bedside care work—whether nursing back to health or comforting the dying—is simply the norm. Barton, despite his stupor, acknowledges these actions, and Gaskell, I believe, means us to do the same. Alice Wilson, who earns her keep as a laundress, offers another example of unofficial doctoring. As her brother explains, "Though she may have done a hard day's wash, there's not a child ill within the street but Alice goes to offer to sit up, and does sit up too, though may be she's to be at her work by six the next morning" (46). Alice, we are told, brings know-how as well as kindness to the sickbed: "In addition to her invaluable qualities as a sick nurse and her worldly occupation as a washerwoman, she added a considerable knowledge of hedge and field simples" (51). We first meet her fresh from gathering medicinal herbs, and their efficacy, we can be sure, surpasses that of the "powerless" potion with which Barton is placated on his visit to the professional druggist (102).

DAILY LITTLE ACTIONS

Barton visits the druggist on behalf of the Davenports in chapter 6. Devoting more than a few pages to Barton's and Wilson's series of microactions (99–102), it is a chapter illustrating Gaskell's third strategy for appreciating unpaid labor, domestic labor in particular: breaking it down and parsing it step by careful step. This time *they* are the compassionate neighbors, hastening to aid a destitute family—the woman even more starved than her children, her unemployed husband dying of typhus, and all of them huddled in a fetid cellar. The thrust of this chapter overall is to give logical and emotional weight to Barton's anger at the social injustice wrought by capitalism. It opens with a pointed observation: the same slow times that bring leisure and pleasure to owners bring layoffs and suffering to workers (95–96). Illustrating this inequity, the chapter goes on to juxtapose the wretched Davenports with a view of the pampered Carsons, enjoying their "luxurious library" and "well-spread breakfast-table" (107). But the contrast between rich and poor is most neatly condensed by the five shillings Harry Carson casually pulls from his pocket and gallantly donates to the Davenport cause. This is, we realize, the exact same amount for which Barton pawned his last valuables—his "better coat" and silk handkerchief—in order to buy the Davenports meat, bread, candles, chips, and coal (99). The difference between these two offerings is in part the relative value of five shillings: what is pocket money for Carson is Barton's last penny on earth. I would point, however, to what I see as an even more significant difference: the fact that Carson gives money only, while Barton's gift includes the personal, domestic labor by which abstract coin is transformed into concrete relief.

The significance of this labor is brought out by means of what I have described as Gaskell's mode of step-by-step narration. In a section largely focalized through Barton, we see him first as a frugal shopper, debating which stores to enter and which items to buy, before returning to the cellar loaded with the makings of "food, light, and warmth" (99). Having lit a fire, his next task is to revive the woman, half dead from hunger. He carries her to the fire, chafes her hands, and raises her head. Lugging the smallest child, he runs upstairs to borrow the neighbor's only saucepan, along with some water. "Then he began," the narrator reports, "with the useful skill of a working-man, to make some gruel" (100). After feeding the woman a drop at a time, he turns to the tossing, delirious man. Over the next twenty-four hours, Wilson, too, takes a turn at soothing and covering the patient while also feeding the child and speaking tenderly to the woman (102).

Barton's errand to the Davenports began with the donation of his own supper, fetched from the very cupboard that, the narrator pointedly reminds us, was "his wife's pride long ago" (97). Transporting us back to the opening tea scene, this simple item of furniture serves to connect two extensive passages that, although opposite in affect, are similar in method. In both cases, Gaskell makes domestic industry visible by means of the hyperdetailed, slow description of spaces and gestures that I identify with shelter writing. Turning now to the well-known tea scene, here Gaskell spends several pages panning around the space and furnishings of the Barton home, from the aforementioned cupboard with its crockery and glass (49), to the deal table displaying a "bright green japanned tea-tray" (50), to the blue-and-white checked curtains, "now drawn, to shut in the friends met to enjoy themselves" (49). As this last implies, the scene is about not only ostensibly static rooms and things but also guests entering a home and hosts bustling around to serve them tea.

Dramatizing what I have stressed is the industrious aspect of daily consumption, Gaskell's description of domestic objects is followed by a narrative of domestic actions: the labor without which there would be no sipping of tea or eating of ham. As Giard explained in "Doing-Cooking," first comes the planning phase, well recognized when it comes to government or business outlays, but often scarcely visible when it concerns the stretching of pennies for daily expenditures. Here Gaskell takes the time to show us Mr. and Mrs. Barton discreetly weighing menu and money considerations before sending Mary off to shop with very specific instructions: the ham must be a nice cut of Cumberland, the milk and bread very fresh, and the rum obtained from a particular merchant (50–51). She is also to invite Alice Wilson and ask her to bring a seventh teacup. Remarking how "well and ably" (52) Mary executes these tasks, admiring her confident "culinary powers" (53) breaking eggs and turning ham, the narrator celebrates the multiple competencies required to host a party of seven on a meager budget with only six teacups.

Mrs. Barton's role is to preside at the tea table. Later, she piles up the tea things but leaves their washing until the morning—a morning, sadly, she will not live to see. We know about the dirty dishes because John Barton, finding them, "was reminded of one of the daily little actions, which acquire such power when they have been performed for the last time, by one we love. He began to think over his wife's daily round of duties; and something in the remembrance that these would never more be done by her, touched the source of tears, and he cried aloud" (57).

A couple of things are evinced by this passage. Because keeping house means, precisely, *keeping*—battling the forces of entropy to maintain a status quo of livability—it is labor most apparent in the omission. Mrs. Barton's daily washing of dishes is thus especially conspicuous at the moment she ceases to do so. It is also, I think, significant that for Barton the enormity of his loss is measured out in this and other such "little actions," the humble rites of their cohabitation. As with Barton's recognition, through his grief, of the neighbor's care work, here readers are once again invited to cherish, because he does, Mrs. Barton's "daily round of duties."

In turning from domestic spaces and things to practices, we seem to have turned from the inert to the active. But just as tea needs to be choreographed, so rooms need to be curated. The hospitable warmth of the Barton home, the sociality it sponsors, is produced by the ruddy fire and also by the considered arrangement of gay-colored oil cloth, bright green tea tray, crimson tea caddy, leafy geraniums, and blue-and-white checked curtains. I promised to say more about these curtains and do so now with the help of Elaine Freedgood, who has taught us to pursue the ideas lurking in things in this and other Victorian novels.[20] Freedgood's important reading of *Mary Barton* begins with the familiar assumption that Gaskell's curtains represent domesticity and that domesticity, in turn, is synonymous with deference to the social order. If the ideological work of curtains is to put up a front of stability and respectability, Freedgood would "show how that work unravels if we look closely at the fabric out of which it is constructed" (62). As she demonstrates, to look closely at checked calico and fustian is to recover a "history of increasingly successful British imitations of Indian cottons, the destruction of the indigenous industry in India, and the subsequent need—an ironic and horrifically consequential one—for India to import cloth from Britain, leading to poverty and famine" (66). It is a history that further includes the use of slave labor to pick cotton in the United States, and the plight of Afro-Caribbean slaves who, in the eighteenth century, were both purchased with and clothed in checked fustian (63).

What Gaskell's curtains implicitly reference, then, are the sufferings of three groups of workers: British, Indian, and West African. Yet the novelist, according to Freedgood, by giving us blue-and-white checks in a domestic context, "would have us experience cotton as a thing rather than as a commodity, as something that is consumed pleasurably rather than produced miserably" (60). For Freedgood, Gaskell's use of cotton in the service of domestic "coziness" effectively suppresses a disquieting labor history—the checkered history, as it were, of checks. My problem with this reading is not how far it goes but that it doesn't go far enough. In accepting a view of domesticity, including working-class domesticity, as no more than pleasurable consumption, Freedgood's history of labor stops abruptly at the front door. My purpose all along has been to bring out Gaskell's rendering of unwaged, typically feminized labor, from child care and sick nursing to amateur botanizing and sleuthing. Accordingly, I would like to observe that bolts of calico, though factory woven, do not come to drape a window without first being cut, stitched, and hung by a capable needlewoman. As illustrated by *The Workwoman's Guide to Cutting and Completing* (1838), Victorian women used various methods to fabricate curtains, depending on the specific kind of fabric, window, and room (figure 2.2).[21]

In this regard, we should also note the prominence in *Mary Barton* of seamstresses. Our eponymous heroine is apprenticed to a dressmaker, through an arrangement that doesn't pay for the first two years. Musical Margaret, as we know, has been earning her keep doing "slop-work"—plain sewing done at home by the piece. In addition to the making, mending, and alteration of clothing, this work would have included sewing sheets, towels, and other items for the home. Chapter 5 gives us a picture of the two needlewomen hard at work. Though weary from sewing all day at the dressmaker's, Mary agrees to help her friend complete a rush job for mourning wear. The family, Margaret confesses, is unlikely to pay; what's more, the black fabric is especially hard on her failing eyes (86). Overworked, underpaid, and losing her sight, the character of Margaret evokes what by 1848 had become an iconic figure: the

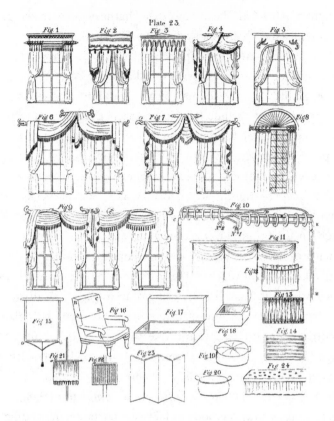

FIGURE 2.2 Window treatments. (From Sarah Josepha Buell Hale, *The Workwoman's Guide* [Birmingham: Simpkin, Marshall, 1838], plate 23)

distressed needlewoman whose sweated labor, detailed in an 1843 employment report, scandalized the public and came to exemplify the plight of female workers in the hungry 1840s.[22]

Taking into account the figure of the needlewoman enables us to read back into the Bartons' cheerful window treatment an additional, more proximate labor history. This includes work by women as well as men; work that may be done inside as well as outside the home; and work that may be paid but is often not. It is work, in short, that challenges a view of the domestic sphere as antithetical to the sphere of immiserating labor. Freedgood herself has written elsewhere about Victorian lace makers, women whose handmade lace, laboriously produced at home, was more highly valued than lace churned out by machine. Yet despite its skilled and arduous nature, Freedman observes that this kind of labor "was and is not always or clearly regarded as work."[23] Like Freedgood on female lace makers, I call attention to the paid labor performed by Victorian women in the domestic sphere, whether in the making of lace, mourning wear, or other marketable commodities. Beyond this, I join Gaskell in further recognizing *as work* the many forms of unpaid, "nonproductive" domestic labor typically performed by women and accomplishing nothing more than feeding, clothing, and sheltering the bodies of children and adults, keeping them alive to see another day.

THE RIGHT TO HABITATION

It is important to acknowledge the troubling conservatism of a class politics valuing unwaged labor while also, as Gaskell seems ultimately to do, discrediting the labor activism of factory workers. The same goes for a gender politics that values women's domestic labor while also seeming at times to discourage or downplay their participation in factory work.[24] Certainly the ending of *Mary Barton* disappoints by implying that right relations in the domestic sphere can substitute and compensate for inequitable ones in the public sphere.[25] At the same time, however, the fact that notions of proper domesticity can be mobilized to paper over social problems should not, and does not logically, implicate the entirety of domestic objects and practices. In *The Ideas in Things*, when Freedgood says that checked curtains "indicate domesticity, and *hence* orderly relations between men and women, children and adults, home and world" (57 [italics added]), she reduces a complex, variable, and often embattled realm of lived experience to a synonym for bourgeois, heteronormative, and imperialist social relations. I have already objected at length to similar moves by scholars on the Left whose politics I share but whose casual vilification of domestic figures, knowledge, and labor strikes me as inconsistent with otherwise progressive analyses.

My central argument has been that Gaskell, for her part, portrays *home* not simply as the site of "pleasurable consumption" but as a workplace in its own right. I have hinted, too, that Gaskell's text serves in other ways to complicate normative formulations of domesticity. Its depiction of home, as we have seen, hardly conforms to images of stability, security, and complacency. Mothers die, aunts tumble, fathers turn to opium and violence, neighbors are felled by typhus or lack of food. And if people are fragile and transitory, so too, in this rendering, are their things. Houses are steadily emptied as objects are pawned one by one. In the story told by "The Oldham Weaver," an unemployed worker and his wife were going downhill fast when the baileys arrived and "whopped up th' eawd stoo" (73) right from under them. Their last stick of furniture confiscated, the couple fall with a tragicomic whack on the floor. Here, then, a stool appears not as a decorative accessory but as the last prop of a weaver's right to habitation. Likewise, when Job quietly rearranges the furniture to accommodate his blind granddaughter (137), furniture and its disposal are not about conspicuous consumption and social control but bespeak instead Job's understanding of home as the sense of being safe and oriented in one's environment.[26]

The baileys' intrusion raises another category often invoked to disparage the domestic sphere—privacy. It is undoubtedly true, as left scholarship generally assumes, that privacy may be no more than a form and function of class exclusivity. But when baileys sweep in, or a detective waylays Mrs. Wilson, or visitors come missionizing, or bodies are exposed by ragged and insufficient clothing, then privacy is a matter not of exclusion but of protection—from the police, from middle-class moralizing, from the weather, and from shame.[27] Finally, over against the reflexive association of domesticity with individualism, I have stressed that the world of *Mary Barton* is emphatically one of interdependent subjectivities and domesticities: from the routine borrowing of teacups and pots of water to the life-and-death kin work spontaneously taken up by neighbors. All of this is to say, in the working-class milieu so thickly described by Gaskell, collectivity functions as a hedge against the precariousness of everyday life. And with stability, ownership, and privacy all in jeopardy on a daily basis, the demand for a modicum of coziness can hardly be dismissed as the mere copping of bourgeois values. Indeed, we might claim it as an expression of protest against these values and their support for unequal living conditions. In this light, returning for a last time to the Bartons' closed, checked curtains, I suggest we recognize them as a record of diverse labor histories as well as, more literally, a domestic boundary asserted for the purpose of keeping the authorities out and working-class camaraderie in.

3

DOMESTICITY BEYOND SENTIMENT

Edith Wharton, Decoration, and Divorce

Moving forward some fifty years, this chapter takes us from the vulnerable dwellings of Elizabeth Gaskell's urban poor—huddled in the shadow of Manchester's textile mills—to the elegant mansion that Edith Wharton designed and built for herself in the scenic countryside of Lenox, Massachusetts. If the former are extreme in their poverty, the latter might seem, at first glance, to be extreme only in its opulence. At the very least, their juxtaposition suggests the vast range of domestic circumstances and meanings. Yet Wharton's experience of home, however stable economically, was tumultuous its own right; by the time she was granted a divorce, she had been living yoked to an incompatible, unfaithful, and mentally ill husband for almost thirty years. In the following discussion of *The Decoration of Houses* (1897), I explore Wharton's strategies during these years, not for leaving home altogether but for remaking it as a refuge from, rather than an emblem of, her marriage. Divorcing her love of domestic matters from love of traditional family life, Wharton supports my argument (continued in chapter 4) that nineteenth-century U.S. domesticity need not be conflated with conservative gender politics.

Chapter 2 defended the right of working-class families to seek privacy from police intrusion; this chapter finds a woman writer desperate for privacy from the intrusions of compulsory heterosexuality. Wharton enables us to revisit and reformulate the issues of domestic instability and privacy raised by *Mary Barton* from the vantage point, in this case, of gender rather than class disparities.[1] In other ways, however, Wharton's domestic values and aesthetic don't revise so much as completely reverse those we have just seen. Gone is the emphasis on interdependence so crucial to survival for the Bartons and their neighbors. Shaped by marital distress, professional ambition, and the prerogatives of wealth, Wharton's domestic vision is as solitary and cold as Gaskell's is crowded and warm. I take its antagonism to cozy family feeling as a pointed rebuff to sentimental versions of domestic life, including that to which *Mary Barton* ultimately defers. Reflecting their divergent aims as well as the dictates of their respective genres, Wharton is also Gaskell's inverse in her treatment of domestic labor. For if Gaskell's realist novel walks readers through every step of having friends to tea, Wharton's famous design manual does the opposite: its photos of idealized, unvisited rooms indulge readers in the fantasy of never lifting a finger. There is one exception, however. Toward the end of this chapter, I turn to an image in *The Decoration of Houses* depicting not manual but mental labor: a woman whose workplace is a secluded room, the tool of her trade a book.

DIVORCING DOMESTICITY

With the publication of Lauren Berlant's *The Female Complaint: The Unfinished Business of Sentimentality in American Culture* (2008), one is tempted to remark that scholarly debates *about* sentimentality, its antebellum formation and subsequent meanings, also appear to be unfinished. Initiated by Ann Douglas in 1977, these debates have explored the linked categories of sentimentality, women's fiction, and the domestic sphere in U.S. texts assembled most often around the prototype of Harriet Beecher Stowe's *Uncle Tom's Cabin* (1852). The story is by now familiar: Douglas's denigrating view of "feminine" culture as banal and consumerist was quickly countered by Jane Tompkins, Nina Baym, and other early feminist critics, whose recuperation of popular nineteenth-century women writers exposed the biases of prevailing critical paradigms. For the next two decades, scholars fell loosely into one of these two camps, with the champions of "women's culture" losing ground by the late 1980s to those who took a dimmer view of this culture's manifold political implications. Gillian Brown, for example, would come to associate the domestic with individualistic notions of American selfhood, while Laura Wexler decried sentimentality as a form of "tender violence" that sugarcoated social control.[2]

The end of the 1990s saw various efforts to mediate between these highly polarized positions. Lora Romero protested that "domesticity" was intrinsically neither progressive nor conservative but likely to have a mix of political valences, depending on local context. In an article appearing the same year, Joanne Dobson made a similar pitch for the variable quality as well as the ideological significance of "sentimental literature." Not long after, Cathy Davidson brought out the influential "No More Separate Spheres!" issue of *American Literature*. As her exclamatory title makes clear, the goal in this case (building on precedents by Linda Kerber and others) was not to complicate dichotomized views of "feminine" domestic culture but to question the axiom of its separateness from the "masculine" marketplace. Pointing (as Romero and Dobson had, as well) to male participation in the "sentimental tradition," the issue overall debunked the separate-spheres model, primarily by implicating middle-class women in various forms of public aggression. As it turned out, by stressing the role of bourgeois domesticity in enforcing "larger" structures of national, racial, and class domination, post-spheres scholarship effectively tipped the balance still farther toward negative views of the domestic and sentimental. Extending into the twenty-first century, notable examples of this tendency are Amy Kaplan, on domesticity in the service of imperialism; Lori Merish (updating Ann Douglas), on sentimentalized consumerism; and Lauren Berlant, on sentimental culture as typically "a love affair with conventionality."[3]

Here I will venture an observation. Whatever scholars of American culture have thought about the "private" sphere—its political coloration, its ties to national and commercial interests—they have generally continued to assume its sponsorship by three ideologically laden and virtually coextensive terms: the *domestic*, the *sentimental*, and the *feminine*. Davidson, for example, groups these terms between parentheses while describing essays that address "the creation of interlocking ideologies of the separate spheres (domesticity, sentimentalism, women's fiction) and other social practices."[4] Kaplan launches her article "Manifest Domesticity" by reeling off the same set of categories, once again presumed to be closely knotted if not synonymous: "The 'cult of domesticity,' the ideology of 'separate spheres,' and the 'culture of sentiment' have together provided a productive paradigm for understanding the work of white women writers in creating a middle-class American culture in the nineteenth century."[5] So, too, for the vast majority of other commentators. Though in some cases the focus is on "sentimentality," in others on "domesticity," the two terms are rarely differentiated and often invoked interchangeably. Consequently, in the skeptical context of recent decades, the pejorative connotations of the former have served to taint the latter.

A primary goal of this chapter is to challenge this habitual, unthinking conflation. I do so by turning to Wharton for a vision of domesticity extricated from sentimental views—split off, in particular, from the sentimental framing of women as selfless, emotional creatures, their devotion to home bound up with their care for others. That Wharton's work poses a challenge to sentimental views of gender and family is hardly news. Kaplan's reading of Wharton as a realist defines her as such in contrast precisely to that popular "feminine" idiom associated with Stowe and later scribblers for the mass market. Yet Kaplan takes for granted (as she does in "Manifest Domesticity") that the home itself is also necessarily aligned with sentimentalized, self-effacing femininity. Narrating the novelist's self-conscious development as a working professional, Kaplan promises to "trace Wharton's effort to write herself out of the private domestic sphere and to inscribe a public identity in the marketplace."[6] My own emphasis, by contrast, is on Wharton's effort to develop a professional identity, in defiance of class as well as gender norms, by writing herself *into* the private domestic sphere. Far from opposing her domestic preoccupations to professionalism, I aim to show that Wharton's house love was crucial to her self-definition in excess of conventional, married womanhood.

Wharton was deeply invested in houses, domestic design, interior decoration, and the everyday routines of housekeeping. *The Decoration of Houses* was her first publication, and the principles of this acclaimed guide to interior design would later be materialized in The Mount, Wharton's beloved home in Lenox. Yet her vision of domestic spaces in *The Decoration of Houses* and The Mount was not, I have asserted, a celebration of sentimental attachments. I read it, indeed, as a form of resistance to these, and specifically as a counter to her unhappy marriage. Elaborating on hints dropped by architectural historian Richard Guy Wilson, my discussion puts Wharton's waxing passion for houses in dialogue with waning passion for her husband, Edward "Teddy" Wharton. Agreeing with critics Judith Fryer and Vanessa Chase, among others, I reiterate the importance of personal privacy to Wharton's carefully theorized design aesthetic.[7] In addition, I offer a new take on *The Decoration of Houses* based on a consideration of its fifty-six illustrations. My analysis places these stark, rather technical images in the context of two adjacent discourses: on the one hand, Wharton's novels of marital dysfunction and, on the other hand, a typical rival design manual, whose sketches of tasteful furniture are aglow with tender feelings for traditional family life. It is my contention that the antisentimental domesticity in *The Decoration of Houses* actually has more in common with the first than with the second.

By adducing Wharton as a revisionary theorist of domesticity, I hope to intervene in the aforementioned scholarly debate. By valuing Wharton's relation to window treatments and washstands, I continue to make my case against the tendency of recent critics simply to demonize the domestic sphere and the broad span of feminized knowledge, practices, and pleasures associated with it. As I have explained, Wharton helps me do so by offering a version of domesticity liberated from the trappings of sentimentality. Divorcing homes and homemaking from scripted spousal and maternal sympathies, she permits us to parse them in more complicated, flexible ways. Anticipating Lora Romero, Wharton's example invites scholars on the Left to recognize and own "domesticity" as a category available for various ideological ends.

CLEAN REVOLUTION

At age eleven, Edith Wharton nervously shared with her mother the opening lines of her very first novel: "'Oh, how do you do, Mrs. Brown?' said Mrs. Tompkins. 'If only I had known you were going to call I should have tidied up the drawing-room.'" Her mother's response to this hopeful bit of dialogue was sharp: "Drawing-rooms are always tidy."[8] Fortunately, as we know, Wharton grew up to prove her mother wrong. Like this early fragment, her mature works of fiction would feature married ladies, polite aggression, and domestic messes that no amount of warning could possibly remedy. Even as a child, Wharton seems to have recognized that stories actually require a certain amount of mess to get them going. From a novelist's point of view, a disorderly family home is dynamic—"narratable," as D. A. Miller would say—while always-already tidy rooms and relationships have nowhere to go.[9] Jane Austen knew this well, launching each of her novels with some kind of family squabble or separation. How then to manage an ending? What Austen illustrates, too, is domestic fiction's usual trick for restoring order: its ultimate recourse, like other comic forms, to one or more marriages. Narratively speaking, weddings have long been an effective way to clean house, to put people and things in their places, polishing up a promise of happy home before gently closing the door.

Of course even in Austen the equation of marriage with enduring tidiness was treated with unmistakable irony. By the time Wharton came of age in the 1880s, a transatlantic women's movement, building for several decades, had increased women's access to higher education, called for women's self-support, and succeeded in expanding divorce as well as property rights. As the century drew to a close, the visibility of "masculine" New Women and "feminine" male aesthetes contributed to the troubling of traditional marriage along with normative gender roles. In the United States especially, the rate of divorce was climbing steadily: between 1880 and 1900 it doubled, and by 1920 it had doubled again.[10] No wonder that far from implying order and stability, the wedded couple in turn-of-the-century stories and plays was just as likely to suggest the disappointing inverse. Edith Wharton joined Henry James, Mona Caird, William Dean Howells, Thomas Hardy, and many others in invoking marriage, especially when women were concerned, not as a pat resolution but, on the contrary, as the messy, motivating problematic of her fiction.

Failed marriages abound in Wharton's most acclaimed novels: *The House of Mirth* (1905) and *The Age of Innocence* (1920). The complex ramifications of divorce take center stage in *The Custom of the Country* (1913)—considered a founding text in the American divorce canon, along with Howells's *A Modern Instance* (1881)—and divorce returns as a theme in *Glimpses of the Moon* (1922) and *The Mother's Recompense* (1925). Besides being an available structure of feeling at the time, the apprehensive and often cynical view of marriage evident across these works had, for Wharton, a painfully personal dimension. As she intimates in her memoir, *A Backward Glance* (1934), and as biographers have thoroughly detailed, Wharton's own marriage in 1885 to Teddy Wharton was a disaster almost from the start—a gross mismatch aggravated by the decline in Teddy's mental health from 1902 onward.[11] Wharton's good friend Henry James simply refused to believe in it, calling the union "an almost—or rather an utterly—inconceivable thing."[12] Wharton nevertheless remained in this implausible (and childless) state of wedlock for twenty-eight years, finally obtaining a divorce from a Parisian court only in 1913. At the same time, as I have promised to show, long before their legal separation Wharton found various practical and psychic means for contriving a life set off from, if not actually shored against, the institution of marriage.

Women's pitiable, brave, sometimes deplorable, and often self-compromising efforts to navigate the shoals of marriage were, as we know, a driving concern of much of Wharton's fiction. Fittingly enough, *The Custom of the Country* appeared just months after her own divorce, but its scathing look at marital instability had been anticipated by such works as *Madame de Treymes* (1907) and *The Reef* (1912), as well as *The House of Mirth*.[13] Moreover, if *what* Wharton wrote demarcated from early on an imaginative space alienated from marriage, so too did the fact *that* she wrote, gaining a professional identity and considerable celebrity in tension with her role as Teddy's wife. Among her many admired publications was one that remains a touchstone not as a work of literature but as a classic guide to home decoration. As I have mentioned, *The Decoration of Houses*, coauthored with architect Ogden Codman and published by Scribner in 1897, was Wharton's first book.[14] With its photographs of elegant and immaculate rooms, its comments on boudoirs and bric-à-brac, and its general reverence for the home, *The Decoration of Houses* would seem to be wholly at odds with the marital turmoil of Wharton's fiction. It might, indeed, strike us as a weak-kneed capitulation to her mother's genteel truism; certainly the drawing rooms pictured in its pages are always tidy. To me, however, this book's apparently complacent domesticity evinces not only a fondness for home decoration but also, like the divorce novels, an implicit rebuke to matrimonial custom. My counterintuitive project in this chapter is to identify *The Decoration of Houses*, along with the actual New England residence Wharton constructed in its image, as texts in dialogue with her larger divorce corpus.[15]

My understanding of *The Decoration of Houses* in particular and Wharton's architectural fervor in general as counterpoints—indeed, antidotes—to her fraught life with Teddy rests on three intertwining claims. First, publishing *The Decoration of Houses* and building The Mount according to its precepts were key to shaping a professional self external to her marriage. This self drew authority from her prowess as both a writer and an expert in domestic and landscape architecture. Second, the layout of The Mount, while attesting to this professionalism, was also designed specifically to foster it. As I have noted, Wharton's architectural vision placed a high premium on privacy. Unlike today's craze for open floor plans, Wharton believed in sharply individuated rooms, including several set apart for the lady of the house. A central feature of The Mount was a separate suite of rooms in which Wharton could write without being disturbed. Third, I suggest that *The Decoration of Houses*'s excessively well-ordered interiors do not simply bow to her mother's conventional standards but have, instead, a rather more oppositional thrust. In my view, it is precisely the impossibly tidy, sterile, and rarified nature of the book's photographic images that serves to critique and correct the affective disorder of traditional family homes as Wharton experienced them. As we will see, these images also functioned to rebut the visual idiom represented by another popular guide to interior design, Clarence Cook's *The House Beautiful: Essays on Beds and Tables, Stools and Candlesticks* (1877).

What I find in Wharton's corpus is thus a bifurcation between messy fictions and neat rooms: between *narratives* exploring the often entropic trajectories of married life and, as if in compensation, *visual images* in which drawing rooms and dining rooms, ballrooms and bedrooms are arrested in time, ordered, and aestheticized. I am proposing that we recognize these two modes, antithetical in formal and affective terms, as ideologically continuous. Glossing Wharton's use of illustrations in *The Decoration of Houses*, along with the professional debut represented by this book and the architectural project it inspired, I hope to show how these forays into domestic design can be aligned with the fiction's more overt revolt against marital and familial norms.

EXTRAMARITAL DOMESTICITY

The 1890s saw a shying away from the aesthetic as well as the family values of the Victorian period. In decorating, the preference was now for lightness over the heavy and somber, and for simplicity over the cluttered and overstuffed. In addition to touting new technologies, the 1893 World's Columbian Exposition in Chicago offered the fair's gleaming neoclassical edifices as architectural fixes for the social problems ailing American cities. Feminists likewise endeavored to address "the Woman Question" in part by redesigning interior spaces. In the coming years, domestic scientists like Sophonisba Breckinridge and Ellen Richards would develop more efficient and hygienic kitchens along with more highly trained housewives, while Charlotte Perkins Gilman would advocate collectivizing and commercializing food preparation and child care.[16] Wharton's recourse to architectural schemes in response to a stifling marriage resonated, then, with the Progressive Era's general confidence that renovated spaces could have a transformative effect on social relations.

Edith Wharton was, I have emphasized, strongly attached to her various homes and closely concerned throughout her life with their design and decoration. As James observed, "No one fully knows our Edith who hasn't seen her in the act of creating a habitation for herself."[17] Such acts were not arrived at casually. Stints in Europe from an early age, a "photographic memory of rooms and houses" (*Backward Glance*, 28), the cultivation of her taste by discriminating mentors, and intensive self-schooling combined to help Wharton achieve an astonishing level of "nearly professional architectural competence," according to Wilson (173). Almost from the start, Wharton seems to have turned to houses as well as writing—and sometimes to writing about houses—for respite from marital disappointment and the chronic ailments she began to experience just a few years into married life. The Whartons, we recall, were wed in 1885, and biographers agree that the couple's intellectual, social, and sexual unsuitability became apparent not long afterward. Until 1902, their primary residence was in Newport, Rhode Island, a playground for the newly rich where Teddy flourished but where, as Shari Benstock puts it, Edith "wilted and grew hollow-eyed."[18] After narrating the unhappiness of the Newport years, possibly sexless and certainly disillusioning, Benstock notes that "soon after her marriage, Edith began to study seriously the history of architecture, furniture design, and house decoration."[19] Wilson is more explicit in proposing that Wharton's marital frustration led directly to her first, serious immersion in domestic design. "By 1890," he observes, "Edith had completed her initial aesthetic education. . . . Certainly she was escaping from an unsatisfying marriage and in a very real sense architecture and decoration became surrogates" (138).

This education provided the basis for *The Decoration of Houses*, on which Wharton and coauthor Codman began work in 1896. Five years later, this text would inform the plans for Wharton's famed house in the

Berkshires, on which she once again collaborated (though not exclusively) with Codman. Wharton herself signed the Lenox property deed in 1901, named it "The Mount" after her great-grandfather's estate, and threw herself completely into the ensuing construction of house and gardens. Notwithstanding the services of Codman and others, Wilson avers that The Mount was ultimately "Edith's own creation" and represents her "most complete realization of a total environment" (164, 172). Wharton herself described it glowingly as "my first real home" and confessed in her memoir, "It was only at the Mount that I was really happy" (*Backward Glance*, 125, 149). In fact, the evidence suggests that if Wharton had long sought out home design and decoration therapeutically, her work on and relocation to The Mount finally effected a lasting cure. The Whartons' removal in 1902 to the house that Edith built marked the end of her chronic nausea and fatigue. As she wrote to a friend that June, "I feel like a new edition, revised and corrected, in Berkeley's best type."[20]

Wharton's correction coincided, unfortunately, with Teddy's further slide into mental illness and marital errors both sexual and fiscal. His affliction undoubtedly placed further strain on an already vexed relationship and would be a decisive factor in the Whartons' eventual divorce. Yet despite this and despite the routinely inverse relationship between one spouse's sickness and the other's good health, Wharton described her life at The Mount as joyful and productive: "There for over ten years I lived and gardened and wrote contentedly, and should doubtless have ended my days there had not a grave change in my husband's health made the burden of the property too heavy" (*Backward Glance*, 125). In addition to the lovely New England countryside, Wharton appreciated what she described as "the freedom from trivial obligations which was necessary if I was to go on with my writing" (125). "The country quiet," she added, "stimulated my creative zeal" (125). Settled into her new house, she developed the habit of "systematic daily effort" required by serial publication and quickly polished off her second novel, *The House of Mirth*. As Wharton put it, the process of writing this best-selling book transformed her "from a drifting amateur into a professional" (209).

How was it that Wharton managed to wrest from the decade culminating in her divorce a sense of beauty and freedom, along with the discipline and aplomb of a professionalized writer? Benstock attributes Wharton's recovery at The Mount largely to the climate, and it is true that Wharton delighted in having "fields and woods of [her] own" (*Backward Glance*, 124). But I concur with those who stress the tonic effect of building a house and garden to her own exacting specifications.[21] Clearly this residence was not, for Wharton, a place of cozy marital and maternal satisfaction; yet neither was it the maddening incarceration of Gilman's "The Yellow Wallpaper" (1899). Thanks to the strategic design of The Mount, Wharton was able to enjoy a domesticity nominally shared with a restless and disordered husband but effectively extramarital. As I began by suggesting, rather than simply rejecting the domestic sphere as confinement to family, Wharton thus managed, with surprising success, to configure it as a refuge *from* family. She accomplished this goal by supplementing the customary privacy of the home with a second order of privacy within the home. James, a frequent houseguest at The Mount, made appreciative note of what he called its *penetralia*: the feature (uncommon in the United States) of having "some part . . . sufficiently *within* some other part, sufficiently withdrawn and consecrated."[22] Practically speaking, The Mount's penetralia enabled Wharton to withdraw in order to write. In more figurative terms, its innermost sanctum represented a domesticity pulled apart from the conjugal, linked instead to Wharton's autonomy and professionalism—also perhaps, as we will see, to a measure of gender pliability and improvisation.

Early in *The Decoration of Houses*, Wharton declares that "privacy would seem to be one of the first requisites of civilized life."[23] As I have mentioned, she believed that rooms should be kept distinct from one another and specific in their uses—protecting the ability of each to comprise "a small world by itself" (22). In keeping with this view, she laments the modern practice of widening doorways—worse still, the "grotesque conceit of putting sheets of plate-glass between two rooms" (23). As Vanessa Chase observes, the book goes on to stress the importance of substantial doors, announcing their ability to exclude as well as admit. In fact, Wharton devotes an entire chapter to doors, and one of her plates features a pair of handsome, chiseled bronze locks "in the French style" (plate XVII). Chase describes the house thus imagined as "a woman's shelter, her barrier against anything or anyone that she does not choose to allow into her life."[24] Still more removed, the shelter within this shelter, was the boudoir. As described in *The Decoration of Houses*, the boudoir ideally is situated between an antechamber on one side and a lady's suite of three additional rooms for sleeping, dressing, and bathing on the other. "In French suites of this kind," Wharton explains, "there are usually but two means of entrance from the main corridor: one for the use of the occupant, leading into the antechamber, the other opening into the bath-room, to give access to the servants. This arrangement, besides giving greater privacy, preserves much valuable wall-space" (170).

As Wharton designed it, The Mount included just such a series of rooms, sequestered on the second level of the north wing. Adjoining but separate from Teddy's, Wharton's quarters were reached by stairs inaccessible from the public rooms below, and it was there, in the remoteness of her boudoir, that Wharton ritually secluded herself every morning to write. As Wilson says of Wharton's well-fortified chambers, "The plan can be interpreted as a series of barriers to protect Edith at her work and yet allow the house to function with visitors and guests" (166).[25] There was, indeed, a constant stream of literary visitors at The Mount— in addition to James were close friends Walter Berry and Bay Lodge, among numerous others. Far from being a social recluse, Wharton played host to a sizable coterie and relied on her guests for the intellectual companionship missing from her marriage (*Backward Glance*, 149–94). Yet as Wilson and others stress, in addition to its gracious public spaces, the house was also laid out to ensure her intellectual solitude. Always socially prominent, Wharton became an ever more public figure as her literary reputation grew. She therefore sought the protection of The Mount in part to escape an intrusive press, whose attentions were particularly unwelcome in light of her marital troubles and eventual divorce. More than this, The Mount afforded the novelist privacy at the most personal level. If Gilman's feminist response to an oppressive private sphere was to flee outward, resituating cooking and child care within expansive, public spaces, Wharton's strategy was to flee inward, taking refuge in a heightened privacy—removing herself even (or especially) from her role as Teddy's wife.

To immure herself more deeply in the house might seem like a project of hyperfeminization, but I propose that Wharton's space apart, the space she claimed for her work, might be thought of instead as liminal in relation to traditional gender categories. Wharton's conservative family and even some critics regarded her authorial prowess as unsexing, and she herself once confessed to an appetite for literary criticism whose ferociousness left her "a little confused about [her] sex."[26] There were, in fact, several ways in which Wharton's revisionary domesticity situated her on conventionally masculine terrain. Most obviously, her professional drive and stature—distinguishing her from Teddy and, in general, from her leisure-class peers—demoted her to the role of bourgeois breadwinner while at the same time promoting her, in effect, to head of household. Indeed, the income from Wharton's writing widened what was already a sizable gap between her large inheritance (allowing her, for example, to purchase The Mount independently) and Teddy's modest personal income. Noting Wharton's superior deftness at managing as well as making money, Wolff asserts that "husband and wife had somehow exchanged roles."[27]

As we have seen, Wharton's professional competence extended beyond literary (and monetary) matters to architectural ones. Here too, in a field prioritizing male knowledge of external structures while relegating women to the separate, subordinate task of interior decoration, Wharton's wide-ranging historical, technical, and aesthetic expertise challenged the usual dichotomies. As a book about interiors, *The Decoration of Houses* might have been expected to comment exclusively on the ornamentation of surfaces, layering on of textiles, addition of small finishing touches, and display of sentimental objects. Wharton chose, instead, to address such large, structural elements as doors, windows, fireplaces, and stairs while advising against insipid wallpapers, heavy draperies, overstuffed upholstery, fussy details, and useless clutter. The introduction of *The Decoration of Houses* sets out to remind us that interiors were historically dictated by architectural attributes and ideals, with careful attention paid to moldings, cornices, and other intrinsic aspects. In keeping with its insistence on "*house decoration as a branch of architecture*," the book promises a return to rooms ruled by classical architectural principles of symmetry and proportion—this "in contradistinction to the modern view of house-decoration as *superficial application of ornament*" (xx–xxi [italics in original]). Poaching on professional territory even today strongly marked as male, *The Decoration of Houses*'s brief for "interior architecture" served at once to legitimate the still emergent field of interior decoration, to further confuse Wharton's "sex," and to contest the received architectural division between "masculine" outside and "feminine" inside.

DOMESTIC STILL LIFE

The Decoration of Houses bolsters its case for interior architecture with fifty-six halftone plates. All but two of them are photographs, and most display the furniture and rooms of Italian Renaissance palaces along with the later Italian, French, and English designs they inspired. In addition to their palatial scale, Wharton's many pictures of rooms are notable for their frozen perfection, undoubtedly due in part to the relative starkness of photography as a medium—this in contrast to the palpable aura and ready intimacy of the charming line drawings or prints typical of earlier decorating texts.[28] But the scenes featured in *The Decoration of Houses* are rendered all the more pristine by having been cleared of people and sentiment. Indeed, it is not only human figures but all signs of human existence, the casual trappings of everyday life, that have been carefully excluded. The rooms on offer are radically impersonal, defined as much by the absence of messy family matters as Wharton's novels are defined by their presence.

The dichotomy in Wharton between messy fictions and neat rooms, evinced by her novels and life story over against *The Decoration of Houses*, is replicated within the book itself by a subtle but comparable disjunction between its written and pictorial registers. The narrative opens with a short history of design, showing how architecture develops in response to human habits and needs (1–16). If people shape buildings, they are also shaped by them; the section on schoolrooms and nurseries argues that children's tastes are influenced by their early surroundings (173–83). Brief consideration is given to those arrangements most convenient for servants (85–86, 105) and to husbands driven to their men's clubs by the "exquisite discomfort" of showpiece drawing rooms (20). In addition to cameo appearances by servants and husbands, architects and decorators are occasionally invoked, as are some other, sadly less discerning, figures: the "amateur" collector, who is apt to overbuy (187–88), or the poor, benighted soul who fails to recognize frames as ornamental elements comparable to moldings (45–46). Above all, there is the discreet persona of the narrator, who still occasionally employs the practical, kindly idiom of advice literature, though more often assuming the impersonal, broadly historicizing voice of a scholarly tome. I will argue shortly that Wharton eschews the cast of family characters and intimate asides of Cook, whose *House Beautiful* preceded her book, as well as the chatty tones of popular authors like Elsie de Wolfe, whose manual *The House in Good Taste* (1913) came after Wharton's.[29] At the same time, I offer this brief overview of the written text to show that Wharton's narrative retains subtle traces of story, characters, and conflict—traces utterly and, I believe, strategically expunged from the accompanying photos.

The introduction to *The Decoration of Houses* offers "to explain the seeming lack of accord between the arguments used in this book and the illustrations chosen to interpret them," a discrepancy Wharton recognizes but understands in terms somewhat at variance with my own (xxii). She is referring here to the gap between her brief for simplicity and her photographs of palatial spaces—Versailles, Fontainebleau, and the like.[30] Such grand homes have the advantage, she insists, of being open to the public and may, in any case, be essentially simple in form, despite their extravagance. Wharton's remark that lay readers might enjoy the chance to actually visit the rooms pictured in *The Decoration of Houses* resonates with a long-standing, constitutive aspect of bourgeois subjectivity: a fascination with aristocratic manners, which might well be indulged by traveling abroad to gawk at European castles and country houses. I propose that our relation to the images in *The Decoration of Houses* is likewise essentially touristic. Wharton's photos appeal to us not because they remind us of home but precisely because they replace familiar rooms with those evoking an exotic country, century, and station. *The Decoration of Houses*'s visual register is thus further distinguished by its heightened association with class privilege and, more generally, with a domesticity on vacation from the mundane.

Of the fifty-six plates in *The Decoration of Houses*, more than twenty are long shots of rooms, halls, and staircases (figure 3.1). Except for three eighteenth-century English rooms, all of these are from Continental

FIGURE 3.1 "Staircase in the Parodi Palace, Genoa. Sixteenth Century." (From Edith Wharton and Ogden Codman Jr., *The Decoration of Houses*, facsimile ed. [1897; New York: Rizzoli and The Mount, 2007], plate XXX)

FIGURE 3.2 "Dining-Room, Palace of Compiègne. Louis XVI Period." (From Wharton and Codman, *Decoration of Houses*, plate L)

palaces dating from the eighteenth century or earlier (figure 3.2). Other plates focus on the ornamental treatment of palace walls, ceilings, doors, and mantels. The remaining photos feature chairs and other furniture of Louis XIV, XV, or XVI vintage, along with a few counterexamples from medieval France or Italy. In keeping with the book's mantra of simplicity and proportion, the spacious rooms are uncluttered and emphatically symmetrical. Their lines are strong; their edges are clean; and the Victorian rage for upholstery and curtains is nowhere apparent. The overall effect is one of ideal order and poise, and though no one would accuse them of being cozy, they are restful as well as elegant. The book's supertidy images permit readers to follow Wharton in imaginative flight from two particular aspects of domestic reality: first, the emotional messiness of family life; and second, the literal messiness of houses whose upkeep is unceasing and always inconclusive. In Wharton's perfect rooms, by contrast, the stain of food, drink, and bodily fluids has been eliminated right along with volatile emotions and un-ruly behavior. And if for Wharton the invisibility of domestic labor is in part a function of her wealth, for the rest of us domestic drudges, its absence is an enormously compelling fantasy.

It is not only laboring housekeepers who are omitted from these pho-tos. With only two exceptions (to be considered shortly), none of these rooms features any people at all, and they give the impression of never having done so. Most of the houses, dating from the sixteenth through eighteenth centuries and long since vacated, are not so much homes as monuments to the glory days of monarchy, and all have the airless quality of museum exhibits, stage sets, or still lifes. The photos of furni-ture are even more denatured. Flawless, regal chairs and tables are typi-cally shot against a perfectly neutral background, making them appear to be almost suspended in space. Except for a museum-style caption—"Dining-Chair. Louis XIV Period," for example (plate LII [figure 3.3])—all possibly debasing context is stripped away. Certainly there is no indi-

FIGURE 3.3 "Dining-Chair. Louis XIV Period." (From Wharton and Codman, *Decoration of Houses*, plate LII)

cation that anyone has recently (or ever) sat heavily on such a chair, found it too upright toward the end of a long meal, or dusted it in preparation for guests. Nor is there even the slightest hint that said chair might once have encountered a table, scraped against a marble floor, or leaned with other chairs against a wall. If the rooms in *The Decoration of the Houses* float above the vagaries of life, these museum pieces, without even rooms to anchor them, are pure Platonic form.

TWO VIEWS THROUGH THE KEYHOLE

While Wharton's lifeless, aristocratic interiors will not seem strange to readers of *Architectural Digest* and other twenty-first-century publications in which glossy photos of unpeopled, upscale rooms are the rule, the significance of their depiction in *The Decoration of Houses* becomes clearer in contrast to one of the works Wharton sought to rival: Cook's *House Beautiful*.[31] Like *The Decoration of Houses*, Cook's popular work was published by Scribner, proceeds through various kinds of rooms, and advocates simplicity over slavishness to fashion. But though Cook was similarly accused of failing to picture the simplicity he preached,[32] the resemblance to Wharton ends there. His "little book" is fondly dedicated to Mrs. Cook: "To her whose happy union of head, hands, and heart, has made one house beautiful through many checquered years." Next comes an epigraph in praise of time-tested marriages and enduring love. "There is nothing can please a man without love." For the man who "dwells in love," his wife is fair and easeful, his home a "sanctuary," his children a source of "joy and comfort." In the pages that follow, Cook assumes a genial, avuncular voice, recommends bookshelves and tableware for spaces far more modest and plausible than Wharton's palazzi, and seizes every chance to invoke, especially in pictures, the cozy family scenes so conspicuously missing from *The Decoration of Houses*.

Cook's volume includes ninety-nine "cuts," pretty engravings featuring tea kettles and cats, like those in a children's book. Many are little cameos set between lines of text and accompanied by captions ranging from the merely descriptive ("Italian Fire-Screen")[33] to the cute, homiletic, or literary ("A Love of a Bonnet-Box," "'T is home where'er the hearth is," "But soft! what light through yonder window breaks!" [293, 116, 182]). Like *The Decoration of Houses, House Beautiful* offers helpful close-ups of recommended chairs and tables. Unlike Wharton's book, however, it is animated throughout by men, women, and children who inhabit Cook's interiors in predictably gender-appropriate ways. The title page, for example, centers on a small, circular vignette of a husband and wife, along with the eponymous bed, table, stool, and candlestick (figure 3.4). The book opens, in effect, with a keyhole view of the master bedroom, immediately locating its treatment of domestic objects in the context of marital intimacy. Logically enough, this bedroom scene is later followed by a picture purporting to illustrate "An Every-day

FIGURE 3.4 Francis Lathrop, vignette for title page. (From Clarence Cook, *The House Beautiful: An Unabridged Reprint of the Classic Victorian Stylebook* [1877; Mineola, N.Y.: Dover, 1995])

FIGURE 3.5 Maria R. Oakley, "An Every-day Mantel-piece, Simply Treated." (From Cook, *House Beautiful*, 125)

Mantle-piece" but actually featuring a mother and babe, seated in a rocker by the hearth (125 [figure 3.5]). Another sketch shows a man at his desk and a woman at her instrument (46). Entitled "The Young Scholar and His Wife," it neatly summarizes the gendering of subsequent images in which men reading are described by captions as "working" (78) or "studying" (176) while "wives" depicted holding books seem less studious than ornamental (108, 165 [figure 3.6]). We are, indeed, encouraged to see them as such both by their placement in public rooms alongside furniture and knickknacks and because the female body's function as decorative object is strongly suggested by the Venus de Milo-type statues hovering nearby.

Marriage and domesticity as happily inseparable; domestic objects and spaces saturated with sentiment; homes divided along strict gender lines between scholarly men and doting wives; women shown to be

FIGURE 3.6 Francis Lathrop, "What do you read, my lady?" (From Cook, *House Beautiful*, 165)

nurturing and picturesque, the more so for their sweet, recreational literacy—all this is conveyed by Cook's little pictures and ruthlessly purged from Wharton's alternative domestic vision. She achieved this by ridding her rooms not only of people but also of anything suggesting the personal or emotional, leaving only the cool, refined shell, the elegant geometry. There are, however, two images departing from this rule, which happen to be the only two historical prints included in *The Decoration of Houses*. One features a social gathering of men and women in a *Salon à l'Italienne* (plate XLII). Its referent is not the Victorian private sphere but eighteenth-century courtier life, and Wharton's point is to endorse its strongly architectural treatment of interior walls, with decorative columns echoing actual ones visible through a doorway. The other exceptional image—a woman reading alone in her boudoir—is more telling for our purposes (plate XLI [figure 3.7]). For if Wharton's other fifty-some plates serve to sweep the home of distracting guests, servants, and family members alike, they may well do so in order to

FIGURE 3.7 "French Boudoir. Louis XVI Period" (from a print by Joseph Barthélémy Le Bouteux). (From Wharton and Codman, *Decoration of Houses*, plate XLI)

install this single figure: the literary woman secure in the penetralia of her private quarters.

I conclude my discussion of *The Decoration of Houses* by taking a closer look at this print. Reading by candlelight in a narrow but high-ceilinged room, the woman sits at a desk whose graceful curves echo the rounded backs of two chairs, the flow of her skirts, and the ornamental globe set high against the back wall. The globe is positioned above the subject's head, as if a kind of "thought bubble" suggesting, from this fixed location, unlimited mental reach. The woman's posture is relaxed (elbow on desk, cheek resting in hand), and the line of her forearm directs our eye from the manuscript up to her illuminated face, highlighting an expression of serene absorption. The emotional state thus indicated would seem to be at odds with the original French caption, which titles her a sad, abandoned lover. If our reader is indeed an exile from romance, she looks to be reasonably content with her cloister. Appearing sheltered rather than confined, she enjoys a privacy that Cook's reading women, on display in the living room, might well envy.

The woman is not quite alone with her book, however, if we count the little dog sitting just beyond the shadow of her skirts. Long a symbol of carnality, the beast is facing the fire, its back pointedly turned on its mistress. As we continue to mine this print for a narrative about the author of *The Decoration of Houses*, how should we interpret this averted animal presence? Was Wharton, in self-exile from her marriage, dogged by desire in the privacy of her boudoir? One hesitates to say whether Wharton's refuge from traditional wifedom should be considered a space of errant sexuality as well as gender-bending professionalism. We know she had a fling in the summer of 1909 with the faithless Morton Fullerton (as Teddy, for his part, dallied with an actress). I am inclined to agree, however, with Wilson's alternative view of Wharton's extramarital proclivities. "Throughout her long and sexless marriage to Teddy," Wilson asserts, "architecture and decoration acted as not just a diversion, but as erotic surrogate" (177). I have argued that *The Decoration of Houses* and The Mount functioned in advance of the law to grant Wharton a de facto divorce—a critical distance from marriage in keeping with the ethos of her novels. Yet we might also, with equal justice, rephrase this dynamic in more positive terms: Wharton's alienation from Teddy coincided with a passionate fixation on the house itself, whose strong contours, graceful symmetries, and carefully discrete parts were also a flattering reflection of her own professional talents.

THE BOOK OF THE HOMELESS

Wharton sold The Mount in June 1912 and ten months later was formally released from her marriage. Following her divorce, she relocated permanently to France, eventually creating two other extraordinary homes for herself. Wharton's first domestic project abroad was not, however, a private residence. Beginning in 1914, she threw herself into war relief work and spent the next five years establishing and overseeing shelters for thousands of European war refugees. Scarcely sleeping at night, Wharton founded and ran multiple organizations, including the American Hostels for Refugees, a rescue committee for Belgian orphans, and two sanitariums for tubercular refugees. As one of her fundraising efforts for these and other charities, she assembled a collection of celebrity works entitled *The Book of the Homeless*, with contributions from Henry James, Jean Cocteau, Sarah Bernhardt, W. B. Yeats, Joseph Conrad, and many more.[34] Published by Scribner in 1916, the volume makes a poignant companion piece to *The Decoration of Houses*.

As I began this chapter by noting, Gillian Brown, Lori Merish, Amy Kaplan, and others have shown us that notions of the "domestic," entwined with the "sentimental," are readily mobilized in the service of individualism, consumerism, U.S. imperialism, and other unattractive ideologies. I do not dispute this. Too often, however, the important left critique of normative domesticity devolves into a wholesale dismissal of domestic rituals and concerns. I have therefore been at pains to insist that domesticity—a category strongly marked as "feminine"—is not necessarily tied to conventional "family values" or, I would add, intrinsically bound up with conservative views of class, race, selfhood, or nationhood. Wharton's devotion to the domestic sphere was sharply severed from sentimental views of gender, marriage, and family. The novels, as we know, bristled with damning instances of wedlock. In addition, Wharton's blueprint for The Mount and illustrations for *The Decoration of Houses* took on the problematics of marriage in a rather different fashion: not by portraying conflict or rejecting domesticity outright but by forcibly reconfiguring "home" as a space of female solitude and serenity, its emotional tenor as restrained and balanced as the classical design of its rooms.

This was, to be sure, an individual strategy, abetted by great wealth, for preserving the sanity and fostering the creativity of a single woman. At the same time, Wharton's dedication over a period of years to sheltering the masses of wartime refugees should remind us of what she apparently

knew: that a degree of safe, stable domesticity, far from being a bourgeois luxury, is a widely shared human need. In response to the large-
scale destruction of French and Belgian homes, Wharton emerged from
her private penetralia, redirecting her introverted domestic energies
outward into public service. Resonating with and overriding her personal dislocation, Wharton's refugee work speaks succinctly enough to
her awareness all along that home—its disruption by conflict, its loss
and rebuilding—is about much more than marble floors and seemly
proportions.

4

BAD GIRLS OF GOOD HOUSEKEEPING

Dominique Browning and Martha Stewart

T he Cult of True Womanhood exerted, as we know, considerable influence over U.S. mores throughout the nineteenth century, and its linking of women to both the domestic sphere and an ideal of chaste, selfless, and submissive femininity is far from obsolete even today. Edith Wharton was not alone, however, in celebrating this sphere even while deviating from the "good girl" mold. Just as the forbidding rooms of *The Decoration of Houses* coded this deviation, so other women both before and after Wharton's time published advice books and magazines whose domestic discourse included or coexisted with defiance of traditional gender norms. This chapter cites a number of such "bad girl" domestic experts from the nineteenth and early twentieth centuries before coming to our own time and taking up my two eponymous figures. Like Wharton, Dominique Browning and Martha Stewart are divorced; in their case, moreover, marital failure has informed and actually enhanced their success as domestic professionals. Further echoing Wharton, both Browning and Stewart are associated with magazines whose photographs of pristine interiors represent an aesthetic and fantasy structure in keeping with—and arguably descended from—that on display in *The Decoration of Houses*. Although the following discussion largely continues that in the previous chapter, there is at least one conspicuous difference: if Wharton's impulse is to plumb the house for the sake of privacy, Stewart's is to mobilize it for the sake of profit and publicity.

REREADING THE SHELTER TRADITION

Is your fantasy space an urban loft—long, clean sight lines and edgy textures? Or do your tastes run more quaintly to log cabins fronted by spills of wild roses? Either way, there is a decorating magazine for you. "Shelter magazines," as the industry calls this women's subgenre, originated in the United States with the founding of *House Beautiful* in 1896.[1] When we include those publications combining beautiful interiors with household instruction, we find an even longer tradition extending back to nineteenth-century American journals and books on domestic advice as well as interior design. *Better Homes and Gardens*, for example, has ties to other shelter magazines and also to traditional "service" magazines for women, a long-standing category focused on home maintenance.[2] Shelter magazines typically circulate less widely and devote less space to running a household. Yet *Martha Stewart Living*, to take another example, juxtaposes photos of immaculate rooms with hints on everything from pies to plumbing, and shelter writing in general may be traced to such works as *The Frugal Housewife* (1829) by Lydia Maria Child.

The class and gender politics of shelter writing would seem to be self-evidently conservative. In an early feminist analysis of women's magazines, Rosalind Coward rightly notes that images of the "ideal home," reflecting an elite aesthetic, are designed to "show off expensive objects to their greatest advantage."[3] In contrast, working-class arrangements of souvenirs and family photos, which display memories rather than wealth, are regarded by shelter publications as the epitome of "bad taste."[4] Coward is also skeptical of the way that immaculate rooms suppress the female labor behind them, along with marital conflicts over women's undue domestic burden.[5] Clearly, there is merit to both critiques. Despite Lydia Maria Child's model of frugality, writers on domestic techniques and decor have long urged simplicity while offering to "improve" taste by touting Italian furniture, Oriental rugs, and other luxury items. The consumerist imperative, of course, has been especially pressing in the case of magazines, whose reliance on advertisers targeting female readers increased steadily, beginning in the 1890s. The result is a tension in shelter magazines, reaching back to the nineteenth century and continuing to this day, between practical, cost-saving advice—including suggestions for clever, do-it-yourself projects—and depictions of exquisite objects and upscale spaces, which cater shamelessly to fantasies of wealth, status, and leisure.[6]

Nor is there any point in denying that much early shelter writing reinforced sentimental views of women as selfless wives and mothers, content to nurture and labor for others in the domestic sphere. Twenty-first-century shelter magazines, too, though read by some men and well aware that most of its female readers work outside the home, still place women primarily inside houses while tying houses primarily to women. Keeping in mind the conservative tendencies of my texts, I would nevertheless argue that those who write and read about domestic interiors may do so in ways that challenge as well as reiterate traditional beliefs about women, marriage, families, and sexuality. The feminist imagination is, understandably, drawn to the open road, to restless women slamming the door on houses that have cramped and infantilized them. As we have seen, my project in this book resonates with another feminist impulse: one that defiantly celebrates domestic spaces, practices, and concerns customarily feminized and, as a consequence, trivialized. Claiming a "private" sphere more often sentimentalized, separated from, and subordinated to the public, my comments throughout are premised on a complex, appreciative view of the home as a site of production as well as consumption, skilled labor as well as taste, utility as well as beauty. More than this, I am interested in representations of zealous domesticity—loving depictions of houses and house knowledge—pried apart from conventional gender arrangements.

Notwithstanding the reflexive linking of high domesticity to marriage and dutiful wifeliness, the two have never been inextricable. The protagonists of this chapter—Dominique Browning, editor of *House & Garden* from 1996 to 2007; and Martha Stewart, founder of *Martha Stewart Living* and Martha Stewart Living Omnimedia—are preeminent domestic professionals, reigning figures in today's shelter world.[7] As I have said, both women not only perform domesticity in the public sphere but also are, quite conspicuously, divorced. Browning has written a memoir describing the emotional aftermath of her divorce, which I take as the subject of my discussion here. Martha Stewart's divorce, sensationalized by multiple biographies and television biopics, is likewise available (indeed, unavoidable) as the backstory to her celebrity as domestic guru and media mogul. Beyond the literal fact of their divorces, Browning and Stewart resemble Wharton in suggesting *divorce* as a trope for the severing of women's domestic expertise from normative marital roles and obligations. In my readings of these two women, domesticity is liberated from protocols of service to others and, more wickedly still, reinvented as service to self.

Browning and Stewart contribute to a store of domestic images, narratives, and advice reaching back more than a century. By opening with a few of their nineteenth- and twentieth-century precursors, I intend to suggest their placement within an extended "bad girl" tradition of American domestic representations. My historical examples anticipate our contemporary figures both by distancing themselves from marriage and by trading on their domestic knowledge to ends more self-promoting than self-sacrificing—for money, as it were, rather than love. Long before the scientizing of housekeeping by the early-twentieth-century home economics movement, the female authors and editors of shelter texts, whether or not they explicitly endorsed wage work for women, were themselves earning incomes and reaching broad audiences as experts in household arts. As authors/editors and sometimes formal educators, the women whose works I cite in this chapter modeled a relation to domestic matters that did not displace but certainly exceeded that decreed by the traditional roles of wife and mother. By professionalizing home maintenance, these decorous women launched the industry culminating today in Stewart's multimillion-dollar "lifestyle" empire.

My readings of Browning and Stewart are further prefaced by some general remarks on the photo aesthetic of contemporary shelter magazines. Ellen McCracken devotes just a few pages to this genre, which she sees as essentially similar to those focused on fashion and beauty: "Although it appears that the ideal homemaker is actively to create her environment here [in the August 1981 *House & Garden*], in fact she is to adorn herself and her home as parallel passive sex objects; the glance of the approving male surveyor is implicit in each of these scenarios."[8] McCracken is certainly right that the *House & Garden* idiom eroticizes household objects and projects, but I disagree that doing so is comparable to preening for the male gaze. Indeed, another oppositional aspect of shelter magazines may be precisely their difference from fashion magazines in this regard. As a rule, not only objectified women but also scrutinizing men and boisterous children have been excised from their pages. Unlike *Vogue* and *Mademoiselle*, with their many pounds of female flesh, the shelter genre features rooms uncontaminated by people, hermetically sealed against the ordinary drama of human lives, and, to a significant degree, extricated from gendered conventions of seeing. Later I will call on Terry Castle, lesbian critic and self-described connoisseur of "house porn," to support my sense that women may study pictures of supertidied interiors not to feather the marital nest but, recalling my discussion of Wharton, to find refuge from marital mess and instability. Perfectly ordered, impossibly beautiful, and carefully evacuated rooms, photographed with precision and tenderness: these images suggest a rejection of domesticity oriented toward (or even including) others. What they evoke instead is a leisured, serene, and sensual experience of home addressed to women themselves.

Interpreting the photographic conventions of shelter magazines, along with the specific examples of shelter pundits Browning and Stewart, and glancing as well toward their nineteenth-century forebears and twenty-first-century readers, I continue to expand my archive of domestic iconography divorced from the ideals of marriage and maternity. My goal once again is to recognize a house culture linked to the very things abjected by these ideals: women who are divorced, widowed, or never married; women who are childless, child averse, or single mothers; women whose domesticity does not preclude and may actually foster professionalism; women who support themselves economically; women who voice their opinions as writers, scholars, and activists; female sexuality veering toward the autoerotic if not the fetishistic—domesticity, in short, elaborated not for husband and children but as a language of female pleasure, self-expression, and autonomy.

CAN THIS MARRIAGE BE SAVED?

There is little question that penning their views of domestic matters has long appealed to women in part because they could thereby purvey (atoning for their failure to observe) conventional notions about the sanctity of marriage and the proper purview of their sex. Yet as I have suggested, there are nevertheless aspects of nineteenth- and early-twentieth-century shelter writing that look forward to the dissenting as well as the conservative implications of our own. More than one study of U.S. women's household books and magazines has stressed the ideological complexity and mixed messages proffered by these texts. Jennifer Scanlon observes that early readers of *Ladies' Home Journal* were sure to have noticed "that much of the editorial and advertising content of the magazine was produced by women who led lives distinctly unlike those they counseled readers to live."[9] Scanlon's history of this journal sets out to show that it functioned not only to dampen women's desires or channel them in consumerist directions but also to register their discontent and validate their aspirations. Nancy Walker shares Scanlon's sense that magazines for women have been more than simply conventionalizing. Introducing her study of the postwar period, Walker notes that "at no time during their histories have women's magazines delivered perfectly consistent, monolithic messages," and she suggests that we therefore "see the domestic as a contested and negotiated concept rather than a proscribed [*sic*] and stable one."[10]

What exactly were female readers dissatisfied with, and what did they long for? Scanlon and Walker agree that a primary site of ambivalence and anxiety was marriage, which popular magazines at once glorified and continually depicted as difficult and precarious. The *Ladies' Home*

Journal, for example, launched a column in the 1940s (long known as "the most popular, most enduring women's magazine feature in the world") that in issue after issue posed the same, seemingly unanswerable question: "Can This Marriage Be Saved?" The counselor's replies aimed to reassure, but Walker is surely correct to infer that "countless articles on achieving marital harmony spoke to widespread disharmony."[11] Earlier indications of doubts about marriage are found in the fiction that once constituted a significant portion of women's service magazines. Scanlon's chapter on stories published by the *Ladies' Home Journal* in the 1910s and 1920s gives numerous examples of narratives dealing with frustrated wives before concluding that "although it warned against careers, divorce, economic and personal independence, and unbridled sexuality, the magazine's fiction acknowledged many of the real problems women encountered, and illustrated that traditional methods did not always suffice."[12]

A volume of stories by Virginia Terhune Van de Water, originally published in 1912 in *Good Housekeeping* and *The Cosmopolitan*, went a good deal further. As its title warns, *Why I Left My Husband, and Other Human Documents of Married Life* is a collection of painfully disillusioned tales, unvarnished renderings of marital alienation from multiple perspectives, including that of a daughter driven from home to escape the cross fire. Some of the couples separate, and some remain shackled to loveless unions for the sake of children or practicality. Either way, far from warning against it, this volume fully rationalizes divorce in moral as well as emotional terms. What interests me here is not just the dark extremity of Van de Water's naturalism (beside which the marital angst in Chopin, Wharton, or James seems almost euphemistic) but also its surprising proximity to texts idealizing the well-maintained home. Van de Water's own mother was the home expert Mary Virginia Hawes Terhune, who published more than thirty housekeeping, child-rearing, and cooking books under the pen name "Marion Harland," several of them coauthored with her daughter. Moreover, just two years before *Why I Left*, Van de Water herself had written *From Kitchen to Garret* (1910), a systematic guide to everything from kitchen floors to laundry hampers, with the usual diatribe against bric-a-brac, a paragraph on training boys to be neat, and several on maternal beauty routines. In Van de Water's family and corpus alike, stories of marital disaster are on intimate terms with discussions of tidy closets and charming tea tables.

In addition to separating out domestic know-how from a sunny view of marriage, this second-generation shelter writer also used house manuals as a stepping-stone to punditry in other areas. As World War I drew to a close, Van de Water wrote two pamphlets published by the jingoistic National Security League: *Women and Bolshevism* and *What the Victory or Defeat of Germany Means to Every American*. Notwithstanding the questionable politics of these latter ventures, Van de Water's spectrum of publications begins to suggest the ideological and generic eclecticism—along with the ambition to opine on matters extraneous to kitchen and garret—that was not unusual among domestic writers. Elizabeth Ellet, to take an earlier example, was the author of *The Practical Housekeeper* (1857) as well as an acclaimed poet and early scholar of women's history. Today she is remembered primarily for *The Women of the American Revolution*, a three-volume work appearing in 1848 and 1850. But Ellet also made headlines for personal reasons: a romantic scandal involving Edgar Allan Poe and the poet Frances Osgood. Clean houses, it seems, have never been synonymous with unspotted lives. Ellet joins Martha Stewart in showing that notoriety as a bad girl does not necessarily undermine one's street cred as a domestic adviser. As we will see, part of Stewart's appeal to female readers may be precisely her status as a "fallen woman" who is wildly successful despite an apparent disregard for so-called family values.

Other early domestic advisers likewise combined shelter writing with self-expression on a range of timely issues, many of them also managing to support themselves through professional activities in or branching off from the domestic sciences. Sarah Leavitt gives ample evidence favoring her contention that American women writing about housekeeping were "connected with the most important cultural dialogues of their day,"[13] making their voices heard on issues from slavery to sanitation. Frugal housewife (and novelist) Lydia Maria Child was an ardent abolitionist, while Sophonisba Breckinridge, coauthor of *The Modern Household* (1912), lent her support to women's suffrage, the protection of children and immigrants, the Women's Peace Party, and the NAACP (10–11, 48–49). Leavitt's book further demonstrates that over the years, women's publications on domestic matters served to increase their access to such professional areas as teaching, architecture, photography, social work, psychology, and the sciences (206). Notable examples include Catharine Beecher, author of *The American Woman's Home; or, Principles of Domestic Science* (with Harriet Beecher Stowe, 1869), who founded the Hartford Female Seminary in 1823 and worked throughout her career to promote, theorize, and fund education for women (16–17); and Ellen Richards, coauthor of *Home Sanitation: A Manual for Housekeepers* (1911), who was the first female graduate of MIT. In addition to teaching at MIT and establishing a women's laboratory, Richards published widely on the topics of domestic sewage and ventilation (47–48).

My final example of bad-girl domesticity in earlier centuries is Harriet Prescott Spofford, whose knowledge of antique tables coincided with frank sympathy for unhappily married women and emphatic support for their political and economic agency in the public sphere. The author of *Art Decoration Applied to Furniture* (1878) as well as articles on medieval, Elizabethan, and later English furniture (Leavitt 16–17), Spofford was also responsible for hundreds of unladylike stories, generally in a sensational vein, most of which ran in the *Atlantic Monthly* and *Harper's New Monthly Magazine* between 1868 and 1893. Virtually unremarked, however, are three feminist commentaries published in the 1890s by the *North American Review*. In 1895, rebutting an article on "nagging women," Spofford itemized common forms of male domestic abuse before concluding, "In reality, there is no sex in nagging. A husband may make his wife as wretched as a wife may make her husband."[14] The following year, Spofford responded forcefully to another article, this one denigrating women engaged in social reform as vulgar, unattractive, and disappointed in love. Defending women who seek an equal voice in public affairs from these all too familiar charges,

Spofford describes them (whether married or choosing to remain single) as fashionably dressed, well groomed, and often beautiful, "neglecting none of the duties and none of the delicacies of manners and of living." Of particular note is her comment that even activists may have "happy homes perfectly kept."[15]

A third piece contends that dowries for daughters would be unnecessary if women became more economically independent. As Spofford explains, fathers and husbands would be relieved, even as women were emancipated, "through the recognition of the dignity of self-support, through the increasing accessibility of professions and crafts, and the occupations of trade, through the growing conviction that it is dishonorable to be supported by the labor of another and that every girl should be reared to take care of herself."[16] Curiously enough, housekeeping is once again adduced to support her point. Spofford argues that along with shortened hours on the job, improvements at home would help women balance family and wage work. I close this brief historical overview with Spofford by way of recapping my central point: that a passion for furniture, a critique of marital wretchedness, a defense of women in politics, care for the "perfectly kept" and modernized home, and a case for female self-support may be, and have been, brought together in mutually informing ways.[17]

HOUSE PORN

Coming now to our own historical moment, I pause first over Terry Castle, best known as the author of *The Apparitional Lesbian* (1993). In an amusing piece originally written for the *Atlantic Monthly* in 2006, Castle goes public concerning her obsession with shelter magazines or, as she puts it, her addiction to "house porn." As "Home Alone" reveals, her usual stash ranges from *Elle Decor* to *Veranda*, though she also admits to making guilt-ridden runs to a foreign newsstand for more exotic fare.[18] Humorously evoking the "autoerotic dimension" of her habit, Castle offers vivid support for a thesis I happen to share regarding trauma and upholstery: idealized rooms as consolation for histories of domestic disaster. As she explains, a fetish for furniture can frequently be traced to a primal scene of decorating—and family—gone terribly wrong. Early-twentieth-century decorator Elsie de Wolfe, for example, was scarred forever by a parental choice of wallpaper so offensive she felt she had been knifed (111–12). For Castle herself, the source of childhood trauma was not only that her mother spray-painted their sofa a "lethal" shade of turquoise (112). It was also that after a harrowing and impoverishing divorce, she migrated with her daughters from their comfortable suburban home to a series of depressing residences: a "dreary seaside bungalow in the UK," a garish pad in San Diego, and, most nightmarish of all, the "dank and malodorous" abode of the man who would become Castle's stepfather (113–14). If divorce and removal are bound up for Castle with demoralizing interiors and the reckless application of pigment, no wonder she would come to find solace and even arousal in images of houses that are tasteful and deliberate. No wonder that her dirty pictures are . . . clean.

Castle's comments rhyme with my own sense that the upheaval of divorce (in this case, her mother's) may cue a special investment in the stability of tables, the comfort of throw pillows. As I have suggested, the allure of shelter magazines for women readers may be tied to their images of pristine family homes unsullied by the presence of family. Indeed, their appeal seems to lie precisely in their explicit, airbrushed photos of depopulated interiors: houses suggesting not marital nest or cozy nursery so much as (like the photos in Wharton's *The Decoration of Houses*) still life, museum, or cloister. In Castle's words, "The ideal room in Shelter-Mag Land is unpeopled—stark, impervious, and preternaturally still" (120). There are, she acknowledges, a few exceptions to this general principle: "*Elle Decor*, for some reason, likes to run pictures of blissed-out property owners" (119). Children also appear occasionally, but only as picturesque blurs, adding local color to flawless stage sets. Castle dubs them "designer" children (just one more accessory to complement the tufted ottoman) while also citing the reproductive yearnings of today's professional women (120). To this compelling description, I would add just a few remarks. As my discussion of Stewart will suggest, if it is true the pictures of children "whizzing by" (119) are wishful, is it possible the wish is less procreative than palliative—the fantasy not of having a child but of having a child *who is just passing through*? Does not the autoerotic pleasure of frozen rooms lie in beauty sealed off from emotional flux and, too, from the never-ending labor of cleaning up after others?

Castle ultimately sees her own confessed tendency to bracket mess in favor of "house beautiful" as morally problematic: an escapist response shared by shelterheads nationwide, especially in these days of global as well as family chaos. In the end, she comes to question the wisdom (and efficacy) of hiding out from entropic realities under high thread-count bed covers (121–27). Castle is right, of course. At the same time, I hesitate to disparage as merely "bourgeois" or "infantile" (125) the longing for domestic spaces that are safe, clean, and bright—a desire that is, after all, both deep-seated and self-preserving. In particular, I feel great sympathy for the women and men who conjure gorgeous, spellbound interiors as antidotes to dwellings made ugly and impermanent by adversity, marital or otherwise.[19] In the memoir to which I now turn, Dominique Browning finds in domestic advice and interior decoration a language not for avoiding but for steering her way through personal loss.

A GOOD COUCH IS HARD TO FIND

Whereas *House & Garden*'s photographs exemplify the home-as-museum aesthetic I have outlined, Browning's nonfiction represents another, rather different shelter idiom. Narrative rather than pictorial, demonstrative rather than stoical, haunted rather than evacuated, it nevertheless further illustrates the logic of shelter texts as therapy: appreciative renderings of home brought on by dislocation, descriptions that cling to house objects and activities in the wake of domestic trauma. Browning's work thus also extends the tradition of home improvement pulled asunder from marriage and repurposed for the woman writer's own benefit. As its title suggests, *Around the House and in the Garden: A Memoir of Heartbreak,*

Healing, and Home Improvement (2003) recounts Browning's mourning for her failed marriage as the story of occupying a house. Composed of forty-one short chapters, with such titles as "Who Gets the House?" "Bed Rx," "Couch Therapy," "Sacred Ordinary," "Repairs Never End," and "Doing the Dishes," the book traces Browning's shifting relation to her domestic space after divorce: letting the house drift and grow ragged; hibernating for a while in this room or that; finding the resolve to change and rearrange the furniture; raising two children under its roof, with flashbacks to her own childhood; musing on the acts of washing dishes or soaking in a tub; securing the house against rain and flies; flinging open its doors while also redrawing its boundaries. And if Browning regains her bearings in relation to concrete, everyday objects and acts— conveyed to us in a realist idiom attentive to things and processes—she also shifts frequently between literal and metaphorical registers. In *Around the House*, home renovation is clearly both physical and spiritual, the genre of how-to merged (as it is for Crusoe, our ur-survivor of domestic wreckage) with the genre of self-help. Throughout this text, the practical, embodied work of home renovation is also a mode of grieving, a trope for persevering, and a blueprint for domesticity reconfigured to suit the single mother.

Around the House opens with an inventory of loss measured out in tables and chairs: "After my husband moved out, I walked from one room to another, slowly, lingering in each doorway. That was where the painting of the ghostly man in the canoe had hung. That was where the armoire had stood, full of china for the next dinner party. Under that table had been a beautiful Persian rug. That was where I had once sat in a big, comfortable armchair and nursed my second son."[20] Recovering a degree of postmarital order and serenity means living with these ghosts while also, one humble item and task at a time, shifting into the present tense and replenishing empty spaces. Purging and purchasing, selecting and arranging, Browning must feel her way via the tactile and visual pleasures of homemaking. As queer phenomenologist Sara Ahmed might put it, Browning must get "oriented," figure out the where and how of her body and things, establish her physical relationship to a defamiliarized dwelling. Orientation, Ahmed would add, involves "registering the proximity of objects and others" and directing one's desiring attention here as opposed to there.[21] To address the sexual despair accompanying divorce, Browning must first become intimate with her surroundings, reinhabiting her body as it moves through the house—touching, adjusting, replacing, and bandaging.

Determined to update the master bedroom, Browning begins by exhorting us: "If your marriage has gone bad . . . burn the sheets. And start over" (29). Rolling up her sleeves, she patches her walls and paints them the elemental color of clay. She splurges on the best mattress she can find, a mile-deep featherbed, and the "softest possible throw" (30). But this bedroom is for more than lounging. Browning forgoes cute, matching nightstands and maneuvers into place a single, generously sized table. Thinking of the table as "command central" (30), she creates a place of pleasure and rest that is also a woman's headquarters. On this table, she assembles a mix of useful and sensuous things. In addition to books, a beloved painting, and a coaster for bottle or mug, she imports "an old crystal goblet (why save the good stuff for dinner parties?), a sturdy lamp, a few rocks from [her] favorite beach, the silver candelabra that certainly wasn't being used in the dining room, an ancient, softly glazed porcelain cup and saucer, and the remote control for the music box" (30). The result is a haven of her own, in which candlelight glances off surfaces polished by time: old crystal, ocean rocks, ancient cup, a woman's face. With music, goblet, and candelabra, the scene is set for celebration as well as meditation, herself the guest of honor.

Self-love is one thing, loneliness another, and at other times Browning's language of interior decoration is invoked to lament the loss of domestic partnership. In the chapter "Armchair Love," chairs nestled together look to her like couples reading side by side in cozy silence. "Whenever I saw pairs of chairs," she confesses, "I began to fantasize about occupying them, pairs of books, pairs of hearts. Every once in a while I would find myself craving that kind of quiet companionability" (108). The personification of furniture is repeated in a chapter about searching for a couch that is "stylish, yet dependable; relaxed, yet elegant; yielding, yet strong; mature, yet companionable" (79). Having flirted with many and settled on none, she is forced to admit, echoing Flannery

O'Connor, that "a good couch is hard to find" (79). Browning is fond of this conceit, in which domestic objects stand in for romantic ones. Returning to it more than once in subsequent columns written for *House & Garden*, she puts the comparison to various ends, in some cases to express her longing for the proverbial good man and in others to mock and redirect this longing.

Browning's editor's column in May 2007, for example, describes attempting to salvage a lonely Valentine's Day by treating herself to a "gorgeous, fluffy, nondenominational white cake smothered in coconut, just a little bigger than a cupcake." Tweaking Charlotte Brontë, the ever-literate editor closes this piece with the ringing apostrophe, "Reader, I ate it all."[22] The next month's column follows suit by narrating a friend's purchase of a table as an earth-shaking romance, radical enough to smash her old aesthetic and inspire a wholesale revamping. Catching sight of the "dark, handsome table," Browning explains, her friend "had fallen in love, the way people do, violently and unexpectedly. And nothing else seemed the same."[23] As with the elusive "good couch," in both of these more recent examples a dessert or antique is likened to a romantic partner. In the first case, it is only with considerable effort that a cake is ultimately enabled to trump a man, thus rewriting the usual "happy ending." In the second case, by contrast, Browning's column opens with, and assumes throughout, the primacy of furniture. To put this another way, whereas the May column invokes a household object in a tale that is really about yearning for heterosexual romance, the June column mobilizes the language of heterosexual romance for a tale that is really about a household object. Vehicle and tenor have now switched places so that this time, Browning's metaphor serves to dramatize the life-changing properties of a table in a love story approaching the fetishistic.

We see a similar oscillation in *Around the House*, in which sometimes a sofa is a figure for a lover, while at other times it remains comfortably inanimate, only to be redeployed as a figure for a woman navigating divorce. A notable instance of the latter occurs in the chapter "The New House." Browning begins by remarking that the best antidote for a spoiled romance is a new one, and she proceeds to tell the story of falling in love with a ramshackle house by the sea, which happens to coincide with a promising new man. "But it quickly became clear," she continues, "that, even while the house was in the most decrepit state possible, and the man at the height of his powers, so to speak, it was the house that was going to be around for the long haul" (94). As Browning observes, "It was the man who fell apart, beyond my repair. So I took on the challenge of bringing the house back to life, and I think at the same time I started to bring myself back to life" (94–95).

All this is to say that *Around the House* begins to propose, however tentatively, that things domestic may not symbolize a mate or even compensate for his loss so much as cheerfully replace him. "The New House" enacts a series of substitutions—from old lover, to new lover, to new house, to new self—mapping Browning's psychological journey to renewal and self-reliance. Another version of this trajectory is suggested by a chapter that opens by declaring, "I love having men around the house. Men with tools" (132). Sure, Browning admits, there are women who know about plumbing and electricity; she just doesn't happen to be one of them. Though her father was a master builder who once gave her a tool set, she never outgrew her dependence on men who could fix things (133–34). But here the chapter suddenly swerves, for while some repairmen in her past have been trustworthy, "others have been scoundrels, or worse, villains" (135). With this about-face, Browning turns, for the rest of the chapter, from missing men who know about gutters and furnaces to excoriating those who prove ignorant and unreliable. "Those guys don't know everything," she concludes, adding that she has finally begun to learn the art of self-repair (136).

Browning clearly cherishes connection. She mourns her ex, misses having a partner, loves sharing space with her two sons, and laments the prospect of an "empty nest." At the same time, *Around the House* asserts above all that Browning's nest isn't empty so long as she is in it. It provides, moreover, a welcome refuge "from others' anger, hysteria, bad behavior" (167). Stressing the importance of boundaries, Browning decides, at some expense, to fortify her yard with a "big, beautiful stone wall" (165), choosing stone because it feels so primal and immovable (167). Whether from an excess or deficiency of maternal feeling, she tells us she is tired of looking at the neighbor children and their plastic toys

(166). Yet the wall, Browning insists, is less to keep people out than to mark off and value what is within (167). The structure she has in mind is no rickety, "Leave It to Beaver" picket but a strong, lasting embrace of stone, built to defend the autonomy and to figure the self-custody of a single woman. "It can be very difficult," Browning says in the last pages, "to believe that you have the right to call what you are now making by yourself a home" (201). With this closing chapter, she affirms the right of all women to walk through the front door while calling out to no one but themselves: "Honey, I'm home!" (202).[24]

DOING IT YOURSELF

Coming now to the rather less introspective figure of Martha Stewart, we find ourselves on a first-name basis with someone I think of as the Hillary of homemaking, the Madonna of domesticity—a smart, hard-working, and strong-willed woman, whose person is synonymous with her high-grossing product and whose extraordinary success inspires equal shares of admiration and derision. A more sensational example than Browning of professional decorating juxtaposed with public divorce, Stewart offers expert advice on household matters against the backdrop of her own infamously disastrous marriage and uneasy motherhood. Unlike Browning, Stewart does not narrate this conjunction herself and would probably prefer to keep the one cordoned off from the other. Yet the proliferation of biographies, biopics, blogs, and general media overload regarding Stewart has made it virtually impossible to peruse the pages of *Martha Stewart Living* (or consume any number of other Martha Stewart products) in ignorance of her tumultuous and even scandalous personal life.[25] Completing my lineup of bad girls renowned as good housekeepers, I offer Stewart as the ultimate example of a woman whose story works to loosen the celebration of domesticity from its mooring in traditional family values.

A woman with a past if there ever was one, Martha is at once genteel and disreputable; high-flying entrepreneur and fallen woman; blonde, feminine ideal and aging divorcée. Her lurid history has been endlessly rehearsed: the Jersey girl who clawed her way up from working-class origins, tyrannized her husband until he left her for a younger woman, neglected her daughter while pursuing fame and fortune, and took the rap for insider trading—only to bounce back from incarceration seemingly undeterred and scarcely rumpled. All this coexists strangely with Martha's role as arbiter of good taste and domestic correctness, a contradiction that has not gone unnoticed. Indeed, there is an entire genre devoted to parodying Martha's homemaking advice as sadistic and delusional.[26] Our awareness of and interest in Martha is thus necessarily double: as much as we respond to domestically correct Martha, we are equally fascinated by her evil twin. Biographers love to play up the latter as a way of undercutting Martha's claims to refinement. For example, Jerry Oppenheimer delights in the irony and potential marketing disaster of her husband's departure in April 1987 at the very moment that Martha was promoting her elegant new book on weddings.[27] In fact, not only did the wedding book make a splash, but Martha's most popular and lucrative projects—the magazine *Martha Stewart Living* (1991), the televisual tie-ins (1993, 1997), the deal with Kmart (1997), and the incorporation of Martha Stewart Living Omnimedia (1999)—all took shape in the coming years, notwithstanding her contentious and well-publicized divorce. My own view, once again, is that Martha's appeal, from the standpoint of her female readership, is actually helped rather than hurt by her status as divorcee.

A primary aspect of her oppositional domesticity, in accord with what we have seen of shelter magazines generally, is the almost complete exclusion of children from Marthaland. Real-life daughter Alexis played one of her mother's sidekicks on Martha's short-lived version of *The Apprentice* (September–December 2005). But Lexi's evident discomfort in this role did little to dispel the public image of Martha as having been no June Cleaver.[28] Representations of sons and daughters alike are also, generally speaking, missing from the pages of Martha's best-known magazine. We recall that Castle mentions the occasional child-in-motion as an exception to the rule of deathly stillness, and tousled blond youngsters do make brief appearances in *Martha Stewart Living*. Overall, however, this publication bears out the logic we have seen in favor of deleting children—"children" being the category most profoundly antithetical to fastidiously curated rooms and tranquil autoeroticism. The same might be said of Martha's notoriously labor-intensive, do-it-yourself projects, which I take to mean projects best attempted in seclusion, beyond the reach of helpful little hands.[29] Fans interviewed in 1998 by ethnographers Ann Mason and Marian Meyers confirm this theory that Martha's projects are, almost by definition, at odds with maternal responsibilities. As these women explained to Mason and Meyers, they value the unbroken concentration and creativity required to paint a windowsill or recover a lampshade precisely because it represents a break from child care and serves to validate their extramaternal selves.[30] One overwhelmed but optimistic mother noted that she clips articles from *Martha Stewart Living* for later years, hoping to eventually have more time for making plum galettes and decorative shade pulls (812). It has often been remarked that Martha's absurdly intricate and unnecessary projects cater to fantasies of infinite leisure based on wealth.[31] While this is certainly true, there may also be something more shameful and subversive at work for female readers of shelter magazines: the fantasy of infinite leisure based on *childlessness*.

In keeping with the photo aesthetic previously described, *Martha Stewart Living* includes extended sections on interior design cleansed not only of children but also of human drama and debris more generally. Its images of white towels stacked thickly in rustic baskets by glistening, claw-foot tubs are positively virginal. In Marthaland, even a laundry room can look achingly beautiful—detergents lined up in matching decanters, dirty clothes stowed in neatly labeled muslin bins. Unlike *Elle Decor* or *Architectural Digest*, however, *Martha Stewart Living*'s untouched interiors are juxtaposed with more general household advice, including directions for hands-on projects like those just mentioned. As a result of its hybrid status (part shelter, part women's service) *Martha Stewart Living* adheres only partially to the shelter-mag ban on human figures.

Reflecting the corporate cult known as Martha, Inc., the person depicted most often in *Martha Stewart Living* is Stewart herself, who makes frequent appearances in its pages as well as on her television show and website, and in ads for her various products. Despite the wide circulation of her likeness, however, neither Martha Stewart nor *Martha Stewart Living* can be accused of pandering to the male gaze. Like other shelter magazines, *Martha Stewart Living* generally forgoes the beauty articles and downplays the beauty ads so ubiquitous in fashion and other publications aimed at women, featuring instead a wide range of activities and products tied to crafts, gardening, cooking, decorating, and home care. Mason and Meyers report that loyal readers of *Martha Stewart Living* specifically cited its varied content as a welcome alternative to the usual, single-minded preoccupation with weight gain and skin care (811–12). Mason and Meyers also found that fans admire Martha's own unfussy and realistic appearance: despite having modeled in her youth, she gardens in a tossed-on T-shirt and jeans, the same thing they themselves wear for working in the yard (816). It is just this eschewal of ingratiating sexiness that seems to have infuriated biographer Oppenheimer, who describes her as a "man-hater" (33) with a "cold and intimidating manner" (66). Yet I am convinced that for many women, Martha's unspoken resistance to compulsory heterosexuality is actually a significant aspect of her appeal.

At times a relatable Everywoman, "Martha Stewart" is also, of course, a marketing logo branding the innumerable product lines that swell her corporate empire, from Martha Stewart Thé (available in Martha's Breakfast Blend) to Martha Stewart Living Cabinets at Home Depot. There was even a special Martha Stewart Summer Edition of Triscuits. Elsewhere, our heroine takes the only slightly more human form of infallible expert: Martha-as-oracle. If we have any questions, magazine and website urge, we need only "Ask Martha."[32] In *Martha Stewart Living*, both personae are in play, disseminating Martha as global brand name while also proclaiming her house-and-garden know-how. Under the rubric "Where to Find Martha," we are directed outside the magazine to Martha on television, Martha on the radio, Martha as the genius behind various spin-off publications and goods. Another regular feature takes us inside: "From My Home to Yours" offers a glimpse of the Ideal that is Martha's Own House (handsomely framed maps massed on the wall, for example, as in her lodge on Mount Desert Island) for possible adaptation to our own shabby quarters.[33] Dominating the domestic sphere and saturating the public, the larger-than-life pundit and entrepreneur represented by *Martha Stewart Living* is a far cry both from the self-displaying mannequins of fashion magazines and from the self-effacing maternal ideal.

The aforementioned features, many of which include photographs of Martha, fall outside the shelter-mag logic of domesticity-without-people while also allowing this logic to function in other parts of the magazine. The same is true for the "how-to" portions of the magazine, which (echoing her televisual demonstrations) show Martha and others teaching us to pit cherries, reweb chairs, or master some other such arcane domestic technique. Magazine photos of this kind are typically framed to show, for example, only an aproned torso and a pair of hands effortlessly de-panning brownies (thanks to Martha's buttered parchment method). These anonymous figures might seem, at first glance, like the "hands" laboring in Victorian textile mills, reduced to instrumental body parts. In this context, however, far from being cogs in a larger machine, they are offered to us as domestic artists—citizens of Giard's Kitchen Women Nation whose skill and creativity we would do well to emulate. I conclude my discussion of Martha's various texts by claiming their obstinately *literal* investment in domestic practices: their step-by-step concreteness, their attention to the craft and sweat expended on small acts of manual labor.[34]

To a degree distinguishing her from Browning and others, Martha gets her hands dirty. Of course she has a large staff of helpers, but Oppenheimer's biography suggests that, behind the image of a woman clipping roses, is a woman attending a power lunch covered with scratches from—that's right—a punishing bout of clipping roses (265). Elsewhere he describes her "maniacally" painting entire houses, hand-mowing huge lawns, gardening at dawn, washing antique linens with lemon juice, stenciling floors until 2:00 A.M., and refusing for many years to hire a housekeeper (144–45). Depictions of Martha putting up fruit, chopping down trees, making paper from scratch, and generally displaying a perverse degree of pioneering spirit serve not only to model the survival of marital loss and the pleasures of an unpartnered domestic life but also to celebrate the artisanal work, physical and aesthetic, performed by all women who keep house.

If Browning explores the domestic largely as an aid to and figure for psychological survival, domesticity in Stewart—scarcely metaphorized, much less psychologized—is rendered in more exclusively material, external terms. Her practical competence reaches from linens to lawns, and, like Wharton, she does not hesitate to encroach on traditionally male turf. Born, according to family legend, with "a sewing needle in one hand and a hammer in the other," Stewart has little use for a housekeeper and none at all for men with tools.[35] A respondent in the Mason and Meyers study says it best:

> A lot of her how-tos are about, like, how to put windows in, how to replace a broken window. I think a lot of her stuff revolves around being single . . . having to do it on your own. . . . I kind of admire her going out and doing stuff on her own like that, instead of just calling somebody to help her. Because I know, being single, you can't depend on somebody. (813)

Having borrowed from Browning's therapeutic tool kit, women on their own look to Stewart for a hammer that is just a hammer.

FELONIOUS DOMESTICITY

These days, our houses may be "smarter," but our notions about gender and domesticity remain largely unreconstructed. For at least two centuries, the category of "home" has been, and continues to be, both feminized and moralized, well-managed domesticity closely aligned with womanly virtues. The proper, bourgeois domicile—clean, attractive, comfortable, and secure—is tied to and essentially code for womanhood idealized as beautiful, nurturing, and sexually contained. As I have argued, traditionalists affirm this construct, while left academics generally deride it, but neither is inclined to question the coupling of domesticity with normative sex/gender values. Frequently, of course, the connection holds true. There is nothing natural or intrinsic about it, however; this chapter has endeavored to claim Browning and Stewart, along with a handful of nineteenth- and early-twentieth-century precursors, for their ungrammatical linking of orderly houses and disordered femininity.

The "badness" of these domestic women lies above all in their flagrant pursuit of happiness for self rather than others. As we have seen, Browning renovates her life-after-divorce by framing her domesticity in increasingly autoerotic terms. With her sensuous boudoir, lust for furniture, love affair with houses, and espousal of baked goods, hers is an appetitive domesticity geared to self-pleasure. Stewart's immodesty, by contrast, takes the form of naked ambition. If earlier housekeepers were driven to market their skills by economic necessity, often to support their families, Stewart is voracious and frankly self-aggrandizing. To many, the jail time she served for insider trading was well-deserved punishment for overreaching; others argued she was singled out because good girls don't compete with boys for power in the public sphere.[36] Either way, the incident offered further evidence of a woman with unstoppable drive. Stewart's aggressive mobilization of domesticity, enacted on the corporate stage, also comes across in the "Ask Martha" imperatives of her magazine. Whereas earlier women offered helpful tips on home maintenance and decor, Stewart—as a matter of temperament reinforced by colossal wealth and status—bullies you into a prettier centerpiece or a better-organized mudroom. As one parody put it, capturing the tone with little exaggeration, "Martha Stewart's *Better Than You* at Entertaining."[37] Greedy, bossy, and boastful, Stewart is anything but ladylike. Her approach to domesticity is ruthless and not necessarily legal. Clearly it's exactly what we need to purge the House, finally, of that musty, iconic Angel.

5

UNDOCUMENTED HOMES

Histories of Dislocation in Immigrant Fiction

hapters 3 and 4 focused on women whose domestic lives had been made by marriage and were later unmade by divorce. Dominique Browning opens her memoir by explaining, "When I was divorced my sense of home fell apart."[1] She was, as we have seen, physically shaken, disoriented and estranged from domestic objects and spaces, pressed to reinvent her relation to tables and chairs, bedroom and front door. Like Edith Wharton and Martha Stewart, Browning was divided by divorce not only from a spouse and familiar modes of everyday life but also from notions of proper womanhood and exemplary domesticity. Yet rather than relinquish a claim to domestic authority, all three of these figures continued to assert it—indeed, declaimed in print, advertised, and professionalized their expertise as home decorators and advisers. Wharton did so with the design manual that launched her career. As I have argued, its museumlike rooms served to conjure, in advance of her actual divorce, a separateness from marital disorder. And if Wharton's domestic vision is unsentimental, Stewart's multinational conglomeration has seemed humorous, if not a little scandalous, in its pairing of napkin folding with empire building. (A *New Yorker* cartoon has her taking over the universe, planning brunch on distant planets.)[2] My aim in both chapters has been to take another shot at killing the Angel in the House—without, however, forgoing the house. I have wanted, instead, to install the anti-angel, to find a place at the table for the bad girl, to acknowledge the work (professionalized or not) of keeping house, to affirm modes of domesticity alienated from conventional family forms and values.

My examples of divorced domesticity serve, in addition, to rephrase the point made by earlier chapters that "home," however invested in stability, is always vulnerable and provisional. Though commonly defined in opposition to travel—the inert beginning and end of expedition—in truth, it is never entirely fixed or singular. We recall that Wharton sold The Mount and reestablished herself in France following her divorce in 1913. With a multiplied, multicultural sense of "home," she has something in common with the fictional characters, the first-person narrators of works by American immigrant writers, to whom I turn in this chapter. Like them, Wharton's experience of living in two countries was crucially informed by gender. She was honored by both the United States and France, yet during her periods of residence could vote in neither. (French women did not gain the franchise until 1944.) At the same time, Wharton's wealth, whiteness, and celebrity significantly cushioned her migration as a woman on her own, as did her origin in the United States and her history of extensive travel to Europe. The author of The Decoration of Houses represents a very particular kind of voluntary migrant: the cosmopolitan American expat, whose travels and eventual settling abroad are underwritten by economic privilege rather than pressure. Certainly, Wharton's version of transplanted domesticity differs dramatically from that of another woman traveling alone— Jamaica Kincaid's eponymous narrator Lucy, who leaves the West Indies for a U.S. household to work as an au pair. As with the other immigrants I'm considering, with family origins in Mexico and Japan, Lucy's new domesticity is informed by the fact that her body and background are categorized as nonwhite. Consequently, while encountering numerous gender constraints, the Angel in the House is not one of them. As an Afro-Caribbean woman, Lucy is eligible to abet but never to embody this Anglo ideal.[3] And if Martha Stewart is a white-collar felon, the domesticity of this chapter's immigrant characters risks being felonious for a rather different reason: by virtue of past and present U.S.

decrees restricting their entry, curtailing their freedom, or sending them "home" through racialized laws of national exclusion.[4]

While all immigrants are outsiders to some degree, the outsiderness of those discussed here is thus heightened both by their own, racially marked bodies and by their ties to groups with histories of subordination in a U.S. and/or British context. In analyzing the challenges of immigrant homemaking, my readings attend to the traumatic backstories of these groups as well as to the foregrounded stories of individuals. Focusing on the relatively harsh physical and psychological experiences of dislocation, nonbelonging, and attempts to remake home, this section harks back to the outcasts of chapters 1 and 2: the fictional Jess Goldbergs and Mary Bartons whose domestic labor and longings are fueled by an extremity of loss in the past and continued insecurity in the present. Although not every text features shelter writing, several include the kind of blow-by-blow process writing we have seen elsewhere, in which characters perform a series of microactions marking their approach to a homier environment. In all of them, the specter of bad homes as well as forced removal impinges on immigrants' efforts to make themselves at home. Examples of tentative, incomplete domestic arrangements—deficient in dreamed-of safety, beauty, autonomy, and belonging—recall my opening chapters and anticipate my turn in chapter 6 to homes in the context of "homelessness."

My inquiry centers on three narratives of dwelling after national dislocation, each written by a woman who shares the immigrant background of her protagonist: *The House on Mango Street* (1984) by Sandra Cisneros; *Lucy* (1990) by Jamaica Kincaid; and *Blu's Hanging* (1997) by Lois-Ann Yamanaka. Published over a thirteen-year period, they represent a body of work appearing in the wake of late-twentieth-century social movements on behalf of women and minorities and coinciding with critical attention to literary contributions by members of these groups. Cisneros and Kincaid explicitly reference the tradition of British women writers recovered by feminist critics beginning in the late 1970s. Invoking this tradition while also offsetting its whiteness, all three books are narrated in the first person by a girl or woman of color. Despite their similarity as immigrant texts of the post–Bernard Malamud period, their renderings of domesticity are differentiated, first of all, by the characters' countries of origin, a factor that includes the histories of particular racial/national groups in the United States. The settling efforts of my immigrant characters are underwritten by such distinct collective traumas as the Mexican American War and ongoing border violence; chattel slavery in North America; the subjugation of Antigua under British colonial rule; and the internment of Japanese Americans during World War II. The characters I discuss are also differentiated by how long they have been in the United States; the circumstances of their emigration and resettlement; their work, education, and other elements of class status; their identities as feminine or masculine; and their position as children or adults. Variations of this kind—especially those of generation, gender, sexuality, and class—play out within as well as among my texts, and Yamanaka takes the further step of dramatizing tensions among immigrant groups.

As I began by noting in relation to Wharton, the effect of considering migrant domesticity is to multiply the meaning of home—and then, contrasting Wharton with a character like Kincaid's Lucy, to multiply it again. The special value of this topic for a book claiming the home lives of outsiders is to insist that domesticity, including nontraditional domesticity, cannot be reduced to a single, unchanging essence (whether negative or positive). Certainly we find recurrent, cross-cultural components—from daily routines to places-for-objects to feelings of security—but the meaning and priority of these components is never the same from one household to the next or even within a single household. The following analyses will, I hope, succeed in bringing out two things: the particularity and special precariousness of immigrant households, along with the larger point that to varying degrees, *all* homes are continuously in flux.[5] As a preface to my readings, I suggest four overlapping ways in which the category of "home" is unstable—each of them intensified and, for our purposes, usefully magnified by migration.

1.   *Homes are vulnerable.* Physical structures may burn, flood, or fall into ruin. Individuals or entire households may remove to a different

neighborhood or distant country, layering new versions of home atop earlier ones. A person's departure or death may have the further effect of disrupting "home" for those left behind. In *Blu's Hanging*, for example, a mother's death throws her family into a crisis that is practical as well as emotional, registered most immediately by the breakdown in routines of cooking and caretaking.

2. *Home cultures are impure.* Domestic practices are hybrid as a result of diverse cultural influences as well as the imbrication of old and new technologies. This is especially, though not exclusively, true of immigrant households. In *Zami: A New Spelling of My Name*, Audre Lorde describes her Grenadian-born mother living in upper Manhattan pounding garlic and spices in a Puerto Rican mortar.[6] Lorde herself, or so I imagine, might employ this same technique for a Westernized Indian curry and later use a microwave for reheating leftovers.[7]

3. *Households of more than one person are heterogeneous.* We tend to forget that multiple perspectives on home may cluster under one roof. The domestic realities of men and women, adults and children, first- and second-generation immigrants, employers and employees are never the same, and they are almost always structured by inequality.[8] One person's leisure at home may depend on another's domestic labor. One person's sense of order at home may feel to another like unbearable constraint. A stark example is offered by Chimamanda Adichie's "The Arrangers of Marriage" (2009), in which a woman from Lagos is married off to a Nigerian living in New York. *His* devotion to American cooking is just one aspect of *her* collision with the demands of an ugly and alien domesticity.

4. *Homes are dynamic.* With the passing of time, whether a day or a decade, domestic life must continually adapt to a host of fluctuating circumstances: physical, affective, technological, economic, and social changes at both the micro- and macrolevels. Dust and clutter accumulate, people and things grow older, appliances are modernized, relationships evolve, landlords die, families are reconfigured, food prices fluctuate, neighborhoods are gentrified. Even a sense of continuity with the past must be actively produced and renewed on a regular basis. It is women,

immigrant or not, who tend to do the work of adaptation, of accommodating change while also creatively mediating between past and present. In Gish Jen's *Mona in the Promised Land* (1996), set in the volatile late 1960s, a first-generation Chinese American mother takes it in stride when the family's flower beds are wrecked by careless drivers: "They can replant. They're the type to adjust."[9] Yet Mrs. Chang also retains her role as unyielding authority on foodstuffs in the old country. "I'm telling you," she informs her daughter Mona, "tomatoes *invented* in China. . . . It's true. Like noodles. Invented in China."[10] She admits, however, to padding her memories of the homeland, and American-born Mona regales her friends with tall tales about Chinese cuisine freely improvised for the occasion.[11] Clearly, it is "China" itself as a foundation for Chinese American domesticity that is invented and revised as circumstances require.[12]

Vulnerable, hybrid, heterogeneous, and dynamic—all these attributes serve to debunk received, naturalized notions of home as inert and one-dimensional. All argue, instead, for the domestic as a site of change and complexity. What they suggest, too, is the invented-ness of domestic life, a process all the more urgent and explicit at the moment of reinvention in a foreign national context. The *doing* of domesticity involves labor that is physical and affective as well as ideological, and women generally get the brunt of it. Ironically, however, housekeepers spend much of their energy sustaining the illusion of sameness, creating the impression that from day to day, nothing much has changed. Preserving the status quo, home maintenance masks itself as the natural result of inaction and restraint. "What did you do all day?" asks the husband returning to a house whose tidiness appears undisturbed. Yet we hardly need Marxist feminists (or Elizabeth Gaskell) to tell us that the illusion of sameness—bodies still breathing, food still edible, rooms salvaged from the forces of entropy, goods flowing in, and waste flowing out—actually requires a never-ending expenditure of effort, tireless running simply to stay in place.[13] Likewise, in first-generation households, the preservation of old-country cultural identity results not from a passive traditionalism or refusal to assimilate but instead from the active, daily regeneration of this identity, usually by women, through physically demanding and affectively charged rituals of cooking, dress, and housekeeping. There are, I think, three conclusions to be drawn from all this, claims that should be familiar from previous chapters but that bear repeating: first, in numerous ways, home is both changeable and multiple; second, home is both a discursive construct and the product of ongoing, often unrecognized labor; and third, however ultimately unstable, home nevertheless takes shape in answer to yearnings for some degree of predictability and continuity.

Drawing on various realist genres for their careful renderings of everyday life—novels, memoirs, house manuals, women's magazines, and ethnographies—a major project of this book overall has been to counter the abstract ideology of domesticity with an insistent domestic materialism. Instead of reducing the actual diversity of houses and housekeepers to conservative ideas about home and family, my goal throughout has been to stress the variability of domestic arrangements; to highlight the gendered labor that produces them; and to legitimate the desire they instantiate for stability and attachment. I am counting on images of immigrant households to help in further depicting this variability and this labor. Affirming a logic we have seen before, the texts examined in this chapter also tell of domestic labor made all the more meaningful by a context of upheaval. For while immigrant homes obviously speak to the instability I have parsed, they also, *for this very reason*, speak to the desire for dwelling as opposed to traveling, for repetition in lieu of change. They offer, if anything, an especially acute version of the impulse to settle in, arrange one's things, develop routines, draw boundaries, form attachments, and achieve a sense of personal security and cultural belonging. The extent to which my immigrant characters succeed in acting on this impulse—one that may include but should not be reduced to the goal of assimilation—varies widely. Nor do my four figures approach homemaking in identical ways or pursue it to the same degree. The effect of their stories is nevertheless similar: to dramatize the value of domestic endeavors even when (or because) they are embattled and experimental.

THE HOUSE ON MANGO STREET:
WHAT ABOUT A HOUSE?

"We didn't always live on Mango Street," Cisneros's girl narrator explains. With these opening words, Esperanza establishes and destabilizes the place she lives. "Before that," she continues, "we lived on Loomis on the third floor, and before that we lived on Keeler. Before Keeler it was Paulina, and before that I can't remember. But what I remember most is moving a lot."[14] Stressing her family's continual dislocation in space, Esperanza also situates their current residence as the last in a historical series. The book begins with domesticity defined as mobile in two senses, with a trajectory spanning time as well as space. In what follows, I will pursue the interest in "before" established by Cisneros's very first sentences, extending it to include a longer, collective history of migration and insecure residency.

The second chapter of *The House on Mango Street* is a celebration of "Hairs": the plurality of hair types in Esperanza's family, from Papa's "broom" and Mama's "rosettes" to Carlos's "straight" locks and Kiki's "fur" (6). Differentiating among family members, the description honors the diversity and hybridity of Chicano and Chicana bodies, evincing centuries of miscegenation among indigenous, Spanish, African, and Anglo peoples. Only in the fourth chapter, "My Name," does Esperanza explicitly mention bilingualism (contrasting the English meaning of her name with Spanish ones) along with her Mexican ancestry (10). But the hybridity of her milieu has already been suggested by "Hairs" as well as by the street names of chapter 1: English "Loomis" and Scottish "Keeler" yielding to Latinate "Paulina" and Mango Street itself, with its non-tropical stand of elm trees (4).

Quickly manifesting the instability and hybridity of Esperanza's home life, Cisneros's novel proceeds to take as its primary concern an exploration of domestic heterogeneity—the differences and possible conflicts among people sharing a space delimited by four walls. Familial variation is, we have seen, lovingly introduced by "Hairs," which closes with "Mama's hair that smells like bread" and the comfort of her body "when she makes room for you on her side of the bed" (7). The very next chapter, however, points to a more negative dynamic within households. "Boys & Girls" describes a gender order that refuses to "make room" for girls. "The boys and girls live in separate worlds," Esperanza complains. Once in public, brothers Carlos and Kiki gang up against girls, leaving the narrator to babysit her younger sister (8). And while this chapter suggests that girls outside the house are ignored, in later chapters ("The First Job," "The Monkey Garden," and "Red Clowns") the public is portrayed as a sphere in which girls routinely risk sexual assault.

As vignettes pile up and Esperanza grows older, the book's feminist protest builds. The denigration of girls outside is bad, but the fate of women locked inside is worse, and adult males prove far more oppressive than brothers. Esperanza's great-grandmother (11), Louie's cousin Marin (27), Rosa Vargas (29), Alicia (31–32), Ruthie (68–69), Mamacita (77–78), Rafaela (79–80), Sally (81, 92–93, 101–2), Minerva (84–85), and Esperanza's own mother (90–91)—all these women are depicted, in chapter after chapter, as suffering variously from domestic servitude, immobilization, frustrated creativity, and violence. No wonder Esperanza repudiates the fate of her great-grandmother, a "wild horse of a woman" forcibly taken and tamed by the man who married her. For the rest of her life, "she looked out the window . . . the way so many women sit their sadness on an elbow." "I have inherited her name," our narrator informs us, "but I don't want to inherit her place by the window" (11). Three generations back, the birthright of an unbridled life was stolen from Esperanza's ancestress. The dilemma facing her namesake is what to do with an empty inheritance.

Of all the abused female characters, it is the narrator's friend Sally whose ordeal stretches most painfully across several chapters of the book and successive phases of Sally's girlhood. It begins with a father who confines and hits her like a dog in an effort to police her emerging sexuality: "He thinks I'm going to run away like his sisters who made the family ashamed. Just because I'm a daughter" (92). Tragically, Sally's struggle to own her body and its desires only occasions further violence at male hands. Desperate for love, she actually fends off Esperanza's intervention when a "game" of teasing in the monkey garden verges on gang rape (96–98). But the ending of Sally's story is saddest of all—she escapes her father only to become the child bride of another violent man. Kept inside and forbidden even to sit by the window, Sally turns for comfort to the trappings of married domesticity: "She looks at all the things they own: the towels and the toaster, the alarm clock and the drapes. She likes looking at the walls, at how neatly their corners meet, the linoleum roses on the floor, the ceiling smooth as wedding cake" (102).

"Ownership" of towels paid for by the loss of personal freedom. Female subjugation in the shape of a toaster. A woman's gaze tracing the outlines of her captivity: walls, floor, and ceiling. Here and throughout *The House on Mango Street*, domestic things and spaces often seem antithetical if not fatal to female development and empowerment. The felicitous house explored by my earlier chapters is particularly elusive in this story of Chicana girlhood and neighborhood.[15] Instead, the portrayal of Sally and others recalls the images of female confinement identified by Sandra Gilbert and Susan Gubar as typical of nineteenth-century British and American writing by women.[16] And if *The House on Mango Street* resonates with *Jane Eyre*'s trope of an incarcerated wife, it shares even more with *Wide Sargasso Sea*, Jean Rhys's rewriting of Brontë's novel from a *mestiza* point of view.[17]

Despite her emphasis on the confines of Mango Street, Cisneros does offer a glimpse or two of liberation from the "gothic" house. Her antidote to enclosure is not, however, adventure on the open road. In Esperanza's imagination, freedom lies not in the absence of walls but in walls that make a refuge rather than a cage. Rescuing Sally in her mind, she pictures her friend walking away from Mango Street: "And maybe your feet would stop in front of a house, a nice one with flowers and big windows and steps for you to climb up two by two upstairs to where a room is waiting for you" (82). The windows would latch, but they would also "swing open, all the sky would come in" (82–83). There would be no laundry to do or patriarchal rules to obey; unlike the monkey garden, there would be safety. As Esperanza concludes, it would be a place to sleep and wake undisturbed and "never have to think who likes and doesn't like you" (83).

In the penultimate vignette, "A House of My Own," the narrator imagines something similar for herself. Her dream of a genuine domesticity was first announced in chapter 1, inspired by alienation from Mango Street: "I knew then I had to have a house. A real house. One I could point to. But this isn't it. The house on Mango Street isn't it" (5). A hundred pages later, her ideal is still defined in part by what it *isn't*: "Not a flat. Not an apartment in back. Not a man's house. Not a daddy's" (108). The need to negate—to dismantle the master's house, rebutting both poverty and patriarchy—is clearly ongoing. But here, at long last, Cisneros also permits her narrator a place she can point to:

> A house all my own. With my porch and my pillow, my pretty purple petunias. My books and my stories. My two shoes waiting beside the bed. Nobody to shake a stick at. Nobody's garbage to pick up after.
>
> Only a house quiet as snow, a space for myself to go, clean as paper before the poem. (108)

As with Esperanza's fantasy for Sally, this is a vision not of travel but of arrival. A girl climbs her own steps onto her own porch and enters a space of beauty and solitude. Her shoes are off, placed neatly by the bed; she is home now and won't be needing them anytime soon. The place is pretty, quiet, and clean, with no one else to mess it up. Head on her pillow, she sleeps as soundly as Sally with her sky-filled windows. This time, however, there is no mention of windows or sky. With its books and stories, its blank page and inward gaze, Esperanza's is a particular kind of house—the meditative house of a writer (figure 5.1).

Suggesting once again the plurality of domesticities, this house differs from Sally's sky-house and from the American Dream house longed for by her credulous parents: big lawn, at least three bathrooms, its color (of course) white (4). As June Dwyer observes, Esperanza's dream house is "not *white* as snow, but *quiet* as snow. It is not *white* as paper before a poem but *clean* as paper."[18] Rather, as suggested by the pretty petunias, its signature color is purple, a color that Cisneros, citing Mexican and Tejano precedents, later painted her own house in San Antonio (on which more shortly).

FIGURE 5.1 Sandra Cisneros in her study, Chicago, ca. 1982. (Photograph by Diana Solís)

In an earlier chapter, Esperanza has her cards read by the "witch woman" Elenita. Unlike Sally's sterile prison, Elenita's home is described as a space of creative chaos: dirty dishes, crazy kids, TV cartoons jumbled together with the accoutrements of prophecy and cure (62–64). I want to double-back briefly to this chapter for its representation of working-class Chicana self-expression in the domestic sphere. As Amalia Mesa-Bains explains in another context, everyday Chicana aesthetic practices may include the curating of home altars, shrines characterized by dense "arrangements of bric-a-brac, memorabilia, devotional icons, and decorative elements."[19] Elenita's refrigerator appears to be topped by just such an assemblage: "holy candles, some lit, some not, red and green and blue, a plaster saint and a dusty Palm Sunday cross, and a picture of the voodoo hand taped to the wall" (63). A *mestiza* space melding voodoo and Catholicism, Bugs Bunny and *los espíritus*, Elenita's home is also the workplace of a female artist and visionary. Yet though Esperanza admires the witch woman's remedies for headache and heartache, she is dismayed by her reading: a "dark man on a dark horse," going to a wedding, losing "an anchor of arms" (63–64). "What about a house," the narrator demands, "because that's what I came for" (64). Between kids fighting and Esperanza doubting, Elenita must repeat her answer several times: "I see a home in the heart" (64). Our narrator, however, has little patience for romantic platitudes. "Is that *it?*" she asks sadly (64).

Lest there be any doubt, returning now to the book's finale, we see at a glance that Elenita's home-in-the-heart, like the crowded house on Mango Street, isn't *it*. Esperanza's domestic ideal—"quiet as snow" and "clean as paper"—seems to be the inverse of Elenita's traditional Chicana one, with its aesthetic of accumulation (kids as well as things). In the purity of its retreat from distraction, along with its rejection of sentimental clichés, this writer's house more strongly suggests a kinship to Wharton, secure in her private penetralia. Geoffrey Sanborn reasons similarly in an essay on privacy in Cisneros. Defending what he calls her "politics of private enjoyment," he links her in this regard to the famously reclusive Emily Dickinson. The most obvious literary comparison, of course, made explicit by the title of this section, is to Virginia Woolf's *A Room of One's Own* (1929). For many critics, the question raised by all such resemblances is whether Cisneros's feminism should be seen as aligned with a tradition of Anglo-American women writers rather than with the Chicano/a community. Those who accept this characterization may do so in appreciative terms (Sanborn) or critical ones (Alejandro Morales). Either way, the upshot is similar: *The House on Mango Street* is read as only marginally interested in ethnic affiliation or else as featuring a heroine who disavows this affiliation altogether.[20]

I have observed that Esperanza is no Elenita, but I would also insist that neither is she reducible to a Dickinson, Wharton, or Woolf. As I am not the first to suggest, Cisneros's gender concerns in *The House on Mango Street* are substantially shaped and differentiated by her background as a Mexican American woman (no less than Woolf's are comparably shaped).[21] If we want to understand why Cisneros closes her novel with a reference to Woolf, we need to focus on how she revises her source text to address the specificity of Chicana girlhood. Taking up this issue, a number of critics have argued that Cisneros extends Woolf's purview (and that of feminism generally) simply by introducing a brown protagonist. In "More Room of Her Own: Sandra Cisneros's *The House on Mango Street*" (1994), Jacqueline Doyle explores the influence of

Woolf's feminist polemic while also stressing its "class and ethnic biases." Cisneros, she asserts, "covertly transforms the terms of Woolf's vision, making room in the female literary tradition for a young working-class Chicana."[22] While Doyle's essay associates *The House on Mango Street* with a more inclusive feminism, Marci McMahon takes us from a pluralistic framing of Cisneros's revision to an intersectional one. According to McMahon's *Domestic Negotiations: Gender, Nation, and Self-Fashioning in US Mexicana and Chicana Literature and Art* (2013), Cisneros revises Woolf by theorizing the identity axis of race as well as gender.[23] *The House on Mango Street*, I agree with McMahon, is less a call to "make room" for Esperanza in Woolf's paradigm than the basis for a new one prompted by Chicana subjectivity.[24]

How, then, should we understand the ethnic particularity of Cisneros's feminist domesticity? We might begin, still following McMahon's lead, by identifying *The House on Mango Street* as a Chicana critique aimed specifically at the gender politics of Chicano nationalism (106).[25] Nationalist discourse, she explains, "valorized male authority in the household" and idealized Chicanas as "mothers of the nation, configuring women as reproducers of conservative and normative constructions of culture, family, and tradition" (111). As we have seen, *The House on Mango Street* strongly rejects the traditional family as the basis for Chicano/a identity and proceeds to reinvent the home as a site of female autonomy and creativity. In McMahon's view, Cisneros's Chicana critique further involves downplaying the concept of Aztlán or Aztec homeland (which roots nationalist demands in ancient territorial claims to the American Southwest) in favor of a trope reflecting her female perspective. "Utilizing the symbol of the house, and not the land," McMahon argues, "shifts from the heroic symbols of Chicano/a nationalism, to represent the ideological, cultural, and economic limits imposed on a young Chicana" (107).[26]

Departing here from McMahon, I take issue with the view that Cisneros's Chicana feminism leads her to displace a nationalist emphasis on "land" with an alternative emphasis on "house." My own argument—bear with me as I set this up—takes us back for a closer look at Cisneros's riff on Woolf's famous title. What exactly is accomplished by her rewording of *A Room of One's Own* as "A House of My Own"? There is, first of all, the unmasking of Woolf's "one" as a false universal, a move in keeping with the feminist wariness, building throughout the 1980s, of language presuming to generalize about all women. Substituting "my" for Woolf's "indefinite" pronoun, Cisneros stakes a definite claim for a girl named Esperanza. The implications of her second change are less obvious and, I believe, more broadly resonant. How does Cisneros transform Woolf's metaphor by substituting "house" for "room"? What is the difference between a "house" and a "room," and what is the relation of each to the third category of "land"?

To answer these questions, we must return to the opening chapter with its oddly dejected announcement of home ownership. As Esperanza informs us, after moving from rental to rental, "the house on Mango Street is ours, and we don't have to pay rent to anybody" (3). "But even so," she continues, "it's not the house we'd thought we'd get" (3), and the chapter ends with Esperanza reiterating that Mango Street is not the "real house" she has been seeking (5). There are several respects in which Mango Street might be seen as "unreal," the first being its decrepit condition and inadequate space (4). (Cisneros means, of course, for us to understand quite the opposite: what's actually unreal are the television dream houses.) Mango Street also feels unreal because Esperanza still recalls the time that a nun, passing her old house on Loomis, doubted its being habitable. "You live *there*? The way she said it made me feel like nothing" (5). The narrator's shame illustrates what Monika Kaup describes as "the power of public norms to disqualify the reality of the houses of poor and nonwhite families."[27] Like Loomis, Mango seems unreal because its poverty weighs on those who live there and also because in another sense, it carries no weight at all—is, indeed, scarcely visible or imaginable to those outside the barrio. (As we will see, the domestic arrangements of the homeless are less visible still.)

This brings me to the last reason the house on Mango Street, though nominally owned, might still feel shaky and illegitimate: the fact that, for generation after generation of Mexican Americans, *ownership* itself has been unrecognized and rendered, effectively, unreal. Because this history is frequently overlooked, I will touch very briefly on some pertinent events. The story of dispossession begins with the U.S. annexation of Texas in 1845, followed by the Mexican American War (1846–1848). Spurred by expansionist fervor—in particular, the desire to take California—the invasion of Mexico was initiated on a military pretext and rationalized by the imperialist logic of "Manifest Destiny." As historian Amy Greenberg has stressed, the war was not unopposed at the time. Among others, Abraham Lincoln (then in Congress) debunked the fiction that Mexico had provoked the conflict by shedding blood on American soil. It was U.S. troops, Lincoln asserted, who took the first step of advancing into Mexico, causing residents to flee and "leaving unprotected their homes and their growing crops."[28] Ulysses S. Grant, serving as a lieutenant, wrote home decrying the atrocities committed by American soldiers and, in later years, condemned the war as "wicked."[29] Despite such sentiments, the U.S. Army continued its advance into California, New Mexico, and as far south as Mexico City. As Howard Zinn recounts in his classic, revisionist textbook, when the war ended, "There were calls among Americans to take all of Mexico. The Treaty of Guadalupe Hidalgo, signed February 1848, just took half. The Texas boundary was set at the Rio Grande; New Mexico and California were ceded."[30]

For Mexicans living in newly ceded areas, the appropriation of Mexican territory was followed by decades of further infringement of their right to landownership. Under the Treaty of Guadalupe Hidalgo, Mexicans in these areas were given the option of U.S. citizenship along with the property rights guaranteed thereby. According to legal scholars, however, by the time the treaty was ratified, it had been carefully modified to dilute and muddle the protection of Mexican land rights. As Kim David Chanbonpin asserts, "The history of the Treaty reveals a desire on the part of the United States to speed the transfer of Mexican-owned lands to Anglo settlers."[31] Bearing out this desire, even those protections specifically promised by the treaty were, in the coming years, ignored at all levels of government. President James Polk downplayed them, and his secretary of state declared them unenforceable (305–6). Courts and other adjudicating bodies found reasons to set aside legal precedent where Mexican claims were concerned (298–99). It was thus no coincidence that land claims filed in the decades after 1848 were settled overwhelmingly in favor of Anglos, effecting the dispossession of Mexican Americans on a massive scale. By the 1870s, Californios, for example, had lost three-quarters of their former lands (306).[32]

Since then, the exploitation of migrant workers combined with recurrent anti-immigrant hysteria and vacillating immigration policies has meant that Mexican and Mexican American people as well as lands have never been secure. The history of personal insecurity, in frequent violation of U.S. and international laws, includes lynching and other forms of mob violence, abusive labor practices, separation of families, human rights violations by immigration officials, and denied or abridged citizenship rights. A particularly egregious example was the forcible "repatriation" of people of Mexican descent implemented during the Great Depression. Legal scholar Kevin R. Johnson estimates that about a million people were removed during this period, 60 percent of whom were U.S. citizens.[33] "Legally," Johnson observes, "the repatriation program violated the rights of persons of Mexican ancestry in almost too many ways to mention. . . . The Due Process, Equal Protection, and Fourth Amendment rights of persons stopped, detained, and deported from the United States were sacrificed" (9). Tying this program to subsequent rights violations, Johnson cites the "deportation of Mexican immigrants and Mexican-American citizens in 1954 in a massive operation known as Operation Wetback" (10); "the militarization of the border that began in the 1990s [resulting] in the deaths of hundreds, if not thousands, of people, almost all of Mexican ancestry" (10); and the use of racial profiling, harassing citizens and terrorizing communities, in recent campaigns to round up undocumented immigrants (10–12).

Internationally recognized borders, the Treaty of Guadalupe Hidalgo, deeds for Mexican land grants, U.S. birth certificates and naturalization papers, the U.S. Constitution—all these legalities have often proved insufficient to protect the right of Mexicans and Mexican Americans to, as it were, stand their ground. Given this sketch of the barrio's extended "before," we can now revisit Cisneros with a fuller sense of why technical home ownership might fall short of feeling safe, stable, *real*. In the experience of Mexican Americans going back to the nineteenth century, title has not always ensured entitlement. Cisneros gives a current example of dispossession at the ur-level of identity in the chapter "Geraldo

No Last Name." Sleeping in rented rooms, working in a restaurant, and sending money back to Mexico, the title character goes to a dance and dies on the way home. Despite being young and pretty in his "shiny shirt and green pants" (66), Geraldo is an all but invisible man—"Just another *brazer* who didn't speak English. Just another wetback" (66)—so anonymous and expendable that his death barely registers on either side of the border. The driver didn't stop, the surgeon didn't show, and the family will never learn his fate. Geraldo typifies, in short, the plight of Mexicans who exist en masse as a source of cheap labor while being effaced as individuals with personal identities, family lineages, linguistic traditions, and cultural affiliations. If Geraldo's death seems to be a nonevent, it may be because the United States has already sentenced him to social death, because he has already been discounted at an ontological as well as civil level.

All this will, I hope, enable us to address my earlier question about why our Chicana protagonist requires not just a room but a house, and it better be a *real* one. As I see it, there are four significant differences between Woolf's and Cisneros's architectural tropes. To consider them one at a time is to mark the originality and specificity of 1980s Chicana feminism, its use as well as its revision of the 1929 text so formative for Anglo-American feminists:

1.   Unlike a room, a house sits on, takes up, and stakes a claim on land. In my reading, Cisneros doesn't oppose "house" to "land" but offers it in lieu of "room" precisely for its inextricability from "land." In this sense, the house ideal doesn't distance itself from the notion of Aztlán; instead, it brings the desire for female autonomy together with the demand for Mexican American turf.

2.   Unlike a room, a house has a title; that is, it has an explicit legal status. In theory, at least, it can be bought and sold, bequeathed and inherited. For a girl doubly disinherited as great-granddaughter and Mexican American, a house is real if the prerogatives of title are real—if both her freedom to leave and her right to stay are truly upheld by law, unimpeachable by family or country.

3.   Unlike a room, a house has an outside as well as an inside. As the book's title and opening chapter emphasize, a house has a public identity in relation to a street. Kaup observes that "Esperanza's education takes

place primarily in the street," and the very "design of *The House on Mango Street* is street-oriented. Its episodic structure follows the movement of street life, where events begin and end suddenly."[34] By embedding the house in a matrix of streets thematically and formally, Cisneros stresses not only the privacy it enables but also the communal spaces it addresses and helps constitute. Identified with a street, a house further partakes of a neighborhood, and though outsiders may be fearful, for Esperanza the barrio spells familiarity and safety. "All brown all around, we are safe," she explains. "But watch us drive into a neighborhood of another color and our knees go shakity-shake" (28). A safe house for Esperanza thus depends on solidarity with her Latino community, even (or especially) if no longer located inside the barrio.

4.   Unlike a room, its widely visible exterior also means that a house beseeches public acceptance. Rooms can go rogue, but houses are often expected, and sometimes required, to comply with local norms. What happens to Esperanza's house if, situated in a predominantly Anglo neighborhood, it embodies a minority aesthetic causing it to stand out from the rest? Strangely enough, a controversy involving Cisneros's own, actual house proved to be a case in point. Fourteen years after publishing *The House on Mango Street*, she was inspired to paint her San Antonio residence a shade of "Mexican" purple, only to have the color vetoed by the Historic Design and Review Commission as "incorrect" for her neighborhood. Cisneros stood her ground, however, demanding recognition for her own purple house and the Tejano residents whose historical presence, real but undocumented, had been omitted from the record.[35] If a house (but not a room) can represent loyalty to a particular ethnic community, this example suggests it can also petition the dominant culture on behalf of that community and its aesthetic traditions.

My argument has been that Esperanza's "house of my own" is a vision of reparation responsive to multiple forms of disinheritance and dispossession. Sheltering a girl who likes to tell stories, it also elaborates on Woolf by claiming for Chicanas and Chicanos a place of their own in the neighborhood and, by extension, the nation. Among the broader conclusions Cisneros enables us to reach are the following: domesticity can give girls room or take it away; each domesticity has a history, which may include forcible as well as voluntary relocation; houses and their streets can be vivid, eponymous characters—dynamic, colorful, and contentious; houses can help us to think through the past as the basis for making demands on the future.

LUCY: SHAKING THE TABLE, OPENING THE BOOK

Like *The House on Mango Street*, Kincaid's novel *Lucy* opens with an arrival at a new address. Lucy has just set foot in the United States, where she has come to be the live-in nanny for a blond, picture-perfect family. Once again, domesticity is immediately in motion, unsettled in space, spread out across time. In this case, however, Lucy's new residence does not extend a familiar series but constitutes (or so it seems) a sharp break with her West Indian past. For Esperanza, Mexico is just a vague memory. For Lucy, it is the United States that has not yet come into focus. As she says of her ride from the airport, "I could not see anything clearly . . . even though there were lights everywhere."[36] In the aftermath of migration, outlines are blurred, and even common domestic objects and actions are defamiliarized. Sitting at a table to eat is no longer the same because, for the first time, Lucy has emerged from an elevator to eat food from a refrigerator (4). Nor will this be the only time in *Lucy* that a table—epitome of stable facticity—will wobble and become strange. One of my aims here is to track the many permutations of a table.

Along with underwear purchased for the journey, Lucy carries with her an old, consoling daydream that going to the United States will rescue her "small drowning soul" (3). But even things brought from home are now experienced as foreign. Lucy's underwear chafes, and the old dream no longer fits: having finally escaped, she finds herself missing the very life she fled (4, 6). As Sara Ahmed stresses, we dwell with all five senses, making orientation to new places a gradual, intimate, and somatic process.[37] Lucy must readjust to her own body as well as to a new environment and an altered relationship between the two. She says she slept soundly her first night in the States, "but it wasn't because I was happy and comfortable—quite the opposite; it was because I didn't want to take in anything else" (4). If the logic of sleep is inverted, so is another seemingly incontestable fact of nature. To Lucy's surprise, the January sun in this nontropical zone fails to provide any warmth. This realization chills and disorients her at an epistemological level: "Something I had always known—the way I knew my skin was the color brown of a nut rubbed repeatedly with a soft cloth, or the way I knew my own name—something I took completely for granted, 'the sun is shining, the air is warm,' was not so" (5). As Lucy's life in the United States continues to unfold, she will find that none of these can be counted on with any certainty: not the warmth of the sun, not the connotations of her skin color, not the knowledge of who she is.

By describing to us an immigrant's first day, *Lucy* immediately estranges the objects and apprehensions of everyday life. In contrast to migration theories tying critical thinking and destabilized truths to travel, Kincaid illustrates the shifts effected by arriving and resettling.[38] Moreover, Lucy's is the perspective of a woman who has migrated for the purpose of *living in*, whose plot as well as setting is domestic. Having shown us the de-naturalizing results of a home-centered lens, *Lucy* goes on to dramatize the heterogeneity and latent volatility present in an apparently harmonious and stable household. More explicitly than Cisneros, Kincaid points to the global forces and collective traumas underlying Lucy's current domestic relations, some recent and others with roots in European colonization and the African diaspora. Showing once again that domesticity always requires a description thick in historical as well as spatial terms, Lucy's arrival resonates with the previous arrivals of millions. The ties and tensions between the Afro-Caribbean protagonist and her white U.S. employers are not entirely shaped by the past but do, Kincaid suggests, inevitably bear the imprint of earlier events.

Mariah and Lewis tell Lucy to regard them as family (7). In this home, everyone has a place at a table that appears to represent perfect equality and freedom. Gathered around it for dinner, the parents neither defer to God nor curb their children's irreverent speech (13). Soon, however, at this same table, they begin to call Lucy the "Visitor" and accuse her of holding back (13–14). This is followed by two stories, along with a reference to Freud that I take as encouragement to probe their political unconscious. In the first, addressed by Lewis to Lucy, an uncle in Canada raised monkeys he loved so much that he came to prefer them to humans. Something about this story prompts Lucy to respond by narrating a dream. In the dream, she is naked and being chased around the house by Lewis while Mariah cheers him on. The ground she runs on is yellow as if "paved with cornmeal." Despite evading Lewis, in the end she tumbles into a hole filled with snakes (14).

We hardly need Freud for "monkeys" raised by an avuncular white man who "loves" them even more than "actual human beings" to suggest an allusion to the scientific racism, paternalism, and concubinage underwriting slavery in the United States and Caribbean. Indeed, Lucy's answering dream quickly rewrites sentimentalized "monkey-love" as a scene of race-gender predation, viewed from the perspective of a terrified black woman fleeing her white master. Her narrative calls out the uncle's "Canada" as an unfree place, paved with the cornmeal that comprised the bulk of slave rations. With Lewis as predator and Mariah as accomplice, Lucy's dream points to New World slavery as a set of relations and feelings that continue, at some level, to inform their current household dynamic. Like West Africans brought in chains to the Americas, Lucy is indeed a Visitor from across the water, and her position as "nanny" to white children cannot help but recall that of "mammy" in the pre- and postbellum periods. Of course slavery is long gone, and Lucy has come to the United States voluntarily. The history of institutionalized race-gender violence shadows her nonetheless. We might say, indeed, that her employers' domesticity continues to invoke this history in exact proportion to Lewis's and Mariah's determination to forget it.

Later in the book, references to Paul Gauguin add another layer to the themes of servitude and sexual exploitation. Introduced to the painter by Mariah, Lucy initially identifies with Gauguin's alienation and flight from his homeland. All migration is not the same, however. As Lucy quickly realizes, "I was not a man; I was a young women from the fringes of the world, and when I left my home I had wrapped around my shoulders the mantle of a servant" (95). Her own artistic ambitions still nascent, Lucy has come not to paint but to serve. Nor has she come to conquer. Rather, her migration typifies the postcolonial pattern by which women and men from the depleted "fringes" must travel for work to the enriched "centers."[39] Reversing the path marked out by conquering Europeans over the course of centuries, these contemporary migrants are an ongoing reminder of that venture. Not that Lucy needs reminding. Her island home, named by Columbus in 1493, was later subjugated by the British for a period lasting almost until the end of the twentieth century.[40] As early as age fourteen, Lucy declared her own independence by refusing to sing "Rule, Britannia!" (135). Yet even now in the United States, she remains "haunted" by the word *minions*, observing that "the place where I came from was a dominion of someplace else" (37). As with slavery, Lucy can escape her small island but cannot completely escape the economic and psychosexual structures of the colonial era. Toward the end of the novel, a photo taken by her American lover Paul freezes her in the role of Tahitian beauty to his Gauguin. Half naked before a stove, Lucy wears the mantle of neither expatriate artist nor migrating servant; as the exoticized object of white men's fantasies, she wears no mantle at all (155).

Lucy's anger at British cultural imperialism—her schooling in and bitterly ambivalent relation to a foreign literary tradition—plays out in relation to Mariah, whose genuine kindness goes along with what Eve Sedgwick has called the "privilege of unknowing."[41] Thanks to this privilege, Mariah glories in daffodils as the heralds of spring, while for Lucy they mean something else altogether: being raised to recite Wordsworth's paean to English flowers in a place where daffodils never bloom; growing up far from England while being drilled in its worldview. For her, Mariah's "beloved daffodils" are inseparable from "a scene of conquered and conquests" (30). In Kincaid's depiction, however, the relationship between these two women is imbued with a complexity that goes beyond mutual incomprehension and serves to trouble any simple opposition between conquered and conquering. Combining difference with similarity, rage with love, and hierarchy with symmetry, the mixed blessings of their bond are most clearly laid out upon a table.

In the dining car of a train, Lucy explains that "we sat at tables—the children by themselves" (32). What strikes her, however, is a different divide: "The other people sitting down to eat dinner all looked like Mariah's relatives; the people waiting on them all looked like mine" (32). A second glance reveals a finer distinction: the African American workers look like but do not act like her own, more caustic West Indian relatives. Mariah, meanwhile, remains serenely oblivious to all such raced divisions of labor. Another table scene, by contrast, is an occasion for connection as well as alienation. On the alienation side, it references (adding to slavery and colonialism) a third global pattern of wealth, labor, and love unevenly distributed, one that speaks directly to Lucy's role as an immigrant nanny in the late twentieth century.

Before coming to our next table, I want to touch briefly on the "feminization of migration," shaped to a large degree by women from poor countries meeting the "care deficit" of wealthier ones.[42] As Barbara Ehrenreich and Arlie Russell Hochschild explain in *Global Woman: Nannies, Maids, and Sex Workers in the New Economy*, millions of women like Lucy travel along well-established routes (usually from south to north) to take up the traditionally female "care" work increasingly ceded by First World women in favor of jobs outside the home.[43] As is the case for whoever does it, the domestic labor of these immigrant women is undervalued and often unrecognized, despite involving, especially for nannies, delicate physical and emotional work at the very heart of their employers' family.

Though hired as a nanny, Lucy sleeps in a "maid's room." She likens the small enclosure to "a box in which cargo traveling a long way should be shipped," adding "but I was not cargo" (7). Or is she? Kincaid's next paragraph recounts a dream that seems to affirm Lucy's status as "cargo" transported to fill a deficit in child care. In this dream, Lucy clutches a nightgown "printed with beautiful scenes of children playing with Christmas-tree decorations" (9). Anxious to discover its origins, Lucy searches "furiously" until finding a label that reads "Made in Australia." She is then awakened by "the actual maid," a woman who claims to dislike Lucy because of the way she talks (9). Unscrambling this dream logic, we might say that Lucy appears to recognize herself as both an imported object and a body emblazoned with images of joyful children. "Made" abroad, she is both different from and similar to the "actual maid": different in her nominally higher status and West Indian origins; similar in being another boxed-up part in the technology of wealthy, white domesticity.[44]

Returning now to our furniture motif, we find Mariah standing at a rustic kitchen table. To Lucy's amazement, Mariah had spotted the table in a Finnish farmhouse and acquired it on the spot (58–59). Our narrator has already commented on the family's ability to shop the world. "From wherever they had gone," she marvels, "and they seemed to have been all over the world, they brought back some tiny memento" (12). (To be sure, their global tourism is itself a mode of consuming other cultures simply for the pleasure of doing so.) With the help of Ehrenreich and Hochschild's *Global Woman*, it's not hard to connect the dots between Mariah's ability to pluck a thing of beauty and utility from a faraway house and Lucy's concern that she herself is cargo of some kind, with a label reading "Made Elsewhere."

At the same time, this particular table scene also occasions a moment of connection. Mariah is arranging a mass of pink and white peonies, and it reminds Lucy of her mother—the things she did not love about her mother but "more and more the parts of my mother that I loved" (59). Lucy's dismay at the table's Finnish origins is actually in parentheses, and as a whole this long paragraph brackets her usual skepticism, so lost is she in admiration for Mariah's domestic artistry. "Seeing Mariah look so beautiful," Lucy says, "I couldn't tear myself away" (59). As she studies Mariah, images of her own, repudiated mother come into sharper, more affectionate focus, until the two figures become a single, inspirational "they":

How many times had I seen my mother surrounded by plants of one kind or another, arranging them into some pattern, training them to grow a certain way. . . . [Mariah's] hands were just like my mother's— large, with long fingers and square fingernails; their hands looked like instruments for arranging things beautifully. Sometimes, when they wished to make a point, they would hold their hands in the air, and suddenly their hands were vessels made for carrying something special; at other times their hands made you think they excelled at playing some musical instrument. (59)

The scene closes with Mariah inviting Lucy to smell the fragrant flowers and laughing uncontrollably when Lucy says she'd like to be naked and covered by petals, absorbing their perfume (60). Imagining a sensuality beyond Lewis's grasp and Paul's gaze, Lucy also notes sadly that this interaction with Mariah "was the sort of time I wished I could have had with my mother, but, for a reason not clear to me, it was not allowed" (60). The remark makes for a poignant end to a table sequence that has been redemptive in three different ways: as Lucy and Mariah bond over blooms of a tropical lushness, their earlier daffodil differences are partly redeemed; as Lucy recalls her mother in a mode of serenity and creativity, their vexed relationship is likewise, temporarily, redeemed; and as Lucy admires both maternal figures—their hands "instruments for arranging things beautifully"—the talents of homemakers across cultures and their aesthetic contributions to daily life are redeemed.

Reaching the middle of the novel, we encounter a table scene as much about loss as the preceding one is about gain. The family is at their summer lake house having dinner. They are finishing a homemade pie when a seemingly minor controversy causes Lewis to explode, violently rending the picture of family togetherness: "He made his hands into two fists, lifted them up in the air, and brought them down on the table with such force that everything on the table—eating utensils, plates, cups in saucers, the empty pie dish—rattled and shook as if in an earthquake, and one glass actually tipped over, rolled off the table, and shattered" (75). Shocked silence and intimations of tragedy follow, the nature of which is scarcely understood by Lucy and the children, though clear enough to poor Mariah. Lucy nevertheless ventures to observe, "In the history of civilization, they mention everything; even the water glass shattered on the floor—something is said about that—but there is not one word on the misery to be found at a dining-room table" (75).[45]

The shaken-table scene is quickly followed by evidence of Lewis's infidelity, confirming that what has shattered along with the water glass is the integrity of this marriage. For Mariah, the violent shattering and disoriented aftermath play out both practically and metaphorically in relation to domestic objects and routines. The last time she and Lucy have dinner, the table itself is gone. The two women eat sitting on the floor, surrounded by "the remains of [Mariah's] marriage: wine and water goblets made from crystal, china plates decorated with real gold around the edges, real silverware. She was giving all of this away" (162). As we saw with Dominique Browning, Mariah's postmarital despair means being out of sorts with these and other landmarks of her old domesticity. Mariah, however, will not grieve among the ruins while gradually refurbishing; and though her plans to go abroad recall Wharton, the domestic future she invokes is a simple and communal one—non-European and, by the sound of it, antidecoration (162).

As for Lucy, the collapse of her surrogate family spells a second dislocation. Losing her live-in job does, at least, give our narrator a chance to shape a domesticity that is actually hers rather than her employers'.[46] In another echo of Woolf, the novel's last pages see Lucy able to declare: "I woke up in a new bed, and it was my own. I had bought it with my money. The roof over my head was my own" (144). Like Cisneros, Kincaid both cites and pointedly rephrases Woolf, reflecting the long history of black women—as slaves and servants, imported and native born—working under white roofs. Lest we imagine, however, that we are hastening to a happy ending, Lucy quickly adds, "that is—as long as I could afford to pay the rent for it" (144). Indeed, as the narrative winds down, contingencies seem to proliferate. Lucy's friendship with her roommate, Peggy, is strained, and she is tired of Paul, her photographer boyfriend. Having achieved the independent, anonymous life she thought would bring happiness, she tells us she feels nothing of the kind (158). Alienated as ever, Lucy gazes out on a world that looks "unreal" and fears she will always be an outsider: "I would never be part of it, never penetrate to the inside, never be taken in" (154).

Still more distressing is Lucy's sense of being an outsider to herself, dissociated from her own name. Her official identity papers—birth certificate, passport, immigration card—list only external facts and so "showed nothing" (148). Among these facts is an inheritance she disowns: a patronym bestowed by the Englishman who owned her ancestors (149). But the key to her self-alienation lies elsewhere, for along with aspects of her social and familial circumstances, Lucy habitually disavows many of her most powerful emotions. Early on she declares, "I didn't want to love one more thing in my life . . . that could make my heart break into a million little pieces" (23), and this reluctance to love is reiterated throughout the book. In my view, the significance of Kincaid's concluding paragraph is that only then does Lucy finally begin to participate more fully in her own affective life, to penetrate the depths of her longings and take in what she finds there.[47]

This is how it happens. Lucy is "alone at home one night. Peggy was on an outing by herself. Paul was on an outing by himself" (163). Lucy suspects they may actually be together. If so, she doesn't care, for their "outings" enable, as it were, Lucy's "inning": an approach to emotions of her own by means of a series of intimate, domestic tasks. As with other examples of shelter writing, Lucy gives us a step-by-step account of "little things" creating a sense of home in her apartment and in her own skin: "I did all sorts of little things: I washed my underwear, scrubbed the stove, washed the bathroom floor, trimmed my nails, arranged my dresser, made sure I had enough sanitary napkins" (163). Climbing into bed, her last actions are to open a journal, take "a fountain pen full of beautiful blue ink," and write her full name along with a single sentence: "I wish I could love someone so much that I would die from it" (164). The admission causes Lucy to weep with shame—perhaps at having this wish but more likely at having denied it—and the result is words blurred by tears (164). By ending her book and beginning Lucy's with a blur, Kincaid reminds us again that home and identity are always blurred by movement and uncertainty. At the same time, as with Robinson Crusoe and Jess Goldberg, Lucy's small steps toward a cozy interior, however provisional, have served to effect as well as to figure a salvaged interiority. Her second migration promises to be a voyage in.

BLU'S HANGING: DOMESTICITY
UNDER THE HOUSE

Blu's Hanging is the story of a working-class Japanese American family on the Hawaiian island of Molokai. Unlike our previous two texts, it opens not with an arrival but with two departures: the death of a mother and the emotional withdrawal of a father. Three children are left to drift alone with their grief, daily needs, and challenges ranging from homework and puberty to racist teachers and sexual predators. The initial burden of homemaking falls to thirteen-year-old Ivah, the conscientious oldest child as well as Yamanaka's narrator. A key turning point involves the youngest, five-year-old Maisie, who has stopped talking since her mother's death. Increasingly, however, the book's search for a safe and caring domestic space comes to focus on the conflicted, precarious, middle child and eponymous character Blu. As I hope to show, it is finally this queer, eight-year-old boy who becomes the agent of a redemptive domesticity swerving away from normative views of family roles and values.

The Ogata parents were born in Hawaii, making their offspring at least *sansei* (third generation); but the children's parentless home feels like a foreign country, and their need to reconcile with the old while inventing a new domesticity is no less pressing than Lucy's. As with Lucy and Esperanza, moreover, the Ogatas' struggle to be at home is informed by the historical struggle of a particular immigrant group to be at home in the United States. The most scarring domestic trauma suffered en masse by Japanese Americans was, of course, the forcible dislocation and internment of 120,000 women, men, and children during World War II. Recalling the 1930s "repatriation" of a million Mexicans, around 60 percent of those herded into "relocation" camps were American citizens. Japanese aliens and nonaliens alike were ordered to evacuate their homes by noon of May 7, 1942. Almost all were residents of the West Coast. By contrast, the 158,000 Japanese living in Hawaii were deemed so crucial to the economy that, after much high-level debate, they were spared mass incarceration. Significantly for our purposes, however, Navy Secretary Frank Knox had initially argued for a Hawaiian internment camp to be located on a remote island.[48]

Critics have commented heatedly on *Blu's Hanging*'s racial politics (more on which soon), yet no one appears to have noticed the specific reference to internment at the heart of Yamanaka's novel, the scarcely hidden secret within the secret of the Ogata family's shameful past.[49] About halfway through the book, Poppy finally reveals to us as well as to Ivah the story behind his mysterious scars. In the Hawaiian pidgin spoken by most of *Blu's* characters, he confesses: "Me and your madda, us had leprosy. I like your promise that you neva call us lepers. Don't eva define us again by that disease."[50] Diagnosed as children, both parents were "yank from the world" (142) at a young age and quarantined in the Kalihi Receiving Station in Honolulu before being further exiled to the Kalaupapa "lepers colony" on Molokai. As Poppy explains, "When the Japs bomb Pearl Harbor, the government came scared that all us leprosy patients was going break out of the Kalihi Receiving Station. So fast kine, one day in May, they 'wen put all us kids on one boat going straight to Kalaupapa" (143).

After the war, both parents were treated with the curative sulfone drug and eventually "paroled" (143–44). Yet the terrible stigma of leprosy lingered, and relatives continued to keep their distance for fear of its taint. Never feeling clean enough, Ivah's mother died of kidney failure from persisting in a sulfone regimen even after she had been cured. Poppy assures Ivah, "We was imprison down Kalaupapa, and now, no mo'" (142). She, however, sees a father still imprisoned by "shame, so much shame under his skin" (145). Despite his admonition to Ivah, Poppy remains defined by "that disease." Putting the various aspects of his narrative together, the metaphor seems clear enough. The self-loathing figure of the "leper" points, first of all, to a process of racialization by which "skin" becomes the basis for an internalized, abject identity. More specifically, the government incarceration of leprosy sufferers in May 1942 as a panicked response to Pearl Harbor ties this theme directly to the wartime internment of Japanese Americans. As a matter of historical fact, most of those exiled to Kalaupapa were actually native Hawaiians; Yamanaka's metaphor downplays the fact that leprosy was tied to stereotypes of slovenly Hawaiians.[51] At the same time, however, as a trope for the dislocation and imprisonment of a feared group, it serves to underline the lasting trauma, humiliation, and sense of domestic insecurity peculiar to immigrants of Japanese ancestry in the postwar period.[52]

Like Cisneros and Kincaid, Yamanaka thus locates the story of the Ogata children—their inherited stigma and shame, their loss of and struggle to remake home—in the context of a distinct immigrant history. She also, however, represents the family and their community in ways that refute blanket assumptions about Japanese Americans and Asian Americans generally. Against the homogenizing "model minority" stereotype, almost every page of this text offers further evidence of the heterogeneity, hybridity, and vulnerability of Asian American children and adults living without privilege on the island of Molokai in the early 1970s. In this milieu, the ethnic pecking order instituted by early-century sugar planters has scarcely altered. "Haoles" (whites) dominate Asians, with the descendants of Portuguese overseers on the lowest white rung, economically depressed but enjoying a modicum of racial privilege. Among Asians there are further distinctions and inequalities, with Filipinos joining native Hawaiians at the bottom. Haole teachers may resent "Japs" (127), but they are even more contemptuous of Molokai's "brown people all on welfare" (121). The predatory Filipino, Uncle Paulo, may get the worst role, but he also gets the best lines dissing a caste system that demeans him: "Fuck, Japs for think they mo' betta than everybody else, fuckas. Especially the Filipinos. Fuck, everybody for spit on Filipinos, shit" (207).[53]

Explaining which students qualify for free lunch tokens, Ivah suggests that racial identity often, but not always, corresponds to economic status, with her own family a notable exception to the rule: "Most of the Japanese and Pakes [Chinese] don't get tokens. Most of the Portuguese, Hawaiians, and Filipinos do. I'm the only Japanese who gets a free lunch token, but I don't care. It's the best meal of the day for all of us" (104–5). With Poppy working as a janitor and his kids living on white bread and mayonnaise, Yamanaka's characters make visible the often overlooked working-class segment of the Japanese American population. The very first chapter shows Blu mocked by his peers for bringing "poor food" on a class excursion; as we saw with Esperanza, Blu's sense of racial stigma is bound up with class shame (6–8). For me, one of this novel's major contributions is to dramatize for mainstream readers not only the diversity, inequality, and occasional conflict that characterizes relations among Asian American groups but also the spectrum of class circumstances, including dire poverty, that exists in a group better known for its economic achievements.

The most pervasive marker of the Ogatas' lower-class status is their use of Hawaiian pidgin or Creole, an idiom that Yamanaka's *Saturday Night at the Pahala Theater* (1993) was the first to mobilize in a literary context. Although Ivah addresses the reader in "standard" English, hers is a thoroughly bilingual narrative driven by dialogue rendered in pidgin. Disparaged by haole teachers as "limited" (59–60), pidgin is the richly expressive language of everyday life for all of Yamanaka's main characters. Mama called Maisie "Pidge" after a cartoon bird (38), and the endearment aptly expresses Yamanaka's own intimacy with and affectionate use of this Hawaiian vernacular. Her work not only respects and relishes pidgin but also invokes it as a language of race-class opposition and pride. The teacher Miss Ito, declaring her own origins in solidarity with the Ogatas, reverts to pidgin in answering her snobbish colleague: "You keep on lifting your haole nose in the air at me and my friends, you going hear worse things than 'haole' come out of this Jap's mout'" (128). Earlier in the novel, Ivah makes similarly pointed use of pidgin to express her outrage at the same woman's cruelty to Maisie: "Why you making my sista scared for, you fuckin' haole?" (46).

Originating as a plantation dialect enabling communication across language groups, pidgin is an English creolized by successive waves of laborers speaking Hawaiian, Cantonese, Portuguese, Japanese, Korean, and Spanish.[54] As such, it offers a particularly vivid illustration of the hybridity (not just side-by-side heterogeneity but the mingling and cross-pollination of cultures) pervading, to an unusual degree, every strata of Hawaiian culture. Domestic as well as linguistic hybridity is especially pronounced in a state in which whites are a minority, diverse Asians are a majority, and almost one-quarter of the population is mixed race. In *Blu's Hanging*, a mélange of white American and Asian American foods appears at almost every meal. The "saimin" noodles Ivah makes, even before the addition of Spam, are a miscegenated, plantation-era food derived from Japanese ramen, Chinese mein, and Filipino pancit (5). Later, our narrator practices for Thanksgiving by frying up Tyson's chicken and arranging it with boiled won bok (Chinese cabbage) (65–66). Mama's Christmas dinner would likewise combine Japanese *sekihan*, turkey with sweet potato stuffing, and a cheesecake with Cool Whip (89). It is true that Ivah's growth is mapped in part by her culinary progress from "white" to Japanese: from meals consisting literally and almost exclusively of white bread (3) to a wholesome pot of Japanese *nishime* with vegetables from the garden (196). But Yamanaka is no purist—on the contrary—and when Maisie finally recovers her voice, she is enabled to do so by the recipe for a Betty Crocker cake.

Focusing in more specifically on the Ogatas' domestic practices, I turn now to the Betty Crocker cake scene because its reliance on step-by-step instructions to compensate for loss makes it another poignant example of shelter writing. Miss Ito, kind teacher and surrogate parent, has invited the children for a sleepover to celebrate Maisie's birthday and encourage her to speak. Pinning up the cake recipe written out in bold letters, she matter-of-factly invites the mute child to read them. Maisie hesitates at first and then, breaking almost a year of silence, reads aloud: "Mix . . . three . . . eggs . . . with two sticks of butter . . ." (130). As with Lucy's performance of "little things," by voicing this simple directive with its humble ingredients and everyday mathematics, Maisie returns to her body as if "from some strange dream" (130). Eggs and butter, mixing and baking, become stays against the disorienting effects of grief. By means of small physical objects and actions, home begins to be rematerialized.

Cynthia Wu objects to this scene on the grounds that it ties "empowerment" to "the iconic figure of the middle-class housewife." "Instead of making a cake from scratch with a recipe that can be tinkered with," Wu continues, "the characters here actualize a pre-packaged, 'easy-to-follow' domesticity that does not invite improvisation but only lockstep adherence." The scene's optimism, she concludes, depends on conformity to "normative gender, sexual, and kinship articulations."[55] Wu's reasoning, however, is precisely what *Extreme Domesticity* sets out to challenge: the reflexive equation of kitchen labor with conventional domesticity, the housewife assumed to symbolize heteronormativity. In fact, as Wu recognizes, Miss Ito isn't married, biologically related to her charges, or even heterosexual, and relying on Betty Crocker doesn't change this. Yet by treating the homemaker in "iconic" terms, Wu is enabled to ignore the specific worker and to overlook cooking as a material practice and mode of production. By now it should not surprise my reader to hear that I defend housewifery and differ from Wu on the meanings of cake mix and easy-to-follow instructions. For one thing (thanks to Martha Stewart among others), by the 1970s it is actually "from scratch" that signifies middle-class refinement and access to leisure time. For another, at least some of the solace as well as the drudgery of housework lies precisely in its routine nature, its *unoriginality*, the easy-to-follow sequence of cooking a meal and washing a pot. From a practical perspective, this kind of repetitive labor isn't "lockstep"; it's the necessary reproduction of daily life. At the same time, while claiming the value of and comfort to be found in domestic routines, I follow Luce Giard in stressing that these leave plenty of room for—and often require—creative improvisation. (In the history of baking, cake mix is itself one such improvisation.) And for those recovering from domestic disaster, both the appeal of routine and the need to improvise are likely to be that much more extreme.

I close my discussion by turning to Blu as the novel's ultimate "tinkerer" with traditional notions of family and home. Images of unusual, alternative, made-up, and makeshift domesticity recur throughout Yamanaka's text. It opens with Ivah invoking the Crusoe-like castaways on *Gilligan's Island*, who somehow manage to eat more lavishly than her own family of hungry islanders (3–4). Dreaming of food, Ivah wishes for a house right under a grocery, with access to unlimited supplies through a secret door in her bedroom (9). Blu later reiterates the castaway theme, pretending he lives in a tree house "kinda like the Swiss Family Robinson" (147). Other examples of a jerry-rigged domesticity include the overnights at Miss Ito's, when she drags her futon into the living room, joining the children in their sleeping bags. As Ivah marvels, "There is one for each of us, real sleeping bags, with pillows and clean-smelling pillowcases, and no blankets with clothespins" (134). On the

Fourth of July, Miss Ito and her partner Big Sis create a similarly cozy camp for the children, this time in the back of Big Sis's truck, outfitted with "foam padding, sleeping bags, pillows, and her Igloo full of Diamond Head sodas and Millers" (241). Here the bedroom and refrigerator on wheels literalize the women's versatile domesticity, quick to improvise sanctuary for Ivah, Maisie, and Blu.[56] Miss Ito's classroom suggests a further alternative to Poppy's stagnant and occasionally violent house. In addition to books and plants, her space has "apple crates for tables and shelves, a couch and rug by a fake but nice cardboard fireplace, lavender gingham curtains, guinea pigs who have smart names like Einstein and Ophelia, parakeets with the best bird toys, a fish tank, and bookcases without any dust on them" (122). All these rigged-up rooms speak to the constructed, provisional nature of home and to Yamanaka's characters as castaways searching for shelter and playfully reimagining its contours.

With its apple crates for tables, Miss Ito's classroom rhymes with another domestic space coinciding, however, with a rather different pedagogy: "Blu tells Maisie perverted things under the house. He says it makes her laugh. Cool, fine dust under the house. Apple crates for tables. Hollow tile for chairs. Today he's the teacher or maybe Mister Rogers" (18). Later Blu describes happiness as taking care of Maisie. "But if you talking real happy, then thass when Maisie and me camp in the living room in the blanket we pin together with clothespins even if in the morning the pins all over, even under our so-called sleeping bag, no, Maisie?" Maisie nods in response. "Happy too," Ivah comments (118). We have seen how admiringly Ivah describes Miss Ito's bookcases "without any dust." Understandably, our narrator revels in "real" sleeping bags and blankets without clothespins. But I would argue that *Blu's Hanging* overall, in contrast to its narrator, stakes an equal or greater claim to Blu's "so-called sleeping bags"; to his subhouse full of dust and dirty words; to caring, happiness, and children sloppily pinned together, at least until morning. Ivah's attraction to order matches the neat arc of her narrative, a trajectory taking her from family chaos and caretaking to the threshold of prep school in Honolulu. Unlike some critics, I applaud her movement *away from* home. At the same time, I believe Yamanaka places equal emphasis on Blu's movement *toward* home—in particular, toward a re-invented home opposed to parental shame, traditional gender roles, and binary views of pollution and purity.[57]

Blu's Hanging is relentless in its attention to our messy, penetrable, incontinent, and sometimes putrid corporeality. It dwells on fluids that embarrass and frighten us with their connotations of sex and death. All the children, in various ways, are shamed by their animal functions: Maisie by wetting her pants, Ivah by getting her period, Blu by his extra-vagant appetite for food and sex. Yamanaka's bodies have a tendency to ooze and fester, portending their ultimate dissolution. Ivah's trench mouth features "white pus and raw. Sores leaking dead juice all over my mouth" (22). Tortured cats dribble brown juice all over the road (28). Sick, neglected dogs have "gray, scaly lesions, bald spots with thick, red liquid" (178). As the novel progresses, however, the body gradually shifts from being a site of shame and injury to being a site of acceptance and mercy. Of all Yamanaka's characters, it is eight-year-old Blu who presides over this shift, his own vexed embodiment leading him to compassion for the fluid flesh of others. He becomes a savior to dying dogs, cradling and blessing their swollen, leaking bodies (178–79, 190). He buys under-wear for Maisie and pads for Ivah, not to deny the flow of urine and blood, but to save his sisters from further humiliation (62, 100–101). Schooling Maisie in his classroom under the house, the giver of under-wear becomes professor of the bodily nether world, poet of underarms: "When people (mostly man) have bushy underarms, look like the purple sea urchin stuck to your underarm" (110). Using his "teacher voice" (230), he defines X-rated words for his rapt student: "Vagina, Reincarnation, and Masturbation" (229). Finding grace in the sexual body, reincarnation in masturbation, Blu undoes the opposition between flesh and spirit, repu-diates the dirty-clean binary that underpins normative notions of bodies and domesticities.[58] "Mostly man," he bends gender not only by staying home to nurture but also by claiming the lower, feminized part of the body-mind duality. Like Esperanza's dream house, his subhouse is not a man's house, not a daddy's, but that of a boy acting as a Mama whose dirty body is clean enough.

6

DOMESTICITY IN EXTREMIS

Homemaking by the Unsheltered

This book began by thinking about castaways and outcasts in the Crusoe mold. Shelter writing, as we've seen, embedded in tales of traumatic dislocation, shows survivors in the step-by-step process of remaking a home. In the course of fashioning a place to live, repeating the little tasks involved in keeping house, they also assemble a sense of self. Out of his smashed-up domesticity, Crusoe eventually comes to reinvent the household arts. After decades of exile, gender outlaw Jess Goldberg does Martha Stewart proud in a cheap New York City apartment. John Barton's compassionate character comes into focus as he shops, cooks, and feeds, restoring order to the Davenport household. Bad girl Dominique Browning, set adrift by divorce, renovates her life as a single mother, room by room. Blu creates a shelter from shame underneath the normative house. The upshot for all such figures is that *home* is no longer natural or given. It must, instead, be made and remade—its boundaries drawn, its outlines filled in, its hominess continually replenished.

Sara Ahmed (whose theories of emotion as well as spatial orientation have been recurrent points of reference) places a similar emphasis on the contingent and constructed nature of domestic spaces. Their contours, she explains, are delineated only in the act of dwelling, as we gradually become oriented in relation to a particular place. Each time we relocate, it takes a while for us to get our bearings before we can feel once again "at home." Migration, as we saw in chapter 5, is therefore "a process of disorientation and reorientation."[1] At first, the confused migrant faces two directions at once: "toward a home that has been lost, and to a place that is not yet home" (10). As a migrant subject herself, Ahmed appreciates this sense of disorientation, but she is more taken by "the ways we have of settling" (10). Like many of us (or like me, anyway), she hates disassembling a household, which feels like "collecting myself up, pulling myself apart." But then, arriving at the emptiness of a new abode: "How I love unpacking. Taking things out, putting things around, arranging myself all over the walls" (10). Esperanza with her books, stories, and shoes beside the bed. Lucy with her scrubbed stove and beautiful blue ink. Blu and Maisie with their apple crates and *Webster's Dictionary*. This, we might say, is precisely the structure of feeling rendered by shelter writing: delight in putting around one's things, marking one's territory, reestablishing oneself—the urgency and enjoyment of these actions increased to compensate for dispossession.

But what about those for whom dislocation is not backstory but main event? Those who, having pulled themselves apart, realize no timely arrival at a place of their own, so that being *not-unpacked* is an ongoing condition? My concern throughout this book has been to recognize that domesticity takes diverse forms, many less than conventional and all built up from the elemental project of sustaining life. Chapters 3 and 4 looked at homemakers flouting "family values" and unsettled by divorce; chapters 1, 2, and 5 explored descriptions of homemaking intensified by conditions of extreme precariousness. This closing chapter sets out to stretch the concept of shelter writing, possibly to its breaking point, by reflecting on domesticity in situations of homelessness. It seemed only logical as well as ethical for a study of domestic outsiders to include those who may be living, quite literally, out of doors. At the same time, as we will see, attending to such figures serves to complicate and test the limits of my shelter paradigm. Is it true that works portraying homelessness show not only domestic trauma but also the compensatory fervor we have seen elsewhere? Are the lives of displaced people ever the occasion for depicting a therapeutic domesticity? Are there, in fact, moments in narratives of serial dislocation and day-to-day struggle when homeless men or women pause to delight in expressions of domestic creativity? Do people disparaged by city planners and tourist bureaus as ugly objects ever have the wherewithal to be purposeful domestic subjects, engineers of everyday beauty?[2]

Certainly there are cases in which the answer is yes. Images of the New York City "tunnel people" reveal cleverly rigged-up kitchens, elaborately painted murals, and a good deal of house pride. At the end of this chapter, I consider a documentary of this well-developed domestic culture located beneath the streets of the Upper West Side. Yet despite a few other such examples of shelter writing, my foray into the ethnographic and autobiographical corpus on homelessness suggests that texts detailing ingenuity and pride in careful domestic arrangements are the exception. Generally speaking, their overwhelming emphasis is not on homemaking at all but on the trauma of dislocation. When they do come into play, domestic spaces are frequently described not as havens but as sites of entrapment and violence. The family home is, indeed, for battered women, exiled gay teens, and others fleeing abusive situations, the original site of violence, first in a series of unsafe lodgings that often includes the homeless shelter as well as the relative's couch and makeshift encampment.[3]

One purpose served by this chapter, then, in a book devoted to the felicitous house, is to remind us of its evil twin, to put the brakes on any tendency simply to romanticize all things domestic. And if the positive domesticity I've been defending is a strongly feminized category, it is equally true that the exploitative aspects of traditional domesticity and the difficulties stemming from domestic insecurity are more pronounced when women are concerned. Needless to say, whether housed or homeless, women are more likely than men to be juggling child care and to be the victims of rape and domestic violence. They are, moreover, held to higher standards of hygiene and propriety, standards closely tied to strictures on female sexuality. Homeless women, who may be literally walking the streets and sleeping around, suffer the added stigma of perceived indecency. In grosser violation of gender norms, they are likely to be seen as more debased than men in comparable circumstances: a dirty woman is dirtier, a female drunk more deviant, a negligent mother worse than an absent dad. Sadly, this view of women's lower status appears to be shared in homeless as well as mainstream circles, gender politics being one of multiple ways that these circles overlap.[4]

Contrary to popular belief, many of the homeless are employed, whether full time, part time, or intermittently, and most others aspire to be. Homeless women, however, are also at a greater disadvantage when it comes to finding work. Many are hindered by the demands of parenting, others by conditions on the street. As opposed to an unwashed man, who qualifies nonetheless for various kinds of dirty labor, an unwashed woman is virtually unemployable.[5] She is immediately shut out from the major categories of low-wage work available to women: food service, housecleaning, child care, and elder care. Despite being seen as debauched, filthy clothes and body disqualify her for sex work as well. Even women enabled by access to bathrooms and laundry to "pass" in the workplace risk being fired once the sullying fact of their homelessness is discovered.[6] Live-in service positions, at times a solution to women's homelessness, are also frequently its cause, since job termination means eviction along with the loss of wages.[7]

Given their real and perceived vulnerability, it is perhaps not surprising that homeless women seek and gain admission to shelters at proportionately higher rates than men do. This is especially true of women with children, whose custody as well as ability to parent is jeopardized by street life. But while women are more apt to be protected from the elements and to benefit from various services, it follows that they are thereby subjected to a wider range of social controls: from shelter curfews, crack-of-dawn departure times, and lack of privacy to restrictions on alcohol use and other unladylike behaviors.[8] Charitable efforts aimed at protection and support may be hard to disentangle from the project of requiring homeless women to cultivate a seemly appearance, behave modestly, and otherwise conform to the compliant, middle-class ideal. Of course men are under pressure to conform as well, but homeless masculinity clashes less (indeed, partly coincides) with a norm that includes ruggedness, originality, freedom of movement, and self-sufficiency. This chapter is a further reminder that gender roles are produced not only by discursive codes devaluing the "feminine" but also by the practical constraints women encounter on a daily basis, all the more so for those who are precariously housed.

Thus far, I have acknowledged the gothic realities of many sheltered spaces while also recognizing the obvious hindrances to homemaking for those living under ad hoc conditions. My goal in focusing on homeless texts is not, however, to reiterate the common assumption that being homeless is the opposite of being domestic. Rather, what I discern in my texts is less the absence of domesticity than a fragmented manifestation of it—domesticity in pieces, shattered under the pressure of homelessness. True enough that the intense, sustained, and savored mode of nesting so carefully particularized by shelter writing is rarely seen. But if we recognize that domesticity comes together from multiple components in the service of various ends—if we consider that it accommodates our things along with our bodies; that it structures our time as well as our relationships—then we are on our way to reconceiving homelessness as an effort to improvise some if not all of these components. My hope in this chapter is to read my texts for evidence of still another unconventional domesticity, hampered and partial but still *being done*: whether by women caring for children in shelters, the man on a bench with his dog, the woman parked on a sidewalk with her shopping cart, or the men sharing a drink around a fire.

The following observations draw on several kinds of nonfictional works. The majority of these texts, for reasons I will explain, were published in the early 1990s. All concern homelessness in the United States, and almost all focus on such major cities as Los Angeles; Washington, D.C.; and New York. Two are in a journalistic vein: one polemical (by social justice writer Jonathan Kozol) and the other personal (by novelist Ann Nietzke). A third major text is a first-person account of homelessness by the writer Lars Eighner.[9] After these, I turn to a cluster of participant-observer studies undertaken by social scientists, and the chapter as a whole is underpinned by additional ethnographic studies cited in my notes. Finally, at the end of this chapter and as part 1 of my conclusion, I discuss two, millennial, works of visual art: Marc Singer's documentary film, *Dark*

Days (2000), and Samuel R. Delany's graphic memoir, *Bread & Wine: An Erotic Tale of New York* (1999).

These diverse texts were chosen in part because they, among many others, particularly moved and educated me. While speaking to me, they also, despite their differences, are in dialogue with one another, comprising part of a broader conversation across genres and media about the crisis in U.S. housing arising at the tail end of the twentieth century. Though not, of course, direct transmissions of lived experiences, as modes of nonfiction they are similarly earnest in their efforts to capture reality and support their various truth claims. Moreover, as a set of stories about experiencing and observing homelessness, they can tell us a good deal about contemporary understandings of shelter and its lack. As with my discussion of Luce Giard's ethnography, I appeal to them primarily as such: less as empirical sources than as depictions adding to my archive of extreme domesticities. The brief history of American homelessness that follows, drawing on the work of Kenneth Kusmer, is intended to provide some context for my inquiry. As I say, my own method remains not historical but textual analysis, with the goal of offering a new framework for parsing images of homelessness and new ways for thinking about homeless lives.

A SUBSET OF THE VERY POOR

Antivagrancy laws in the United States, which date back to the seventeenth century, indicate both the visibility of "vagrants" or "wandering beggars" in the colonial period and the long-standing criminalization of their status. According to Kenneth Kusmer, the major causes of preindustrial vagrancy were dislocation by war or natural disaster, the arrival of destitute immigrants, and unemployment. By the eighteenth century, the insecurity of poor laborers had been heightened by recurrent bouts of recession, causing a noticeable rise in homelessness, particularly in urban areas.[10] As industrialization took hold, mechanization as well as economic fluctuation magnified the problem, displacing some workers and injuring others. Public responses during this period ranged from alms and soup kitchens to prisons and workhouses. Between 1823 and 1826, New York City's solution to its growing number of vagrants was yoking them to a treadmill. By midcentury, many cities had introduced the only somewhat less punitive measure of using police stations to corral the homeless, a population encompassing single women and abandoned children as well as men (22–25).

The end of the Civil War, followed by a severe depression from 1873 to 1878, ushered in an era of still more widespread homelessness. The 1870s also saw the transfer of public animus from the urban beggar to the emergent figure of the "tramp." As Kusmer explains, tramps were unemployed itinerant men, including a significant number of veterans, riding the rails and foraging for food in a manner continuous with military life (35–38). In the bourgeois imagination, they would come to represent everything at odds with stability and respectability. Their poverty and reputation for defiance triggered a damning association with strikers and organizers of the burgeoning labor movement.[11] Demonized in class terms, the figure of the tramp was further decried as savage, drunken, animal, criminal, and probably foreign, making him a veritable compendium of mainstream fears (43–51).[12]

Not until the early twentieth century were these vilifying images of the homeless challenged by more sympathetic and contextualizing ones. In-depth studies such as Robert Hunter's *Poverty* (1904) and Alice Solenberger's *One Thousand Homeless Men* (1911), along with the newly professionalized field of social work, argued against simply blaming the depravity of individuals. Turning their attention to contributing socioeconomic factors, they also began to identify the differing circumstances leading to homelessness (Kusmer 91–95). For obvious reasons, such views gained credence during the Great Depression, when the rate of unemployment rose to 25 percent and many of the homeless were transient families moving from place to place in search of work. Among the relief programs established as part of the New Deal was the Federal Transient Service, which Kusmer identifies as the first agency ever charged with addressing homelessness at the federal level (210–15).

With the improvement of economic conditions, popular perceptions of the homeless quickly regained their predominantly negative cast. Well before the end of World War II, the face of homelessness had changed from traveling families to aging, alcoholic men crashed in single-room occupancy (SRO) hotels. Written off as hopelessly derelict (despite actual evidence that many SRO occupants were or had been workers), this population was all the more easily caricatured and ignored for being largely confined to specific urban neighborhoods (Kusmer 224–28). Stationary rather than wandering, moral failure rather than economic victim, the "Bowery bum" of the 1950s and 1960s was defined more by the marginal nature and location of his shelter than by the absolute absence of it.

To call such a man "homeless," as we might say today, would therefore be something of a misnomer. But the same is true of those Kusmer describes in his conclusion as the "new homeless," a population whose numbers began rising in the late 1970s and continued to climb throughout the 1980s. In the current era, many of those without stable housing are not actually on the street but are circulating among friends and family; living in motels or transitional housing; squatting in abandoned buildings; occupying semipermanent camps or shantytowns; spending nights in emergency shelters, hospitals, or jails; or sleeping in their cars. All the more reason, as I see it, to ask not how people manage in the absence of domesticity but how aspects of domesticity are replicated under these widely varying circumstances. Note, too, that while some may be chronically homeless, the majority will be rehoused within two years, some within a matter of months.[13] Such great diversity in the kind and duration of experiences should make us wary of generalizing about *the* homeless. Yet among the constants throughout U.S. history has been a reliance on crude generalizations lumping together a subset of our poorest citizens in a category safely removed from the rest of us.

Even contemporary census takers, social workers, and scholars bent on describing homeless people in precise and respectful terms may have trouble identifying and enumerating them with any accuracy. Given the variables just listed, many clearly are missed when counting only those in shelters and on the streets, and counting heads on a single night yields lower figures than counting everyone who has been homeless for some part of a given year. Nevertheless, there is widespread agreement that the rate of homelessness spiked dramatically during the 1980s in response to a number of Reagan-era developments. In addition to drastically reduced social services, these included a stagnating minimum wage combined with rampant gentrification and a nearly 70 percent reduction in federal housing subsidies.[14] Two other factors are frequently cited to account for this increase: the deinstitutionalization of mental patients beginning in the mid-1950s and the crack epidemic of the mid-1980s. In fact, the fastest-growing group of homeless during the Reagan administration was small children.[15] For while addicts and the mentally ill are indeed disproportionately represented, numerous studies have confirmed what the historical record appears to suggest: that the rate of homelessness is closely correlated to fluctuations in jobs, wages, and housing costs; that its root cause, in short, is economic. The crisis of the 1980s is thus most readily explicable as a simple matter of mathematics—elevated rents combined with dwindling incomes.[16]

A marked increase in the homeless population—especially to an extent that spills over into the neighborhoods and troubled awareness of those with homes—is invariably followed by an outpouring of works endeavoring to represent homeless characters and circumstances. Reports in the popular media are likely to appear first, along with analyses by charitable and governmental agencies. More scholarly contributions come later and range from quantitative studies to those aiming to capture the texture of homeless life through participant observation or transcription of oral histories. As John Allen recounts in *Homelessness in American Literature* (2004), Meridel Le Sueur wrote documentary works based on stories told to her by homeless women during the Depression.[17] Somewhat less common are first-person narratives by people with homeless relatives or with their own, direct experience of homelessness. Jack London's account of his days as a hobo belongs to a cluster of tramp autobiographies appearing between 1890 and 1940.[18] Conditions in Victorian England and the United States also inspired a number of well-known fictional works on the topic. Charles Dickens's *Oliver Twist* (1838) and Stephen Crane's *Maggie: Girl of the Streets* (1893), for example, helped shape a novelistic subgenre extending into the contemporary period with such works as Alix Kates Shulman's *On the Stroll* (1981) and Russell Banks's *Rule of the Bone* (1995).[19]

As I have mentioned, most of the homeless texts I draw on belong to a spate of works appearing between 1988 and 1996 (several in the single year of 1993). Their proliferation in the early 1990s can be directly attributed to the increasing visibility of homelessness in the 1980s, and many are explicitly framed in relation to this fact.[20] A few focus on a single figure; others describe a group or subculture. All aim to break with historical patterns of blithely indicting the homeless. To this end, they work hard to demonstrate the particularity of individuals along with the role of environmental factors, from domestic violence and job loss to slashed housing subsidies and the demolition of SROs. Some also take issue with the centuries-old charity model in which certain of the poor are deemed "deserving" of aid, while the rest are disparaged as "undeserving." As sociologist David Wagner says of this model, to be "deserving" typically means conforming to traditional patterns of family and work.[21]

Allen's study of literary representations interrogates two other prevalent myths, corresponding to realist/naturalist and romantic genres. Whereas the first depicts homeless characters as wholly abject and downtrodden, overstating their lack of agency, the second portrays them as free-spirited hobos, overstating its extent.[22] As Allen argues, both versions misrepresent the complexity and variability of being without secure shelter, one by reducing people to victims and the other by assuming they simply prefer a homeless "lifestyle."[23] To this I would add that the "romantic" myth is further problematic in idealizing men seen as liberated from a feminine domestic sphere and emasculating work environment. I find it ironic that several insightful critiques of the charity model imply a similarly gendered logic. Disparaging the acceptance of aid as complicit with the status quo, they end up romanticizing the antishelter homeless as class rebels defying the bourgeois order. However much I concur with a class analysis of homelessness, I am wary of a view that denigrates strategies of survival more often practicable for women, especially those with children, by way of affirming those more easily available to single men and consonant with norms of potent masculinity.[24]

In the pages to come, I hope to avoid romanticizing homeless lives while also building on efforts to counter stereotypes of deficiency and dysfunction. Like those who point to signs of class resistance among homeless people, I am committed to bringing out evidence of agency, competence, imagination, and community in contexts more often assumed to preclude these. What interests me, however, is not agency in opposition to domestic comforts and values but, on the contrary, agency on their behalf. My own recuperation focuses not on "masculine" forms of home leaving but on forms of homemaking marked and undervalued as "feminine." In keeping with this book as a whole, I do so in defense of such domestic virtues as privacy, safety, stability, coziness, quiet, beauty, intimacy, and routine—qualities important to men and women both, especially when they cannot be taken for granted. As I have argued throughout *Extreme Domesticity*, rejecting these qualities in relation to conventional, sentimentalized notions of home should not mean, as it so often does, rejecting them altogether. Privacy and safety, for example, may indeed take the grotesque form of a gated community. True, too, that privacy can work *against* safety in situations of domestic violence, allowing it to remain hidden. At the same time, for those of the poor most susceptible to harassment and assault in public spaces (women, racial minorities, children, and queers), having a private refuge may be key to sanity as well as safety.[25]

Reading my texts for their insights into homeless domesticity, I hope to counter entrenched views of unsheltered people as *them*, alien beings located at the greatest possible distance from *us*. Although the women and men portrayed by my texts are, of course, different from one another and from the well housed, I believe their stories can help us to recognize and claim a common ground of daily domestic needs, practices, and desires. Reviewing the scenarios offered by my texts, I have found it useful to parse them in terms of six overlapping categories: privacy, storage, adornment, routine, intimacy, and kinship. Each suggests a major component of domestic life—here, pried apart, imperiled, and reinvented as an effect of homelessness. Though sometimes derived from the baseline requirements of physical survival (for example, the need to store food), generally speaking they are precisely what exceeds such requirements, what constitutes the dense culture of domesticity peculiar to us as human animals. One advantage of looking at this culture in the context of homelessness is de-familiarization. The ultimate goal, however, is re-familiarization as we come to identify its basic outlines as our own.

Returning to the example of *privacy*, now barely afforded by crowded shelter or dark alleyway, we soon find that it no longer references ownership and exclusivity but instead involves the ability to shit, wash up, change clothes, have sex, study, dream, get high, get a good night's sleep, and more, shielded from the gaze, interference, and moralizing of others. Likewise with *storage*. Not supersized, walk-in closets but simply a secure, accessible means of stashing and/or carrying objects, keeping them safe from pilfering and weather—the provision, as Gaston Bachelard might say, of privacy for one's things. Among the amenities typically offered by shelters are individual lockers or storage bins, each labeled with a name and perhaps a number. For people without an address, such units at least provide a much-needed address for their stuff.[26] Storage, of course, may be short term or long term, a pack tucked behind a bush or a rental unit stacked with furniture. In addition to food, bedding, and clothing, the vast assortment of items likely to be stored includes toiletries, medications, diapers, pet supplies, books, photographs, instruments, mementoes, and assorted trinkets.

When items are treasured as a means of dressing up one's body or decorating one's space, then we are in the area of *adornment*, an aspect of the domestic that, I have noted, may be only thinly evinced, at least where decor is concerned. As one of Jackson Underwood's subjects put it when describing his encampment under a Los Angeles bridge, "I don't have doilies and that kind of crap laying around. My way of life is, 'Stay warm Jerry.'"[27] At the same time, we will see that homelessness does not preclude "doilies" in every instance, and even Jerry wants to "tidy up a LITTLE bit" before the anthropologist comes to call.[28] In addition to organizing space, domestic practices are a way of organizing time. People who are homeless, like those who are not, are apt to develop *routines*. Rituals and rhythms from home may be echoed and adapted as conditions permit: reading the paper, visiting a soup kitchen at a certain time, cooking dinner on a hotplate or over a campfire, sharing a bottle of Thunderbird after a long day of panhandling, getting a kid from shelter to school. Especially for those without children or regular work, domestic routines can be helpful as a stay against boredom and drift.

Intimacy is perhaps the most elusive of my categories, since I invoke it to encompass not only physical/emotional closeness to other people but also the sense of coziness and warmth to be had from tactile contact with a pet or even a comforting object. This brings us to *kinship*, by which I mean a web of ties both looser and more extensive than those with intimates: something like an extended family, but with affiliations based on choice supplementing or replacing those based on biology.[29] Flexible as well as intentional, kinship in my lexicon is really another word for community. Linking people together as neighbors and fellow travelers, kinship speaks to the open, networked nature of domesticity. Expressions of kinship among those without homes recall the neighborliness we saw in *Mary Barton*: the sharing of resources by those with little to spare; acts of charity by those assumed to be on charity's receiving end. Kinship may also, in some cases, be the basis for political solidarity and activism.

For those of us leading sheltered lives, most if not all of these domestic components are enjoyed unconsciously, taken for granted as the least of our entitlement as citizens and members of the human family. Because they are so readily and fully available, they may be largely invisible (or else, derided as signs of bourgeois propriety and consumerism, hypervisible). But if my own experience is any indication, reading about people for whom domestic life is a daily struggle can reboot our respect for domesticity at its most elemental level: the need to secure ourselves and our things; the impulse to beautify; the comfort of going about daily rounds; the importance of warm, tactile connections; the sense of belonging and obligation to a tribe.

SHELTER DREAMING

Jonathan Kozol is a prize-winning writer on issues of poverty and race in the United States, known especially for his efforts on behalf of school reform. In *Rachel and Her Children: Homeless Families in America* (1988), he turned to the issue of homelessness with a scathing and timely critique of shelter conditions in New York City in the late 1980s. Part I introduces us to the lives of residents being warehoused in the Martinique Hotel. My own focus is on the chapter "Grieving for a Lost Home," in which we meet a woman whom Kozol refers to as "Annie Harrington."[30]

Annie, her husband, and their three young children seem to be dying a slow death on the fourteenth floor of a shelter hotel infamous for its squalor (though apparently not the worst of its kind): broken elevators; peeling lead paint; leaking sewage; infestations of rats and roaches; whole families crowded into small rooms, sitting on the bed to eat meals cooked on a hotplate. For many, the food is insufficient. Kids are lethargic from hunger, and poor nutrition contributes to an infant mortality rate among residents that is more than twice the national average (30). Held hostage by an arbitrary and inefficient bureaucracy along with draconian cuts in aid, Annie and her neighbors spend entire, demoralizing days waiting in lines, filling out useless forms, and pounding the streets for housing that doesn't exist within their budget.

Rachel and Her Children is so full of obscenities—children getting arrested for shoplifting a chicken, panhandling to buy Cheerios, running a gauntlet of offers to pay for sex (75–77)—that it can make for difficult reading. For reasons both factual and polemical (like his books on education, this one is lobbying for changes in policy), Kozol keeps the focus on domestic deprivation and suffering. Annie does her best without either kitchen or table. She manages to serve her son Doby hot cereal and tea, bundle him up against the cold, and pack him off to school with his homework (45). Clearly there are routines and intimacy to be had. But the complex logistics of meals, laundry, bathing, and sleeping are nonetheless exhausting, embittering, and divisive. While this family manages better than many, it is hard to dispute Kozol's conclusion that "a place in which a parent cannot cook a meal is, to begin with, something different from a home as most of us would understand that word" (49).

Needless to say, I am grateful for Kozol's exposé of shocking conditions and failed policies. I do, however, wish to experiment with a shift in affective tenor. What happens if we note not only the loss of home in this chapter but also its persistence in a dream Annie had—a dream of having a beautiful apartment—which she describes as "so real I keep on thinking that I went there in my sleep"? (43). Having traveled there in her sleep, she returns for a second time in the telling: a lovingly detailed, room-by-room tour enabling Kozol and the reader to share her vision. Her description (shelter writing, really) illustrates what I mean by domesticity not wholly disappeared but, in this case, dispersed across time: drawing on memories and fantasizing about the future, Annie calls on her dream of a perfected domesticity as a resource for the present. Here is her account:

> My daughter had her own room, pink and white with something up over the bed. A *canopy* is what it's called, I think. . . . The boys, they had to share a room. I painted that room blue; there was a spread over the bed that Doby slept in. It had football pictures on it. My kitchen had a phone, a stove, refrigerator, toaster, all of those nice things. My dining-room table was glass and it was simple, plain and clean. In my living room I had a pretty couch and lots of books, a big bookshelf, and there were plants beside the window, and the floor was what I call a *parquet* floor and it was waxed. My bedroom had a nice brass bed, a lot of books there too, and pillows covered with fresh linens, and the drapes were nice bright colors. Yellow. Like the linens. And the neighborhood was clean. The neighborhood was nice. The neighbors liked me. And the landlord liked me too. He said that we could use the backyard, so we bought a grill to barbecue outside on summer nights. (43)

Before commenting on this passage, I want to address its relation to Kozol's overall project. Throughout the chapter, Annie is clearly being mobilized for the book's systematic counterattack on negative images of the poor. As David Wagner might observe, the Harringtons serve to debunk these images precisely insofar as they conform to normative rather than "deviant" models of both family and work. Kozol is thus at pains to stress that Annie is married to a loving husband who is present, employed, and taking computer classes. Annie herself, despite severe asthma attacks, is prayerful, sexually contained, and bent on being a good mother. The entire portrait seems calculated to serve as a point-by-point refutation of the stereotypical "welfare queen," traipsing around on the government dime and popping out kids by different dads. In Kozol's most explicit formulation, the Harringtons are defended as "good people: clean and honest. Diligent too. They love their children and each other. Nothing I've read about the culture of the underclass comes near the mark" (42). "Clean" in this case functions as code for sexual/marital propriety (especially on Annie's part), while "diligence" checks the work-ethic box (especially on her husband's part). As we know, this approach to redeeming the pathologized "underclass" has a long-standing history, and up to a point it is effective. The problem, I agree with Wagner, is that it deems the Harringtons worthy according to a set of narrowly conservative values, reinforcing the terms by which others will continue to be shunned as unclean and indolent.

Annie works particularly well for Kozol's purposes because she herself is equally invested in legitimating herself and her family, employing a similar moral vocabulary to do so. In Annie's idiom, the qualities of propriety, diligence, and general worthiness are summed up by the word *nice*. Her quiet daughter and studious son are, she insists, "*nice* kids," who deserve to be the family's first priority (41). Other people and places are also approved as "nice," and what interests me here is how often this praise coincides with Annie's being approved in turn. Of a potential landlady, Annie explains, "I believe she took a liking to me. So I was excited. . . . A nice lady. And you see—you do forget what is your *situation*. You forget that you are poor. It's like a dream: This lady likes me and we're going to have a home!" (42). The same holds true of the dream scenario, in which a "nice" neighborhood is one whose residents take a liking to Annie: "The neighborhood was nice. The neighbors liked me. And the landlord liked me too." In effect, nice people nicely situated, by liking Annie, certify her as likable—someone whose niceness matches theirs. As niceness migrates from them to her, Annie is transformed from a person excluded by her *situation* to a woman welcomed into their midst as a tenant and neighbor.[31]

Looking more closely at the details of Annie's dream apartment, there's little question that it conforms in most ways to conservative, middle-class ideals of family and home. The kids' bedrooms are strongly gendered not only by color and football but also, more subtly, by means of the daughter's private room and canopied bed, identifying her with the kind of precious femininity (privileged, white, and pure) that deserves to be protected. Annie herself first enters the picture in relation to her kitchen, complete with "phone, a stove, refrigerator, toaster, all of those nice things." Yet this nice kitchen is hardly overequipped (even for the 1980s). Like the "simple, plain" dining table, it is becomingly modest in keeping with the frugality of a family that gives winter clothes instead of toys for Christmas (41). Annie's taste, even in her dreams, is neither gaudy nor greedy but precisely "deserving": middle class in its reticence, working class in its humility. A desire for cultural capital is likewise discreetly evident in the emphasis on books—lots of them, overflowing from living into bedroom—as well as in Annie's shy use of tony words like *canopy* and *parquet*.

Three more qualities are essential to Annie's vision, all of them familiar to us by now from earlier examples of shelter writing: safety, cleanliness, and beauty. The first is invoked by Annie's description of the neighborhood as "clean" and "nice," conventional code for the absence of street crime. Safety is suggested, too, by the backyard, available to tenants for grilling on summer nights. Contrasting this to actual conditions in the shelter, with fearful families barricaded inside, we realize that domestic security needs to include access to a safe exterior. Cleanliness—in addition to sometimes coding pernicious notions about gender, sexuality, class, and race—literally and more innocently denotes a degree of order and sanitation. Mentioned twice explicitly, cleanliness is further evoked and aestheticized through references to freshness ("fresh linens") and shininess ("waxed" floor and "brass bed"). Fresh and gleaming, Annie's dream space is beautiful as well as clean. Pleasure in adornment, evident throughout, is made explicit by her vision of a "pretty couch" and bedrooms aglow in cheerful colors (pink, blue, and especially yellow).

As usual, I hesitate simply to dismiss this dream as corrupt bourgeois fantasy and would like to propose an alternative reading. To start, I am willing to claim safety, cleanliness, and beauty as generalizable goods—

values not specific to the wealthier classes. A safe, pretty apartment is not, per se, complicit with the dominant culture. I would also distinguish Annie's underclass longing from middle-class complacency. From her perspective, even the official poverty level denotes unimaginable wealth: "That isn't poor. That isn't no way near where I am at" (44). Viewed from so far below, Annie's image of the good life, in its utter remoteness and unreality, exposes the American Dream as a poor person's pipe dream. More important, her longing is arguably, in the end, not about things at all but about personhood. Connection to nice people, rooms, and neighborhoods serves, I have suggested, as a way for Annie herself to be recognizable as nice. In her dream, the freshness of linens works to freshen Annie herself, removing the stain of homelessness. Unlike Kozol's ideological embrace of normative family, I see Annie's as a personal project invested less in propriety than in visibility. What I take from her dream is not complicity with bourgeois values but an outcast's fantasy of inclusion, a dirty woman's fantasy of being clean.

As this last point indicates, Annie's dream is a specifically feminine one. Before moving on, I would call attention to another gendered aspect of her account: a second domestic yearning in tension with Annie's poignant aspiration to proper womanhood. For despite the reference to children's rooms, Annie's pristine rental is no more animated by rambunctious children than are the tranquil country homes and palaces I discussed in relation to shelter magazines and Wharton's *Decoration of Houses*. Further recalling my reading of Wharton is the glaring omission of a single reference to poor Mr. Harrington. Annie's repetition of *my* ("my kitchen," "my dining-room table," "my living room") extends even to "my bedroom." Cheerful and comforting with its brass bed, fresh linens, pillows, and plentiful books, this personal retreat is detailed with no less care than Dominique Browning's sensuous haven in *Around the House*. I close this section with the suggestion that—like Browning's headquarters, Wharton's boudoir, and Esperanza's "house quiet as snow"—Annie's perfect apartment may represent not only stability for her family but also, *over against* family, a privacy of her own.

HOBO DOMESTICITY

My next work is *Travels with Lizbeth: Three Years on the Road and on the Streets* (1993), Lars Eighner's account of being homeless in the late 1980s. The author of gay erotica as well as a novel, Eighner remains best known for his memoir of unsheltered life, one of the few we have from a professional writer.[32] The chapter "On Dumpster Diving" has been anthologized, and the book as a whole has garnered a fair amount of attention. John Allen's *Homelessness in American Literature* places *Travels with Lizbeth* in the tradition of texts romanticizing the "tramp." As we will see, while I agree in finding *Travels with Lizbeth* significant, my reasons for citing it are rather different.

During the years covered by this narrative, Eighner occasionally crashes with friends and makes a few trips to Los Angeles hoping to find work, but most of his time is spent in makeshift camps in and around Austin, Texas. True to the title, wherever he goes, his beloved dog Lizbeth goes too. As with most homeless people, Eighner's loss of shelter comes on the heels of an extensive employment history. For fifteen years, he held a variety of jobs in health care: bookkeeper for an NGO, director of a suicide-prevention and drug-crisis center, and advocate for the mentally ill and patients with AIDS.[33] Even as a homeless man eating out of dumpsters, Eighner donates extra canned goods to an AIDS food bank and gives up his sleeping bag to a homeless man dying of AIDS (109–10, 202–3). Such neighborly acts of care are not unusual among the homeless. Far less common is Eighner's status as a writer. He actually completes the script for an adult video, sells a story, and begins to draft his memoir all during his time out of doors. For Eighner, the daily routine of scavenging in dumpsters, finding an unobtrusive campsite, securing Lizbeth and his gear, making their bed on a patch of level ground, and sharing out their food might also conclude with settling in to write.

Early on, Eighner tells of hitching a ride with a reckless young drunk who commutes between Phoenix and Los Angeles, shoplifting from convenience stores (27–40). Puzzled to explain why he tolerated such company, Eighner muses, "As bad as things had been I cannot deny there is a romance of the road" (32–33). On the face of it, Eighner's story of a footloose man and his dog would seem to partake of the hobo-adventure genre described earlier—a genre, I agree with Allen, that puts a deceptively positive spin on male homelessness. As Allen explains, reviewers have reinforced the myth that homeless men are adventurers or philosophers by comparing Eighner with the travel writer Eric Newby or even Henry David Thoreau.[34] Citing the "romance" remark, Allen further suggests that Eighner himself "seems not to resist the association with romanticized, adventuresome notions of homelessness."[35] If so, then *Travels with Lizbeth* might be said to invert the gender logic of our last text, replacing the mother who dreams of domesticity with the man who abandons it for a life on the road. This, however, is not my understanding. Eighner himself specifically asserts: "My object was not to explore homelessness but to get off the street" (x). Indeed, having noted the appeal of a wandering lifestyle, Eighner proceeds to spend most of his time *off* the road, making every effort to contrive a reasonably safe, stable, and comforting domesticity for himself and his canine companion.

As we have seen, Eighner finds elements of home both in charitable expressions of kinship and in establishing something of a routine. Privacy for himself and his gear proves harder to come by. Like most of those living outside, he is continually hounded out of his various nests, and even Lizbeth can't protect his things from repeated theft.[36] There is, however, a notable period lasting about a month when Eighner fashions a hideaway for himself and his belongings, furnishing it with a DIY fervor worthy of Robinson Crusoe or Martha Stewart. Eighner's own intertext for this project is *The Swiss Family Robinson*, which he cites as introduction to a blow-by-blow description of making a home in a stand of bamboo. Excerpted here, it is a vivid, rather rapturous description that, like Annie's account of her dream, surely qualifies as an example of homeless shelter writing:

> I found shower curtains and learned to layer them to keep the rain off
> our heads. I rigged several of them on bamboo poles so they could be
> lowered down the bamboo walls; I was planning against the winter

winds, although it was July. I camouflaged the shower curtains over-head to prevent their being seen by aircraft. I installed cushions and a foam mattress on them. I put in makeshift bookshelves. I found some large fresh dry cells and wired them to a radio so I did not have to change the batteries every hour as I listened to the news. When I satis-fied myself that light in our camp would not call attention to us at night, I discovered how to make lamps that would burn on cooking oil, a commodity that was always available in abundance in the Dump-sters. . . . I could see no reason I might not bathe in the bamboo, and I set out vessels to catch rainwater for this purpose. I always had some little project. (250–51)

I have several observations to make about this passage. There is, first, the obvious concern with protection from intrusion as well as from the elements. Camouflaging the roof and keeping his lights low, Eighner might seem to be preparing for battle. Bizarrely enough, he is finally chased out because a woman, looking down from her mansion on a hill, imagines she sees the encampment of "a well-armed paramilitary op-eration" (257–58). Contrary to gender expectations, however, Eighner's is not a military but a domestic exercise. His jungle hideaway is not about defending the home front; it *is* the home front. With its plastic sheet-ing and Lizbeth as a deterrent to rats, raccoons, and possums, his nine-by-four room is neatly cordoned off from the wilderness and fitted up for domestic convenience. As in Annie's apartment, cushions and books add touches of comfort and culture, and the sum of these various de-vices, beyond the literal provision of shelter, is a place to dwell. Proving his agency, productivity, and ingenuity, Eighner counters the stereotype of men who, in their homelessness, are shunned as lazy and ineffectual, impaired if not actually disturbed. Like Crusoe, his adventures in home improvement are twinned with self-improvement. As Eighner "rigs" and "installs," he also "learns" and "discovers." Domestic life is shown to have its own demands for labor and creativity, its own rewards of dis-covery and pleasure. And if homelessness can have a softening, disori-enting effect on time as well as space, defining the contours of his little room also enables Eighner to periodize the drift of his days.

A reading of domesticity in *Travels with Lizbeth* would be incomplete without consideration of the eponymous pup. Just as Lizbeth, by warding off rodent (and other) intruders, helps mark the boundaries of Eighner's fragile "indoors," so his domestic efforts are partly on her behalf. In keeping with the title, man and dog travel toward domesticity together, providing aspects of home for each other. As Eighner explains a bit defensively in his introduction, "I often write or say *we*, meaning Lizbeth and I. Some people find this peculiar, but I fail to see why. I do not say *we planned, we hoped*, or *we thought*, because I do not think that way. I do say *we walked, we camped*, and *we slept*" (xii). Theirs, in short, is an emphatically physical companionship, based on sustained, bodily proximity as they move through space, fastened together at leash length, negotiating the ups and downs of each day. Proximity, too, as they climb wearily into a sleeping bag at night. Sometimes, when the temperature drops, Lizbeth ventures to claim one more degree of closeness. Camped on an incline outside Los Angeles, Eighner reports: "The night turned chilly and again Lizbeth . . . climbed up into the down jacket with me" (55).

I have said that Lizbeth is a cocreator of domestic conditions. Beyond this, James Krasner's valuable work on the tactile dimension of hominess points to a sense in which for Eighner, Lizbeth *is* domesticity.[37] Bringing theories of embodiment to bear on our experience of home, Krasner asserts that "while the home is both a cultural formulation and a building, it is, more than either of these, a cluster of tactile sensations and bodily positions."[38] What happens, then, when home-as-building is removed from the equation altogether? Krasner addresses this question in a chapter on "homeless companions" with reference to Eighner: "Because the homeless cannot participate in traditional conceptions of home, they undertake to create somatic homes in motion; their corporeal interchanges with their dogs fulfill those aspects of embodiment fundamental to domesticity."[39]

In Eighner's case, "corporeal interchange" with Lizbeth is often managed by wrapping her leash around his waist, leaving his hands free. This arrangement, combined with the fact that Eighner relies on Lizbeth's keener senses as if they were his own, leads Krasner to conclude that she is "less a partner than an appendage, an actual element of Eighner's body."[40] And this is where my analysis differs just slightly from his. For while Krasner means to illustrate the bond between two creatures, by seeing Lizbeth's body as part and parcel of Eighner's, he ends up collapsing two into one. Such a conflation negates the *with* of Eighner's title and likewise the *we* so lovingly and self-consciously woven throughout the text. To me, the tethering of man and dog suggests not a single composite body but the touching entanglement of two discrete bodies. Recalling primal ties, overlapping with ties to lovers met along the way (and eventually triangulated by a man named Clint), the intimacy between Eighner and Lizbeth evokes for both creatures the reassuring coziness and tactile familiarity of being at home.

BAG LADY DOMESTICITY

Pawing through dumpsters for objects worth scavenging, Eighner reflects on the meaning of so many discarded things. In addition to seeing what people throw away—"abandoned teddy bears, shredded wedding books, despaired-of sales kits" (121)—he has lost his own possessions to theft many times over. Schooled in "the transience of material being," he takes what he needs but no longer "invests objects with sentimental value," no longer accumulates for accumulation's sake (124–25).

The same cannot be said for "Natalie"—the filthy, psychotic, profanity-shouting antiheroine of my third text, parked on a sidewalk with her overflowing shopping cart in Ann Nietzke's *Natalie on the Street*.[41] Nietzke had published one novel and was holed up struggling with another when Natalie entered her life and prompted a detour into nonfiction. In the funny-sad book that resulted, Nietzke recounts her experience one autumn in Los Angeles when, coping with frustration and isolation of her own, she attempted to befriend an elderly homeless woman who had come to rest on her apartment doorstep. Among other things, *Natalie on the Street* is a candid meditation on the pity, guilt, and fear felt by the housed when faced with those who are not.

Centered on the spectacle of a woman and her stuff, Nietzke's text explores not only the challenges and meanings of storage but also the complex issue of personal privacy for women on the street. Like Annie Harrington, Natalie (as Nietzke calls her) is strongly identified with her belongings. Unlike Eighner, hindered but not immobilized by his, Natalie is both sustained and chained by her overloaded cart and auxiliary bags. *Her* travels take the form of a laborious shuffle: "That's what that officer told me. . . . Keep moving, see. As soon as I quit moving is right when the trouble starts" (4). The trouble has apparently started when Nietzke finds Natalie run aground completely, laid out with her baggage at the base of a palm tree. Demonstrating once again the gendered nature of homeless domesticity, the narrative invites us to consider a cluster of social beliefs about women and their containers, women and containment, women and the specter of incontinence.

As we saw with Eighner, storage is an ongoing problem for people living outside, who must stash and/or carry their gear and whose possessions are continually being rained on, stolen, and confiscated.[42] Aside from the practical necessity of storage, a private place for one's things may serve, I have suggested, as a trope for one's own privacy and security. If containers of stuff do this metaphorically, they may also do so literally. In the absence of walls, they may be set down to mark off territory, indicate personal boundaries—a makeshift, open-air version of what Ahmed means by "putting things around." Finally, however, storing one's things in public has a self-defeating quality. However boxed and bagged, homeless belongings are not contained so much as laid out for all to see. The same goes for their proprietor who, surrounded by possessions, isn't walled off but even more conspicuous. For women, charged with keeping domestic objects, including their own bodies, properly ordered and contained, the consequences of such exposure can be especially catastrophic.

While the category of "bag man" simply makes no sense, we are all familiar with the abject figure of a "bag lady," and even well-off women are known to joke nervously about becoming one.[43] As Natalie illustrates, with her shopping cart brimming with parcels, the bag lady inverts respectable femininity while also performing a caricatured version of it.

Invoking women's role as designated shopper and keeper of stuff, the lady with bags points further to the lady *as* bag—to the role, that is, of women's bodies as receptacles for both sexual and reproductive purposes. In normative terms, the good woman is a sound, tightly sealed container and possesses a certain value as such. But once she is no longer seen as young, desirable, and fertile, her worth declines rapidly until she is used up, useless, the proverbial "old bag." Worse still than a container past its prime is the woman regarded as sexually incontinent. Female bodies seen as compromised (whether by sexual assault or their own sexual agency) are bodies whose boundaries, once breached, need no longer be respected. "Bag ladies," old and defiled both, are the most tattered, tainted, and despised of all.[44]

Quintessential "bag lady," poor Natalie is almost entirely lacking in boundaries. Without roof or walls, she is physically bared to the weather and the neighborhood gaze. As we see in the following rant—freely mixing delusion and reality, obscenity and banality—she is further unprotected from bodily violation.

> I mean his *joint*, Ann, right up in the bowel so that whatever comes out comes out. You could call, you could scream, or not, because he won't give a you-know-what what you do, anyway, if he likes it or doesn't like it or calls you every name in the book doesn't matter. If you talk back is when they got out that pipe. But I used to get those coupons and try to use them at the store, you know, but it never quite worked out. (67)

Whether memory, delusion, or a mixture of both, the image of anal rape evokes a number of ongoing, verifiable assaults on Natalie's body, privacy, and dignity. These include the humiliation of having to defecate in public; constant vulnerability to theft, rape, and assault; and continual intrusion by police, neighbors, psychiatrists, and social workers. In light of these facts, we are forced to pause before dismissing her recurrence to such violent scenes as simply paranoid. And if Natalie's fear of violation has at least some basis in reality, I would add that for women in general, the juxtaposition of being raped and going to the store is not incredibly far-fetched.

In the preceding scene, Natalie's screams may be unheeded and "talking back" punishable, but in the role of narrator she would seem to have turned the tables through her use of radically uncensored, "unladylike" speech. Confused in her thinking, Natalie is brazenly transgressive in her utterings. Though her person may be violated, it is tempting to claim as a kind of freedom her own violation of verbal and other rules of feminine etiquette. Looking more closely, however, I am surprised to realize that having barked out "joint" and "bowel," Natalie then resorts to such euphemisms as "you-know-what" and "every word in the book." To me, the most touching aspect of Nietzke's account is quite possibly this dramatically incontinent woman's effort to retain her dignity by continuing to invoke the cultural signs of correct femininity. In addition to skirting "bad" language, Natalie combs her hair, rejects a sweatshirt as too masculine, and reaches into her bra for a lipstick (7, 35, 38). Above all, she responds to her embarrassing lack of domestic boundaries with a number of strategies for creating them. She sheaths her body and belongings in plastic. In lieu of closets, drawers, and cabinets, she packs her cart with bags, boxes, and mysterious bundles. The cart serves further as a barrier both literal and symbolic, claiming a patch of sidewalk as Natalie's own. As Nietzke explains, the cart "had become her traveling *apartment*, which she used to set herself *apart* from her environment on the street" (5–6 [italics in original]). Donated cushions are used in a similar fashion as "boundary markers for her camp rather than as a bed" (160).

If Natalie deploys her cart to contain her body as well as her things, she also aspires to the gendered ideal of the body *as* an intact container. To that end, she avoids drinking water, fearing that "what goes in must come out, you know" (29). Likewise, for reasons that appear psychological as well as logistical, she tells Nietzke, "I've got to learn to control these bowels" (28). When that measure fails, her next tactic is to recontain and hoard her stool. Securing it in covered cups, jars, and boxes, she fiercely resists Nietzke's best efforts to seize, rewrap, and dispose of these containers. A similar tussle occurs around the garbage that Nietzke attempts to wrest from her friend. "Each day," Nietzke reports, "it's an ordeal to get Natalie to let me throw away some trash" (27). Given the women's shared goal of containment (producing a humorously similar obsession with plastic bags [94]), we might be surprised that the issue of disposal creates so much conflict. Yet what appears perversely unsanitary on Natalie's part is not wholly irrational. As she quite rightly recognizes, there is a difference between managing her own waste and Nietzke's efforts to do so on her behalf. In fact, these projects are at cross-purposes: whereas Natalie expresses a wish for privacy and autonomy, Nietzke aims to respect this wish but ends up doing the opposite—invading Natalie's privacy and threatening her autonomy.

As Nietzke herself explains, despite the emotional tie that develops between them, her campaign to get Natalie cleaned up—to bag her shit, bathe her body, and, ultimately, remove her from the street—is often experienced by its object as continuous with other kindly acts of trespass by neighbors and officials. Nietzke notes, for example, that following a supervised bath, Natalie is particularly sensitive to further intrusion (32–38). It is also true that even the best-meant efforts to repair Natalie can scarcely help reiterating the gendered logic by which is she seen as ruined in the first place. Sadly and perhaps inevitably, the more determined Nietzke is to protect her friend, the more clearly she enacts and imposes her own—our own—anxiety about deviance from decorous femininity.[45] By now it would be useless to deny my personal investment in tidiness as well as my wish to redeem it ideologically. Yet Natalie's story should remind us of how fraught the category of cleanliness can be: a generalizable good and self-affirming goal when pursued by a Natalie or an Annie Harrington herself, but also a heavily moralized category deployed with great efficacy to police female behavior and rationalize hierarchies of race and class as well as gender.

I do not say this as a criticism of Nietzke. Her acts of caring go far beyond what most of us would hazard, and Natalie benefits greatly from her gifts of food, clothing, conversation, and understanding. Moreover, it is Nietzke herself who explains how easily "protection" devolves into violation. She hints throughout at the possible legitimacy of Natalie's wariness when offered transportation to a shelter: "I'm better off in the open air. . . . They gave me lye in there, you know. Put it all the way down my throat" (10). Worried that she herself may be forcing "normalcy" down Natalie's throat, she comes to question her own motives for pursuing hospitalization (144). Nietzke certainly doesn't celebrate life on the street, nor should we, but neither does she ignore Natalie's attitude toward being institutionalized: "I'm already home free now, honey" (18). No wonder that Nietzke's feelings, and ours, are so mixed when a hospital van finally arrives and forcibly separates Natalie, "yelling her head off," from the cart and bags that made up her sidewalk domesticity (167–68).

BRIDGE PEOPLE

Natalie on the Street documents the genuine but troubled and short-lived friendship between a reclusive apartment dweller and an unusually isolated homeless woman. Eighner, too, though closely bonded with Lizbeth, spends most of his time out of doors isolated from others. In this penultimate section, I call on three participant-observer ethnographies to illustrate a different pattern: not occasional acts of neighborliness but sustained, reciprocal ties of kinship as they function in particular homeless communities. Countering the assumption that having no housing means having no social ties, all three studies explore the shared spaces, practices, loyalties, and belief systems of what amount to highly elaborated subcultures. I take my subtitle from the first of these works: Jackson Underwood's *The Bridge People, Daily Life in a Camp of the Homeless* (1993). Underwood's reference is to a specific site: the bridges in downtown Los Angeles arcing over a cluster of homeless encampments. My own reference is looser and more abstract, meant to suggest the practical and affective bridges built up among homeless individuals residing as a group. Another, shakier bridge interests me as well: the one separating/joining the unsheltered and the sheltered. In the pages that remain, I consider texts that explore if not a bridging then at least a narrowing of the gap between housing haves and have-nots.

The Bridge People originated as a research project sponsored by the Department of Psychiatry at the University of California, Los Angeles.

Conducted by Underwood in the late 1980s, it undertook to study a group of homeless men (and one woman) living in Los Angeles under the aforementioned bridges.[46] With a few exceptions, the majority fit the "skid row" demographic: the average resident is a white male, forty or older, who drinks moderately or heavily and is no longer employed in the formal economy.[47] Underwood becomes particularly close to two residents he calls "Jerry Michaels" and "Tom Kinkaid." Jerry is initially partnered with "Suzi," and Tom dotes on some kittens (268), their tactile intimacy resembling that between Eighner and Lizbeth. But while forms of sexual and nonsexual intimacy certainly exist, Underwood's primary concern is with the broad matrix of relationships constituting a "people." Comprising several camps with a dozen or so individuals rotating among them, this is not a group of transients.[48] At the time of the study, most had lived in the area for years, and some had long-standing friendships. Their collectivity takes many forms, including collaborative labor, the sharing of resources, mutual caretaking in cases of sickness and injury, enjoyment of one another's company, and, as in all societies, occasional conflict. The following sketch revisits aspects of homeless domesticity previously discussed, from routines to privacy, but places special emphasis on expressions of kinship.

Though officially jobless, the Bridge People work hard. Underwood documents in detail the routines of "panning" (panhandling) and "canning" (collecting cans), often pursued as methodically (with specific hours, techniques, and turf) as more legitimate work (255, 305–6, 319–20). Divisions of labor are well established. When Jerry and Suzi go canning, he does more of the fishing in dumpsters, and she does more of the carrying (94–97, 205–6). Back at the camp, Tom breaks up pallets for firewood and fetches water while Jerry does the cooking (87). In addition to work routines, the Bridge People have well-developed social routines centered on eating, storytelling, smoking, and drinking.[49] To a surprising degree, they keep up with sports and news by listening to the radio and reading the newspaper (27, 80, 254), and Tom is something of a bookworm (108). Although "Larry" is known to keep a tidy camp, we recall from Jerry's earlier "doily" remark that beautification is not a top priority among the Bridge People. Because furniture and other domestic items are frequently confiscated or stolen, there is little incentive to fix things up (261). For the same reason, storage on site is provisional at best (21–22). While privacy inside the camps is scarce, locations are chosen to provide at least a modicum of protection from outsiders. Underwood describes the transition from one world to another achieved by climbing over a three-foot wall, stepping through a hole in a fence, and scrambling up a few more steps to enter "the camp proper" (20).[50]

The anthropologist comments on "the irony of going to see if my homeless friends were at home, but that's the way they referred to their camps too" (68). And why not? They may not be clean, well appointed, or perfectly safe, but the camps are homey for the simple reason that your friends might be *at home* there. Among themselves, moreover, these are friends who behave in many ways more like extended family—sharing food, drink, cigarettes, clothing, and cash. Jerry's rule is that "any food that comes in over the fence [from donors] belongs to all of us, but any money belongs, the money belongs to anyone they give it to unless they specify to divvy it up" (182). Likewise, when Underwood asks if anyone "owns" a particularly rewarding dumpster outside an Italian restaurant, Jerry replies, "No, we share" (156). Extra food and surplus of any kind is always passed along to others, and drinking alone is considered rude (201). Underwood observes that "small amounts of money were constantly being loaned and borrowed" (312). The men also prop one another up, sometimes literally. After Jerry drains a bottle given to him by "Mack," he stands behind "Big Joe," placing his hands on the larger man's shoulders; Joe then leads him down the hill as if he were a child while "John" coaches. On another occasion, when Jerry has a violent case of dysentery, John dashes over to his own supplies, digging out toilet paper and a pair of clean pants (43). When Mack is hit by a bus and lying on the ground, it is Jerry who panhandles until he has enough money for a cab to take him to the hospital (26). And when Jerry and Suzi are sick, the same Mack brings them breakfast every morning: scrambled eggs, ravioli, or grilled cheese (120).

All this helps explain why Jerry might actually prefer living under a bridge to living in a voucher hotel. As he tells Underwood, the hotels are dingy and roach infested, and "there's nothing in them for you to do, except to sit there and look at four walls. . . . You can't have no company. If anybody comes to visit you, you've got to go outside to meet them." The street, he goes on to say, affirms his place in a lively social network: "Since I've been down here so many years, I know people, you know. And they'll stop by and say hello. And how ya doin' and everything else. And so, I don't know, my friends are out here" (32).[51]

Notwithstanding its attractively communal aspects, we romanticize life in the camps at our peril. Filthy conditions and alcoholism take a tremendous toll on health; the daily barrage of mainstream hate and harassment is even more painful and debilitating (11, 59, 73, 117). Nor can we ignore the conflicts and outbreaks of violence among the men (27, 138, 157). Underwood, suddenly less discerning when it comes to gender, comments on the "paradox" of interdependence combined with macho assertions of individualism (139). But this is less a paradox, as I see it, than a clear case of cause and effect. Insecure, aggressive masculinity plays out in other ways as well. Jerry, an endearing wit when sober, is a brutal drunk whose continual fights with Suzi often end with his beating her (87, 109). Here, on the treatment of women, Underwood is especially blinkered. He actually begins a paragraph asserting that "life under the bridges was largely egalitarian" (307) before going on to report that Suzi is routinely abused by others besides Jerry. To this he adds all too casually, "when she passed out, she was occasionally raped" (307).[52] For all these reasons, I see little basis for Underwood's comment that he "envied the social connectedness of the Bridge People" (296). I myself remain unconvinced that any aspect of Bridge life is enviable, especially if you're a woman. At the same time, I find much to appreciate in this study—above all, the compassionate picture it paints of the Bridge People's complex humanity, difficult domesticity, and strong sense of group identity.

David Wagner's *Checkerboard Square: Culture and Resistance in a Homeless Community* (1993), published in the same year as *Bridge People*, echoes its claim that many homeless people have strong subcultural affiliations. For Wagner, moreover, homeless subcultures may serve implicitly if not explicitly to articulate a radical critique of mainstream society. As we recall, Wagner describes the "deserving" poor as those who can be aligned with conventional norms of work and family. His project in *Checkerboard Square* is to champion those labeled "undeserving" by virtue of their alienation from and, in some cases, active resistance to these norms. Findings are based on participant observation and interviews conducted between 1989 and 1991 with a cohort of street people in a "medium-sized New England city." The book's first half calls on this cohort for its interrogation of the traditional work ethic and ideology of family. The second half describes the involvement of this community in various alternative actions and institutions (for example, the "Drop-In Center" and other service agencies).

Wagner breaks the street community down into five, loosely organized subcultures, schematized as follows: Street Drunks (a demographic similar to that of the Bridge People), Street Kids (both sexes, ages 13–18), Young Turks (former street kids, now ages 19–27), Social Club (women predominant, ages 30–45, advocates for alternative mental health care), and Politicos (both sexes, 30–45, radicals, hippies, and mystics).[53] All these formations support Wagner's attack on "the dominant portrayal of the homeless as vulnerable and dependent people worthy perhaps of sympathy but judged to be socially disorganized, disaffiliated, and disempowered" (3). Like the Bridge People, each group illustrates the presence of familylike ties among those alleged to be cut loose from the social fabric.

For our purposes, three more things can be gleaned from Wagner's study. I would point first to the subgroup of kids on their own, most of them refugees from neglectful, abusive, or unstable homes. Needless to say, as with survivors of domestic violence and/or divorce, their stories speak to the destructive rather than creative possibilities of domestic life (155).[54] But I would also note the inspiring example of two groups whose domestic concerns become the basis for political activism. The subculture Wagner calls "Politicos" led a highly successful action that took place in 1987: a tent city lasting about two months, which won improved welfare and shelter policies as well as increased participation in city government (23, 137). Members of the "Social Club," motivated by a "deep sense of social solidarity with all homeless people" (163), also played a leadership role in the tent city action, speaking out especially on behalf of homeless women and the mentally ill (138–39, 163).[55] Politicized tent cities of this kind (including those of the twenty-first-century Occupy movement) insist on the public reasons and remedies for homelessness. Domesticity not only is outed as a matter of public responsibility but also—in the defiant, visible form of the tent city—is mobilized as an emblem and weapon of left political protest.

This brings me to my third point of interest: *Checkerboard Square*'s examples of affiliations serving to bridge the divide between homeless and housed. Wagner's account includes several instances of robust, reciprocal relations, not between himself and his informants, but between homeless and housed members of the communities he is studying.[56] As a direct result of their activism, the Politico and Social Club subcultures interacted frequently with formal organizations, mainstream as well as nontraditional. Politicos worked shoulder to shoulder with other community organizers and had contact with media figures as well as public officials (165). Social Club members clustered around the Friendly Center, a "consumer-run alternative to the medical model" (128) for treating mental illness. Committed to close relations between "consumers" and "staff," the Friendly Center hired street people themselves as employees, with the effect of clouding differences between those dispensing and those on the receiving end of "friendliness" (129). The same was true of the Drop-In Center, a popular day shelter offering such services as breakfast, a mailing address, lockers, and support groups. Here, too, staff and clients mingled and overlapped: clients helped serve breakfast, staff members were involved in political organizing, and all jumped in to help when there was an emergency (126).

Arrangements like these recognize the competencies of people on both sides of the homeless-housed divide. By illustrating mutually beneficial relationships between the sheltered and unsheltered—genuinely collaborative labor on political and domestic fronts—Wagner's study challenges the hierarchy between benevolent patron and needy recipient as well as that between respectable home dweller and pathological drifter. I call on my final ethnography along with Singer's documentary film to expand on this challenge. These last two texts intervene in terms of not only content but also method. Both offer images of domestic spaces shared by someone nominally "sheltered" with others identified as "homeless." The effect of these hybrid residences is to trouble the usual opposition between those deemed rich and poor in the essentials of dwelling. In addition, by engaging their "informants" as virtual equals in the process of representing homeless domesticity, both authors deliberately blur the distinction between researcher and researched. Staging the authorial powers of homeless subjects, the scholar and the filmmaker also reveal the limitations of their own.

Elliot Liebow's *Tell Them Who I Am: The Lives of Homeless Women* (1993) is still another early 1990s, participant-observer study of homelessness, this time focused on single women in emergency shelters not far from Washington, D.C. Between 1984 and 1988, Liebow volunteered four or five days a week, rotating between a day shelter and one of three night shelters. From November through March, his evening shifts were at a place called the Refuge, where twice a month his duties included spending the night. Liebow describes the women's evening routines in detail[57] and even includes a floor plan of the Refuge, showing us the cots, cubbies, and dining tables arranged in a U (6). Sharing meals, sitting around with them, driving them where they needed to go, Liebow spent thousands of hours in conversation with a group of women he soon came to enjoy and admire. The result is an exceptionally nuanced portrayal of what his companions thought about a range of issues from daily relations with shelter staff to jobs, family, sex, and God.

While all this might seem consistent with a typical study, Liebow's is distinguished by the fact that despite his training and national reputation as an ethnographer, it didn't actually begin as a study.[58] Instead it began when Liebow was diagnosed with terminal cancer and, for reasons perhaps only partly conscious, quit his job, gradually increased his hours as a volunteer, and effectively chose the company of transient women for the final transition of his own life. The women knew about his condition. When his health held and he reverted to his habit of taking notes, they also knew he was working on a book. Given their knowledge, Liebow insists they were more than his "research subjects." He considered many to be friends and adds, "They could just as well be considered collaborators in what might fairly be seen as a cooperative enterprise" (xvi). Pointing out that the women had met members of his own family, Liebow describes it as "essential" to his project "that relationships be as symmetrical as possible, that there be a quid pro quo; the women needed to know as much about me as I knew about them" (xii).

Liebow makes good on the goal of symmetry by having two of the women (and one of the shelter directors) comment on his manuscript, and he includes their remarks as notes at the bottom of pages (xvii). Many of these remarks confirm or build on his claims, but some disagree or even poke fun. Kim: "I take strong issue with Elliot's portrayal of shopkeepers, and especially police and security personnel, as generally sympathetic" (159); "Caution: I would not rely too much upon Elliot's description of a particular individual as 'pretty' or 'beautiful'" (153). Grace: "I did not see that much caring, kindness, or courtesy by paid staff or volunteers, as Elliot reports" (129); "Elliot lives in a dream world. He thinks all those staff people and volunteers were around to give love and help. . . . The way people in authority treated you sometimes, I thought they were just out to rob me of what little I had left of my self-esteem" (160). The result is a dialogue in which "Elliot" is the object as well as the author of commentary. And perhaps it is not surprising that he shares both authority and domestic space with these women, given what they all knew: that his own vulnerability and uncertainty about the future—his own transience—was equal to, if not greater than, theirs.

LIKE FAMILY

Shifting genres once again, I conclude this chapter with a slightly later work driving home the aforementioned point: if the homeless share a degree of domesticity with the housed, so do the housed inevitably share a degree of precariousness with the homeless. Building on the still photographs and first-person accounts of Margaret Morton's *The Tunnel: The Underground Homeless of New York City* (1995), Marc Singer's *Dark Days* (2000) portrays daily life in a shantytown located in abandoned Manhattan train tunnels. The film's happy ending shows community members bustling around clean, bright apartments and speaking with disbelief about their former "dark days" (in some cases more than ten years) residing underground. Singer began the film hoping for such an eventuality, and when Amtrak threatened eviction from the tunnels, he teamed with the Coalition for the Homeless to make it happen.[59] The heart of the film, however, is an appreciative portrayal of tunnel domesticity. Despite evidence of rats, garbage, addiction, arson, and emotional trauma, Singer's overwhelming emphasis is on agency, resourcefulness, and interracial camaraderie.

Scene after scene shows friends at ease in homemade surroundings. Someone is cooking on a hotplate, noting the merits of buttermilk in cornbread, or eggs and mustard in meatballs (figure 6.1). As Dee puts it,

FIGURE 6.1 Margaret Morton, *Bernard and Bob.* (From *The Tunnel: The Underground Homeless of New York City* [New Haven, Conn.: Yale University Press, 1995]. Photograph by Margaret Morton © OmbraLuce LLC 1995)

"We're homeless people, but if you know how to cook, cook right." Having tapped into the power grid, the tunnel people have a ready supply of free electricity for cooking and for such things as shaving and watching TV. Sometimes there is running water from city pipes. We see a dartboard on a wall, a toaster oven, a clothesline, a TV stand, and an ingenious security system involving pans, pencil, and tripwire. We see routines of sweeping, painting, brushing teeth, shaving, and getting ready for work canning or reselling found goods. Several households have dogs. One of the most touching scenes shows two men grinning widely as one holds up photos of his various tunnel pets—two cats, a bird, and a gerbil named Peaches. "Miss Peaches was all right," he says wistfully. More than most homeless, including those in temporary shelters, the people in this community have security for themselves and their things, thanks to wooden structures with locks on the doors. Unlike those in shelters, they keep their own hours and are proud of the homes they have built. An especially ambitious man, though modestly deferring to another as having "the nicest house," is always at work on upgrades to his dwelling. In short, the tunnel subculture stands out as having versions of all the domestic elements previously mentioned, including kinship. As one resident put it in response to Amtrak's threat, "I mean we're already down here, you know, by ourselves, my friend. Like family, alright? Now you gonna break up the whole family?"

In an interview for the *Austin Chronicle*, Singer describes feeling "awe" at the mix of people in this particular tunnel and what they had accomplished: "I had so much respect for them because I used to think, 'If I was homeless, would I be able to do the same thing?'"[60] As luck would have it, he was given the chance to find out. Singer himself became homeless while shooting the film and wound up living in the tunnels for several years. What started as a matter of convenience became a matter of necessity. "It was a give and take," Singer explains. "If I had money, everybody was going to eat good. But if I didn't have money, they would help me. There was a six-month stretch where, if they didn't feed me or I hadn't gone out and gotten food with them, I wouldn't have eaten."[61] Besides coming to occupy the status of his "research subjects," the opposite was true as well. Without a crew, budget, or prior experience as a filmmaker, Singer opted to recruit his subjects as gaffers and grips for the project.[62] Henry (adept at tapping into city power) provided lighting for the set. He also rigged up a dolly to run along the train tracks, and the idea to make a film in the first place was Ralph's.[63] Singer's refusal to take sole credit for *Dark Days* was therefore more than usually justified.

Clearly the tunnel people were intrinsic to the production process, filming as well as being filmed. Even more than in our previous examples, cohabitation and collaboration at every level served to bridge the gap between Singer and his "subjects" and to put the categories of "sheltered" and "unsheltered" on a collision course. Taking this a step further, the film itself features a powerful visual trope that neatly upends our usual equation of mainstream life with stability, homeless life with instability. *Dark Days* opens with an Amtrak train leaving Penn Station and is punctuated throughout by the recurrent image of a train roaring through the darkness with its freight of unseen, anonymous passengers. It is an image inviting us to contrast the frenzied mobility of commuters with the settled lives of tunnel people—innovative homemakers gathered like family to eat, joke, argue, tidy up, feed the dog, and lock the door.

CONCLUSION

Dwelling-in-Traveling, Traveling-in-Dwelling

James Clifford has written famously about "traveling cultures." Pointing to instances like our Amtrak commuters or the peripatetic members of a traditional village, he calls our attention to what's missed when anthropologists focus on the stationary aspects of a culture to the exclusion of those involving travel. *Begin with hotels*, he advises more than once, calling on hotels as exemplars of "transient digs," way stations along routes branching out from the domestic center.[1] Clifford stresses that he is not proposing a model of decenteredness and does not intend to deny the importance of dwelling (24–25): "This is not nomadology" (36). Rather, what he urges us to notice is the traveling coincident with our dwelling—and, he adds, the dwelling that persists in our traveling (36).[2]

While Clifford admits to a fuller understanding of the former (44), my previous chapter might be seen as an effort to demonstrate the latter: to show the bits of dwelling that are carried, along with our bags of stuff, when we sign into a shelter, camp under a bridge, or park ourselves on a sidewalk. Traveling-in-dwelling, dwelling-in-traveling—the housed and unhoused cross paths in the liminal spaces associated with both these categories, from train stations, bus stations, and airports to campsites and Occupy actions. These particular sites serve as crossroads for reasons that are practical as well as metaphorical. Homeless people congregate there because in locales where everyone is toting bags, it is easier to blend in. Thanks to the presence of mainstream travelers, there is the further advantage of amenities like public bathrooms, coffee shops, reading material, and places to sit down.[3] Hotels, too, are spaces where temporary travelers overlap with temporary dwellers. In addition to welfare hotels like the one described by Kozol, motels represent still another category of interim shelter for those who have lost their homes. As I make my way toward a conclusion, I will be tweaking Clifford's admonition to *begin with hotels*. The following section will end with one.

DOMESTIC I

Bread & Wine: An Erotic Tale of New York (1999) is a graphic memoir by Samuel R. Delany with illustrations by Mia Wolff. Best known as a prolific, award-winning writer of science fiction, Delany's corpus includes and combines multiple genres from queer cultural studies to pornography and memoir.[4] In *Bread & Wine*, Delany (who goes by "Chip") tells the beautiful, unlikely tale of his friendship, courtship, and eventual long-term partnership with Dennis, a homeless man he meets on the corner of Seventy-second Street and Broadway. Appended to the graphic narrative, an afterword features a conversation in which Dennis, Delany's daughter Iva, his friend John, Mia, and Chip himself share their thoughts about the work. The dialogic effect is not unlike that created by Kim's and Grace's metacommentary in Elliot Liebow's *Tell Them Who I Am: The Lives of Homeless Women* (1993). Here, too, those who are represented—and Dennis in particular—have a chance to tell their side of the story, assuming a coauthorial role.

There are many other things to be said about this rich, rule-breaking text. I might start with the hybridizing choice to graft title and passages from Friedrich Hölderlin's *Bread and Wine* (1800) onto an illustrated tale of contemporary gay romance. There is also the fact that the text's coupling of a light-skinned, African American professor of comparative literature with a bookselling, begrimed street person of Irish descent flips and twists stereotypes of class and race beyond all recognition. One of its more humorous and illuminating moments is when Dennis tells of investigating Chip's background before agreeing to visit him in Amherst: "I was checkin' you *out*, man, 'cause you *could* have been . . . a crazy *psycho* cuttin' me up in little pieces."[5] This seems, at first, like a hilarious reversal—until we realize that Dennis is, of course, the far more vulnerable party to their arrangement. How could this not have been obvious to us? Other subversive details include the depiction of Dennis organizing his cart and backpack with hypermeticulous care (25, afterword), and the fact that getting together means working around *his* schedule: employment watching a storeowner's illegally parked car until nine at night (10). I also appreciate that there are books on both sides of the equation. Dennis sells them, and Chip buys, teaches, and writes them. Not that there is symmetry by any means. Early on, Dennis is aware that his friend is a writer, "He just wasn't sure what writers actually did" (33). Similarly, although both men have kin ties, the graphic narrative pays more attention to Iva and John than it does to Dennis's circle of street friends. In the afterword, Chip regrets this omission, at which point Dennis chimes in, and the book concludes with the couple collaborating on a story about Dennis's beloved friend Lester.

For our protagonists to come together thus requires rejecting the assumption that Chip has everything to bestow while Dennis has nothing to lose, no routines or affiliations of his own. Affirming a tie based on mutuality, the story hastens to a happy ending: "Dennis came up to Amherst in March of 90. We've been together ever since" (36). Yet Delany is not quite finished with us. Somewhat unexpectedly, the narrative goes on to describe the time Chip got hit by a truck, broke a rib, but felt better when Dennis got home. "Just his big warm hands on my side made it hurt less" (41). That night, they ate pizza and watched TV with Iva and John (41). In the coming months, Dennis bikes around Amherst, and in later years, he begins collecting skull rings, loading up the oversized hands that first attracted Chip's attention (43). The closing picture of a sheltered domestic life, with its shared quotidian comforts, is joyful. But by including Chip's accident (echoing one that killed Dennis's father) along with Dennis's collection of *mementos mori*, the narrative seems

FIGURE C.1 Mia Wolff, "Then We Held Each Other . . . for a Couple of Days." (From Samuel R. Delany, *Bread & Wine: An Erotic Tale of New York* [New York: Juno Books, 1999]. Copyright © Samuel R. Delany and Mia Wolff. Courtesy of Fantagraphics Books [fantagraphics.com], Seattle)

to insist that even the most cozy and secure domesticity is essentially precarious.

I have promised to end this section with a hotel, and to do so we must page back to the scene in which Chip and Dennis first have sex in the Skyline. I return to this scene in part because Dennis's precoital series of baths produces a tubful of "India Ink" (16), in keeping with my sense that he (having figured out by the afterword what it is that writers do) will put his own authorial stamp on the work. I pause here also because the depictions of tenderness and fellatio are equally explicit, showing the lovers joined in a spectacular intimacy (figure C.1). And I end here because it would be hard to find another image that so perfectly suggests a momentary bridging of the housed-homeless divide, the interpenetration of temporary traveler and temporary dweller—the transience we all share figured by two men's embrace.

DOMESTIC II

Recalling many of this book's concerns, Delany's lovers not only queer the domestic but also—joining Robinson Crusoe, the Fab Five, John Barton, Blu Ogata, Lars Eighner, plus the male Bridge and Tunnel dwellers—reiterate the point that men are no more inherently creatures of the road than women are creatures of the house. Chip and Dennis serve as well to fold the sheltered into the unsheltered, inviting us all to claim the "extremity" of our home lives. By the same token, they invite us to own the *desire for nonextremity*—for safety, comfort, and belonging—evident across divergent domestic efforts and arrangements. Having focused on "extreme" homemakers as a way of troubling normative notions of home, in the end I offer my subjects, quite simply, as homemakers. In doing so, I follow the lead of an artist whose vision has inspired me throughout the writing of this book: photographer Catherine Opie. While Opie's body of work spans an exhilarating range of subjects and formats, home is a pervasive theme. Among her most powerful images are portraits of queer families and households—portraits insisting at once on the beauty of their difference and the beauty of their ordinariness. Like my own project, her images confront received versions of home while also referencing a common language of longing for domestic rituals and ties. It seemed only fitting to close this book by appealing to one of her photos.

Joanne, Betsy, & Olivia, Bayside, New York (1998) is from a series shot over a three-month period when Opie drove across the country exploring the many permutations of lesbian domesticity (figure C.2).[6] As the title suggests, this particular family consists of three females. I turn to it after Domestic I in part to remind us that as a matter of lived reality, it is women who have been the primary homemakers, and one of my

FIGURE C.2 Catherine Opie, *Joanne, Betsy, & Olivia, Bayside, New York*, 1998. (Chromogenic print, 40 × 50 inches. © Catherine Opie. Courtesy of Regen Projects, Los Angeles)

goals throughout has been to value their particular contributions. But if woman-at-home is the norm, not so these two white mothers and Asian American child. We cannot know if the child has been adopted from across the globe or closer to home, but either way she appears to have entered this family enclave from elsewhere. Combined with the horse she holds and the car at her feet, the girl both anchors the threesome and opens up the frame of their domesticity to life beyond Bayside. There is some traveling in this dwelling, not least because the interracial, lesbian family has already come some distance from Main Street. A large bay window, filling about one-quarter of the overall image, is a literal opening onto a leafy outside, whose greenery is echoed by the leafy tablecloth. The window also serves to frame a plastic dollhouse sitting on the windowsill. Evoking the American Dream House so enticing to Esperanza's parents and Kozol's Annie Harrington, the pink-and-white toy suggests traditional gender as well as class roles. In this case, however, the dream house is both miniaturized and patently fake. Framed by the window, it resembles a picture in a book or an ad on TV. Instead of looming large, it is dwarfed, contained, and contextualized by the real house and real people—no way these large figures and the furniture of their lives could ever fit inside.

It is tempting, then, to assert the irrelevance of this conventional house to Joanne, Betsy, and Olivia, but I hesitate to do so for several reasons. Few of us are wholly immune to its allure, nor is everything about it indefensible. Moreover, despite its small size, it actually occupies the middle of this scene and appears to claim a place in the family circle. If the normative house lingers as a fantasy, we may also scout its influence in the way this family is configured: one woman overlapping with daughter and dining table, the other seated apart in her comfy dad's chair, arm outstretched in an unrequited effort to join in the play. The Bayside family is far from the Angel in the House ideal with which this book began, but neither is it an entirely Other ideal of lesbian family bliss. To me its sippy cup, uncleared table, coordinated colors, cabinet of stuff, and family photos conjure the imperfect—taxing as well as soothing—doing of domesticity: the routines of meals, playtimes, and bedtimes; the labor of caring, ordering, and adorning; the rhythms of concord and discord among family members; the continuities and changes from day to day; the repetition and creative improvisation; the ongoing effort to make a home that is recognized and validated as such. In the end, this household is neither unusual nor extreme. As Opie's one-word title for the series puts it so well, and as I hope this book has managed to show, it is best described as nothing more or less than *Domestic*.

NOTES

INTRODUCTION

1. Virginia Woolf, *The Death of the Moth and Other Essays* (New York: Harcourt Brace, 1942), 238.
2. Betty Friedan identifies the myth of the "happy housewife" in "The Happy Housewife Heroine," in *The Feminine Mystique* (New York: Dell, 1964), 28–61. Sara Ahmed notes the race/class bias of Friedan's formulation while also suggesting the myth's continuing, subtly coercive function, in *The Promise of Happiness* (Durham, N.C.: Duke University Press, 2010), 50–87.
3. My thanks to Chip Tucker for pointing out the double meaning of "extreme" to reference what is extrinsic and what is intrinsic to domesticity.
4. Gillian Brown, *Domestic Individualism: Imagining Self in Nineteenth-Century America* (Berkeley: University of California Press, 1990).
5. Laura Wexler, "Tender Violence: Literary Eavesdropping, Domestic Fiction, and Educational Reform," in *The Culture of Sentiment: Race, Gender, and Sentimentality in Nineteenth-Century America*, ed. Shirley Samuels (New York: Oxford University Press, 1992), 9–38.
6. Amy Kaplan, "Manifest Domesticity," *American Literature* 70, no. 3 (1998): 581–606.
7. Lori Merish, *Sentimental Materialism: Gender, Commodity Culture, and Nineteenth-Century American Literature* (Durham, N.C.: Duke University Press, 2000).
8. Lauren Berlant, *The Female Complaint: The Unfinished Business of Sentimentality in American Culture* (Durham, N.C.: Duke University Press, 2008). For a prime example of early work, see Carroll Smith-Rosenberg's landmark essay "The Female World of Love and Ritual: Relations Between Women in Nineteenth-Century America," in the inaugural issue of *Signs: Journal of Women in Culture and Society* 1, no. 1 (1975): 1–29.
9. Nancy Armstrong, *Desire and Domestic Fiction: A Political History* (Oxford: Oxford University Press, 1987), 204.

10. Ibid., 8.

11. Other criticisms of Armstrong include Patricia Yaeger, "Review: Beyond the Fragments," *Novel* 23, no. 2 (1990): 203–8; and Leila Silvana May, "The Strong-Arming of Desire: A Reconsideration of Nancy Armstrong's *Desire and Domestic Fiction*," *ELH* 68, no. 1 (2001): 267–85. Important alternative accounts, stressing the complexity of Victorian domesticity, include Mary Poovey, *Uneven Developments: The Ideological Work of Gender in Mid-Victorian England* (Chicago: University of Chicago Press, 1988); and Elizabeth Langland, *Nobody's Angels: Middle-Class Women and Domestic Ideology in Victorian Culture* (Ithaca, N.Y.: Cornell University Press, 1995). In "Strategic Formalism: Toward a New Method in Cultural Studies," *Victorian Studies* 48, no. 4 (2006): 625–57, Caroline Levine also disputes the "critical consensus about the politics of the family" dating from Armstrong's brief for "the repressiveness of the discourse of domesticity" (648). Levine's reading of Elizabeth Barrett Browning's "The Cry of the Children" (1843) points instead to multiple, conflicting models of the family. Like me, Levine stresses the variable politics of such depictions, depending on their effects: "In different contexts, the figure of domesticity works both for and against nationalism, both for and against racism, both for and against women's confinement to the home" (650).

12. For analyses of the gender politics implicit in work by Edward Said, Andrew Ross, and Lee Edelman, see Susan Fraiman, *Cool Men and the Second Sex* (New York: Columbia University Press, 2003). For a feminist critique of contemporary animal studies, see Susan Fraiman, "Pussy Panic Versus Liking Animals: Tracking Gender in Animal Studies," *Critical Inquiry* 39 (2012): 89–115.

13. Edward Said, *Culture and Imperialism* (New York: Knopf, 1993).

14. See, especially, Andrew Ross, "No Question of Silence," in *Men in Feminism*, ed. Alice Jardine and Paul Smith (New York: Methuen, 1987), 85–92; and his introduction to *Microphone Fiends: Youth Music and Youth Culture*, ed. Andrew Ross and Tricia Rose (New York: Routledge, 1994), 1–16.

15. Lee Edelman, *No Future: Queer Theory and the Death Drive* (Durham, N.C.: Duke University Press, 2004).

16. See, for example, Langland's *Nobody's Angels*, which analyzes the contradictory class-gender meanings of the role played by middle-class domestic women in the Victorian period.

17. There are, of course, numerous materialist studies of diverse domestic formations once we look beyond English to the fields of architecture, history, and anthropology. Classic examples include Dolores Hayden, *The Grand Domestic Revolution: A History of Feminist Designs for American Homes, Neighborhoods and Cities* (Cambridge, Mass.: MIT Press, 1981); and Leonore Davidoff and Catherine Hall, *Family Fortunes: Men and Women of the English Middle Class, 1780–1850* (Chicago: University of Chicago Press, 1987). More recent texts include Deborah Cohen, *Household Gods: The British and Their Possessions* (New Haven, Conn.: Yale University Press, 2006); Daniel Miller, *The Comfort of Things* (Malden: Polity, 2008); Victoria Kelley, *Soap and Water: Cleanliness, Dirt and the Working Classes in Victorian and Edwardian Britain* (London: Tauris, 2010); and Lisa Goff, *Shantytown U.S.A.: Forgotten Landscapes of the American Working Classes* (Cambridge, Mass.: Harvard University Press, 2016). While I have certainly learned from these and other such works, my primary interlocutors are scholars in my own field of literary and cultural studies.

18. Judy Giles, *The Parlour and the Suburb: Domestic Identities, Class, Femininity and Modernity* (Oxford: Berg, 2004); Victoria Rosner, *Modernism and the Architecture of Private Life* (New York: Columbia University Press, 2005); Douglas Mao, *Fateful Beauty: Aesthetic Environments, Juvenile Development, and Literature, 1860–1960* (Princeton, N.J.: Princeton University Press, 2008). Thomas Foster also stresses the significance of home for writers from Emily Dickinson to Gertrude Stein and Zora Neale Hurston, in *Transformations of Domesticity in Modern Women's Writing: Homelessness at Home* (New York: Palgrave, 2002). For Foster, this corpus is innovative insofar as it deconstructs "home" as a bounded, gendered space. My reading, by contrast, explores domesticity's persistence as a relatively distinct, feminized domain, one with positive as well as negative aspects for people of all genders.

19. Michel de Certeau, *The Practice of Everyday Life*, trans. Steven Rendall (1974; Berkeley: University of California Press, 1984), xiv–xv.

20. Ibid., xix.

21. Ibid., 98.

22. Laurie Langbauer, "Cultural Studies and the Politics of the Everyday," *diacritics* 22, no. 1 (1992): 47–65; Rita Felski, "Introduction: The Everyday," in "Everyday Life," special issue, *New Literary History* 33, no. 4 (2002): 607–22; Sara Ahmed, Claudia Castañeda, Anne-Marie Fortier, and Mimi Sheller, eds., *Uprootings/Regroundings: Questions of Home and Migration* (New York: Berg, 2003).

23. Felski, "Introduction," 610–13. She likens Certeau to his avant-gardist predecessors for whom "the quotidian is prized insofar as it resists the imposition of order, repetition, coherence" (612). "The modernist horror of routine," she adds, "has much to do with its feminine connotations" (612). For more on the linking of repetition to women and the modernist ethos as "anti-home," see Rita Felski, "The Invention of Everyday Life," in *Doing Time: Feminist Theory and Postmodern Culture* (New York: New York University Press, 2000), 77–98. See also Sara Ahmed, *Queer Phenomenology: Orientations, Objects, Others* (Durham, N.C.: Duke University Press, 2006); and Lorraine Sim, "Theorising the Everyday," *Australian Feminist Studies* 30, no. 84 (2015): 109–27.

24. Felski is one of the few humanities scholars to underline Giard's contribution to everyday life studies, praising "Doing-Cooking" for its "materially embedded and thickly contextualized description" as well as its attention to gender ("Introduction," 612). Ben Highmore also takes up Giard in "Homework: Routine, Social Aesthetics and the Ambiguity of Everyday Life," *Cultural Studies* 18, nos. 2–3 (2004): 306–27, and includes an excerpt from "Doing-Cooking" in his edited volume, *The Everyday Life Reader* (New York: Routledge, 2002). These are exceptions, however; though somewhat more visible in the area of food studies, Giard's work, generally speaking, has been almost entirely subsumed by Certeau's. Occasionally recognized as a lesser collaborator, Giard is best known as the posthumous editor of his work.

25. Luce Giard, "Doing-Cooking," in *The Practice of Everyday Life*, vol. 2, *Living and Cooking*, by Michel de Certeau, Luce Giard, and Pierre Mayol, trans. Timothy J. Tomasik (Minneapolis: University of Minnesota Press, 1998), ix. Subsequent references are cited in the text. But Tomasik, the translator of volume 2, takes this rationale at face value. In an opening note, Tomasik attributes the particular difficulty of translating Giard to the French concept of *terroir*. Whereas Giard invokes this concept in its narrow sense, to reference the regional specificity of cheese and other food products flavored by the land, Tomasik broadens it to suggest the regional specificity

of *texts* ("discursive *terroir*"), which frustrates the translator attempting to uproot them from their native soil (ix–x). Tomasik develops this argument in "Certeau à la Carte: Translating Discursive *Terroir* in *The Practice of Everyday Life: Living and Cooking*," *South Atlantic Quarterly* 100, no. 2 (2001): 519–42.

26.   Certeau includes shopping and cooking among his examples of everyday practices that are "tactical in character." As such, they are occasions for "victories of the 'weak' over the 'strong' (whether the strength be that of powerful people or the violence of things or of an imposed order, etc.), clever tricks, knowing how to get away with things, 'hunter's cunning,' maneuvers, polymorphic simulations, joyful discoveries, poetic as well as warlike" (*Practice of Everyday Life*, xix). See also Daniel Miller's valuable discussion of women's grocery shopping as both unrecognized labor and "an act of love, that in its daily conscientiousness becomes one of the primary means by which relationships of love and care are constituted by practice" ("Making Love in Supermarkets," in *The Everyday Life Reader*, ed. Ben Highmore [New York: Routledge, 2002], 342).

27.   This tension corresponds to what we used to call (in the parlance of 1980s women's studies) "difference" versus "equality" feminism. Put simply, while the first redeems modes traditionally devalued as "feminine," the second demands equality in traditionally "masculine" terms. General emphases rather than mutually exclusive positions, each has its uses and risks depending on the specific context. Despite some qualifications, my own argument in this book clearly leans in a "difference" direction. That said, I would emphatically distance myself from the so-called New Domesticity and its resistance to consumerism through a full-blown, unqualified, resentimentalized return to artisanal domesticity. For more on feminism's long-standing ambivalence toward domesticity, see Dana Heller, "Housebreaking History: Feminism's Troubled Romance with the Domestic Sphere," in *Feminism Beside Itself*, ed. Diane Elam and Robyn Wiegman (New York: Routledge, 1995), 217–33; and Leslie Johnson and Justine Lloyd, *Sentenced to Everyday Life: Feminism and the Housewife* (Oxford: Berg, 2004).

28.   Harriet Jacobs, *Incidents in the Life of a Slave Girl: Written by Herself*, ed. Jean Fagan Yellin (1861; Cambridge, Mass.: Harvard University Press, 1987); Charlotte Perkins Gilman, "The Yellow Wallpaper," in *The Charlotte Perkins Gilman Reader*, ed. Ann J. Lane (1892; New York: Pantheon, 1980), 3–19, and *The Home: Its Work and Influence* (New York: McClure, Phillips, 1903); Arlie Russell Hochschild, *The Second Shift: Working Parents and the Revolution at Home* (New York: Viking, 1989); Barbara Ehrenreich and Arlie Russell Hochschild, *Global Woman: Nannies, Maids, and Sex Workers in the New Economy* (New York: Holt, 2002). Novels in this tradition include Virginia Woolf's *To the Lighthouse* (1927) and Marilynne Robinson's *Housekeeping* (1980), among many others.

29.   Gaston Bachelard, *The Poetics of Space*, trans. Maria Jolas (Boston: Beacon Press, 1994), xxxv.

30.   When I speak of *precariousness* in relation to women, queers, the poor, and those disenfranchised by race and/or immigrant status, my meaning is largely coextensive with Judith Butler's definition of "precarity" in *Precarious Life: The Powers of Mourning and Violence* (New York: Verso, 2004). I also (less often) invoke the universal vulnerability of bodies that Butler calls "precariousness" (in contradistinction to the unequally distributed nature of "precarity"). In addition, my discussion of insecurity due to intermittent employment and underemployment (especially in chapters 2 and 6)

calls to mind the narrower, contemporary use of "precarity" to reference the plight of contingent workers in the twenty-first century. Though mindful of these pertinent conversations and allied with their goals, for the sake of clarity I have chosen not to deploy a term laden with such specific theoretical and political meanings in other contexts.

1. SHELTER WRITING

1. In addition to Judith Halberstam, *Female Masculinity* (Durham, N.C.: Duke University Press, 1998), other discussions of *Stone Butch Blues* include Jay Prosser, *Second Skins: The Body Narratives of Transsexuality* (New York: Columbia University Press, 1998); Cat Moses, "Queering Class: Leslie Feinberg's *Stone Butch Blues*," *Studies in the Novel* 31, no. 1 (1999): 74–97; and Kathryn Bond Stockton, "Cloth Wounds: Queer Aesthetics of Debasement," in *Aesthetic Subjects*, ed. David McWhirter and Pamela R. Matthews (Minneapolis: University of Minnesota Press, 2003), 268–84. For my own remarks on Jess's butch maternity, see *Cool Men and the Second Sex* (New York: Columbia University Press, 2003), 148–55.

2. Leslie Feinberg, *Stone Butch Blues* (New York: Firebrand, 1993), 234.

3. Ibid., 236–37.

4. Pat Rogers, "Crusoe's Home," *Essays in Criticism* 24, no. 4 (1974): 375–90. Also relevant here is Cynthia Wall, "Details of Space: Narrative Description in Early Eighteenth-Century Novels," *Eighteenth-Century Fiction* 10, no. 4 (1998): 387–405. Wall's fine book on novelistic interiors, *The Prose of Things: Transformations of Description in the Eighteenth Century* (Chicago: University of Chicago Press, 2006), argues that these were rendered rather sketchily—as needed for plot purposes—in the early eighteenth century, with furniture accumulating and descriptions thickening only as the century progressed. In this essay, however, Wall singles out Defoe for his precocious attention to "topographical" details, whether of rooms or streets. See also her helpful remarks on description as forwarding rather than countering narrative ("Details of Space," 391–95). Lydia Liu, in "Robinson Crusoe's Earthenware Pot," *Critical Inquiry* 25, no. 4 (1999): 728–57, takes a less benign view of Crusoe's domestic production: in the context of economic rivalries, his homemade "English" earthenware implies a slap at imported Chinese porcelain.

5. Daniel Defoe, *Robinson Crusoe* (New York: Penguin, 1965), 91.

6. Michal Peled Ginsburg and Lorri G. Nandrea share my interest in what they call the "home maintenance" language of novels such as *Robinson Crusoe*. Like me, they tie prose describing such everyday tasks as finding food and making pots to Crusoe's dire situation in which immediate survival is paramount. Their emphasis, however, is on the limitations of such language within plots pulling toward the long-range goals of an increasingly comfortable middle class. As Nandrea and Ginsburg explain, despite the novel's specialization in prosaic matters, the physical routines of keeping house quickly become too "low" (in their banality and class connotations) to remain within the purview of novelistic realism. See Michel Peled Ginsburg and Lorri G. Nandrea, "The Prose of the World," in *The Novel*, vol. 2, *Forms and Themes*, ed. Franco Moretti (Princeton, N.J.: Princeton University Press, 2007), 244–73; and Lorri G. Nandrea, *Misfit Forms: Paths Not Taken by the British Novel* (New York: Fordham

University Press, 2014), chap. 3. My own work, by contrast, identifies the persistence over time of home maintenance/shelter writing precisely because some novels continue to focus on "shipwrecked" figures (for whom survival cannot be assumed) and to narrate the series of small, hands-on actions by which they make a place for themselves. Other studies that consider the role of domestic detail in the novel's development (the British novel, in particular) include Wall, "Details of Space" and *Prose of Things*; and David Trotter, *Cooking with Mud: The Idea of Mess in Nineteenth-Century Art and Fiction* (New York: Oxford University Press, 2000).

7. To speak of "dwelling" naturally brings to mind Martin Heidegger's well-known remarks in "Building Dwelling Thinking," in *Poetry, Language, Thought*, trans. Albert Hofstadter (New York: Harper Colophon, 1971), 143–61. While I don't engage directly with this text, I do find it suggestive for my project. Loosely speaking, I take from Heidegger an emphasis on the following: the value of dwelling as part of what makes us human; its role not merely in providing physical shelter but also in orienting us, giving us a place in the world; its role in affiliating us with our neighbors/community; and the active, thoughtful nature of dwelling, which involves both productive labor and the "nonproductive" labor of cherishing, preserving, nurturing.

8. For a collection of essays theorizing descriptive writing, see Jeffrey Kittay, ed., "Towards a Theory of Description," special issue, *Yale French Studies* 61 (1981).

9. Michel Beaujour, "Some Paradoxes of Description," in "Towards a Theory of Description," ed. Kittay, 28–31.

10. In "No Place Like Home; or Dwelling in Narrative," *New Literary History* 46, no. 1 (2015): 17–39, Laura Bieger shares my sense that uncertainty regarding home results in a textual pull toward orientation and belonging. But while Bieger ties uncertainty to the modern human condition, I tie it to the special vulnerability of certain groups; moreover, while hers is strictly a narratology, I locate the desire for dwelling in *descriptive* passages as they operate within narratives of loss.

11. Philippe Hamon, "Rhetorical Status of the Descriptive," in "Towards a Theory of Description," ed. Kittay, 11–14.

12. Jeffrey Kittay, "Introduction: Towards a Theory of Description," in "Towards a Theory of Description," ed. Kittay, i.

13. Beaujour, "Some Paradoxes of Description," 58–59.

14. Gaston Bachelard, *The Poetics of Space*, trans. Maria Jolas (Boston: Beacon Press, 1994), xxxv. Subsequent references are cited in the text.

15. Ben Highmore, "Homework: Routine, Social Aesthetics and the Ambiguity of Everyday Life," *Cultural Studies* 18, nos. 2–3 (2004): 311.

16. Feminist criticism on domestic spaces as imprisoning for women includes Sandra M. Gilbert and Susan Gubar, *The Madwoman in the Attic: The Woman Writer and the Nineteenth-Century Literary Imagination* (New Haven, Conn.: Yale University Press, 1979); Kate Ferguson Ellis, *The Contested Castle: Gothic Novels and the Subversion of Domestic Ideology* (Champaign: University of Illinois Press, 1989); Valerie Smith, "'Loopholes of Retreat': Architecture and Ideology in Harriet Jacobs's *Incidents in the Life of a Slave Girl*," in *Reading Black, Reading Feminist: A Critical Anthology*, ed. Henry Louis Gates Jr. (New York: Penguin, 1990), 212–26; and Catherine Golden, ed., *The Captive Imagination: A Casebook on "The Yellow Wallpaper"* (New York: Feminist Press, 1992).

17. Needless to say, obligatory unpaid or low-wage domestic labor, often in someone else's home—housework as a servitude shaped by inequities of gender/race/class—

belongs to the gothic house that haunts my own more consolatory space. In addition to Jacobs's slave narrative, novels addressing the particular role of African American women in producing domesticity for whites include Toni Morrison, *The Bluest Eye* (New York: Holt, Rinehart and Winston, 1970); and Barbara Neely's "Blanche" mysteries (1992–2000), whose detective-protagonist is a housekeeper.

18. Bill Brown, *A Sense of Things: The Object Matter of American Literature* (Chicago: University of Chicago Press, 2003). See also Bill Brown, ed., *Things* (Chicago: University of Chicago Press, 2004), a collection based on a special issue of *Critical Inquiry*; both works helped launch the interdisciplinary field of "thing theory" or "object studies." In chapter 2, I take up another influential contribution to this area, Elaine Freedgood, *The Ideas in Things: Fugitive Meaning in the Victorian Novel* (Chicago: University of Chicago Press, 2006).

19. Brown, *Sense of Things*, 139.

20. Ibid., 141.

21. Michel de Certeau, *The Practice of Everyday Life*, trans. Steven Rendall (1974; Berkeley: University of California Press, 1984), 117–18.

22. For this reason, among others, the roving gypsies in *Emma* represent the ultimate Other for Jane Austen, their exclusion key to delimiting the world of her characters. On the racial/national work accomplished by the gypsies' abjection, see Michael Kramp, "The Woman, the Gypsies, and England: Harriet Smith's National Role," *College Literature* 31, no. 1 (2004): 147–68.

23. Rita Felski, "Introduction: The Everyday," in "Everyday Life," special issue, *New Literary History* 33, no. 4 (2002): 612.

24. Luce Giard notes a similar logic at work in relation to the scarcity of food, lists of delicacies generated in the context of deprivation: "These worn-out litanies of words used to evoke food that is lacking is a game taken up again thousands of times . . . in soldiers' barracks, in the prisoner's cell . . ." ("Doing-Cooking," in *The Practice of Everyday Life*, vol. 2, *Living and Cooking*, by Michel de Certeau, Luce Giard, and Pierre Mayol, trans. Timothy J. Tomasik [Minneapolis: University of Minnesota Press, 1998], 174).

25. For references to works elaborating these views in American studies, see the introduction, notes 4, 5, 6, 7, and 8. For an account of their development beginning with Ann Douglas's *The Feminization of American Culture* (New York: Knopf, 1977), see chapter 3.

26. Tania Modleski, *Loving with a Vengeance: Mass-Produced Fantasies for Women* (New York: Methuen, 1984); Naomi Schor, *Reading in Detail: Aesthetics and the Feminine* (New York: Methuen, 1987); Bonnie Zimmerman, *The Safe Sea of Women: Lesbian Fiction, 1969–1989* (Boston: Beacon Press, 1990).

27. On Radclyffe Hall's housekeeping, see Laura Doan, " 'Woman's Place *Is* the Home': Conservative Sapphic Modernity," in *Sapphic Modernities: Sexuality, Women and National Culture,*" ed. Laura Doan and Jane Garrity (New York: Palgrave, 2006), 91–108. Doan comments on two fascinating "good housekeeping" interviews with Hall that appeared in the *Daily Mail* (May 11, 1927, and July 16, 1928). For Doan, Hall's praise of polishing "with beeswax and turpentine," her "housewife's" eye for dust, and her love of roses are invoked strategically if not disingenuously. Doan disparages Hall's self-described mania for cleanliness as retrograde in gender terms, complacent in class terms, and hypocritical in sexual terms—an effort to "sanitize" her lesbianism. I, of course, am far more willing to be seduced by Hall's housekeeping language.

Especially relevant is what Doan herself describes as Hall's erotic pleasure in domesticity, about which more later.

28. Charlotte Brontë, *Villette* (1853; New York: Penguin, 1979), 585.

29. Defoe, *Robinson Crusoe*, 76–93.

30. For an alternative aesthetic, in addition to Trotter, see Eleanor Kaufman, "Living Virtually in a Cluttered House," *Angelaki: Journal of Theoretical Humanities* 7, no. 3 (2002): 159–69.

31. Elizabeth Gaskell, *Mary Barton: A Tale of Manchester Life* (1848; New York: Penguin, 1970), 49–50.

32. Radclyffe Hall, *The Well of Loneliness* (1928; New York: Avon, 1981), 323.

33. Ibid., 321. For a discussion of queer spaces in *The Well*, especially that of the war front, see Victoria Rosner, "Once More into the Breach: *The Well of Loneliness* and the Spaces of Inversion," in *Palatable Poison: Critical Perspectives on "The Well of Loneliness,"* ed. Laura Doan and Jay Prosser (New York: Columbia University Press, 2001), 316–35. James Krasner's *Home Bodies: Tactile Experience in Domestic Space* (Columbus: Ohio State University Press, 2010) is also relevant here; Krasner will come to the foreground in chapter 6, where I cite his views on companion animals in the context of homelessness.

34. Doan, "'Woman's Place *Is* the Home,'" 91–108.

35. For comments on *Queer Eye for the Straight Guy*, see the short essays in Chris Straayer and Tom Waugh, eds., "Queer TV Style," *GLQ* 11, no. 1 (2005): 95–117. In general, these pieces accuse the show of commodifying a desexualized white queerness, the better to moisturize the metrosexual market. Jaap Kooijman, however, notes its reliance on actual gay men (as opposed to actors anxious to clarify their off-screen straightness), and Sasha Torres agrees with me that the show usefully suggests a crisis in heterosexual masculinity. Andrew Gorman-Murray offers a helpful overview of scholarship on gay men and domesticity as depicted by *Queer Eye* and similar "lifestyle" shows, in "Queering Home or Domesticating Deviance? Interrogating Gay Domesticity Through Lifestyle Television," *International Journal of Cultural Studies* 9, no. 2 (2006): 227–47. Contrasting two Australian examples, he goes on to argue for the contradictory politics represented by such depictions.

2. BEHIND THE CURTAIN

1. Friedrich Engels, *The Condition of the Working Class in England*, trans. and ed. W. O. Henderson and W. H. Chaloner (Stanford, Calif.: Stanford University Press, 1968), 131.

2. Raymond Williams, *Culture and Society: 1780–1950* (New York: Columbia University Press, 1983), 88–89. Subsequent references are cited in the text.

3. Catherine Gallagher ties Mary to the genre of the working-class domestic tale predominant in the book's second half, in *The Industrial Reformation of English Fiction: Social Discourse and Narrative Form, 1832–1867* (Chicago: University of Chicago Press, 1985), 78–83; Patsy Stoneman identifies the Mary material with a working-class ethic of caring evinced by nurturing fathers, in *Elizabeth Gaskell* (Bloomington: Indiana University Press, 1987), 68–86; and Rosemarie Bodenheimer likens Mary's narrative to John Barton's, both involving a burst of public action and speech,

in "Private Grief and Public Acts in *Mary Barton*," *Dickens Studies Annual* 9 (1981): 195–216.

4.   Bodenheimer, "Private Grief and Public Acts," 197.

5   Gallagher, *Industrial Reformation of English Fiction*, 79.

6.   Luce Giard, "Doing-Cooking," in *The Practice of Everyday Life*, vol. 2, *Living and Cooking*, by Michel de Certeau, Luce Giard, and Pierre Mayol, trans. Timothy J. Tomasik (Minneapolis: University of Minnesota Press, 1998), 149–247.

7.   Elizabeth Gaskell, *Mary Barton: A Tale of Manchester Life* (1848; New York: Penguin, 1970), 39. Subsequent references are cited in the text.

8.   In addition to Stoneman, *Elizabeth Gaskell*, see Lisa Surridge, "Working-Class Masculinities in *Mary Barton*," *Victorian Literature and Culture* 28, no. 2 (2000): 331–43.

9.   On *industry* as a "key word" indicative of social changes beginning in the late eighteenth century, see Williams, *Culture and Society*: in addition to referencing individual diligence, it emerged at that time as "a collective word for our manufacturing and productive institutions" (xiii). Gaskell, I am suggesting, isn't so much reverting to the original sense as illustrating a third sense: domestic industry as a structured set of practices among the poor, an institution in its own right. My reading echoes Stoneman's view that throughout her corpus, Gaskell "highlights working women," from factory workers and seamstresses to farmers and housewives. Anticipating my own concerns, Stoneman praises Gaskell's attention to physical detail and cites two Sunday-school stories that "bring home the sheer effort required to produce the simplest results—a cup of tea, for instance—in the working-class homes of the 1840s" (*Elizabeth Gaskell*, 46).

10. To put this in Marxist terms, Gaskell is concerned with both the production of things and the production and reproduction of people and everyday life. Citing Engels on this "dual project," Heidi I. Hartmann notes that Marxists have, however, traditionally proceeded to explore the first at the expense of the second, in "The Family as the Locus of Gender, Class, and Political Struggle: The Example of Housework," in *Feminism and Methodology*, ed. Sandra Harding (Bloomington: Indiana University Press, 1987), 113. Beginning in the late 1970s, she and other Marxist-feminists sought to address this neglect by tackling the class-gender politics of housework as well as paid labor. For references to some key texts, see chapter 5, note 13.

11. As Hartmann observes, "That portion of household production called housework consists largely in purchasing commodities and transforming them into usable forms. Sheets, for example, must be bought, put on beds, rearranged after every sleep, and washed" ("Family as the Locus of Gender," 114); so even in an era of ready-made products like sheets, additional labor is required in order for them to be "usable."

12. Bodenheimer discusses Gaskell's attention to "manners in close quarters: how the Wilsons pretend not to hear the Bartons' negotiations about buying food for their tea-party; how Margaret Legh can tell from the sounds in the apartment below, when it would be appropriate to knock at Alice Wilson's door" ("Private Grief and Public Acts," 198).

13. Mary Poovey, *Uneven Developments: The Ideological Work of Gender in Mid-Victorian England* (Chicago: University of Chicago Press, 1988); Elizabeth Langland, *Nobody's Angels: Middle-Class Women and Domestic Ideology in Victorian Culture* (Ithaca, N.Y.: Cornell University Press, 1995); Cathy N. Davidson, "Preface: No More Separate Spheres!" in "No More Separate Spheres!" ed. Cathy N. Davidson, special issue,

American Literature 70, no. 3 (1998): 443–63. Influential historians of Victorian domesticity include Martha Vicinus, Leonore Davidoff, Catherine Hall, and Carol Dyhouse.

14. See, for example, Louise A. Tilly and Joan W. Scott, *Women, Work, and Family* (New York: Holt, Rinehart and Winston, 1978); Judith Walkowitz, *Prostitution and Victorian Society: Women, Class, and the State* (Cambridge: Cambridge University Press, 1980); and Anne McClintock's chapters on Arthur Munby and Hannah Cullwick in *Imperial Leather: Race, Gender and Sexuality in the Colonial Contest* (New York: Routledge, 1995). Tilly and Scott, interested in whether industrial-era wage earning by women improved their lives, explicitly specify: "We did not include strictly domestic activity—child care, cooking, housekeeping—in our definition of work, except when it was performed for pay by domestic servants" (introduction to *Women, Work, and Family* [New York: Methuen, 1987], 5). However valuable, these studies exemplify the tendency to downplay the unpaid domestic activity of Victorian working-class women. Exceptions that come to mind include Ellen Ross, *Love and Toil: Motherhood in Outcast London, 1870–1918* (New York: Oxford University Press, 1993); and Victoria Kelley, *Soap and Water: Cleanliness, Dirt and the Working Classes in Victorian and Edwardian Britain* (London: Tauris, 2010).

15. The "second shift" is Arlie Russell Hochschild's term, introduced by her influential book on the unequal division of labor in late-twentieth-century households: *The Second Shift: Working Parents and the Revolution at Home* (New York: Viking, 1989).

16. Elaine Freedgood points out that Gaskell omits the most confrontational stanza, in "The Novelist and Her Poor," *Novel* 47, no. 2 (2014): 210. Reading *Mary Barton* as utterly conservative in its class politics, this article reiterates Freedgood's general judgment of this novel in *The Ideas in Things: Fugitive Meaning in the Victorian Novel* (Chicago: University of Chicago Press, 2006). Later I discuss the Bartons' checked curtains as well as my alternative view of these and other things domestic in *Mary Barton*.

17. On the development of fire insurance, see Robin Pearson, *Insuring the Industrial Revolution: Fire Insurance in Great Britain, 1700–1850* (Aldershot: Ashgate, 2004). On *Mary Barton*'s abiding concern with risk management, overlapping with the discourse of fire insurance, see Paul Fyfe, "Accidents of a Novel Trade: Industrial Catastrophe, Fire Insurance, and *Mary Barton*," *Nineteenth-Century Literature* 65, no. 3 (2010): 315–47.

18. For a thorough account of the historical and political context leading to the passage of the Metropolitan Police Act, see J. L. Lyman, "The Metropolitan Police Act of 1829," *Journal of Criminal Law and Criminology* 55, no. 1 (1964): 141–54.

19. For a study of the professionalization of medicine in early-nineteenth-century England, focused on the northern city of York not far from Manchester, see Michael Brown, *Performing Medicine: Medical Culture and Identity in Provincial England, c. 1760–1850* (Manchester: Manchester University Press, 2011).

20. Freedgood, *Ideas in Things*. Subsequent references are cited in the text.

21. Sarah Josepha Buell Hale, *The Workwoman's Guide, Containing Instructions to the Inexperienced in Cutting and Completing . . . ; Also Explanations on Upholstery . . .* (London: Simpkin Marshall, 1838), https://books.google.com/books?id=spIQAQAA MAAJ&printsec=frontcover&source=gbs_ge_summary_r&cad=0#v=onepage&q&f

=false. Chapter 8, on upholstery, includes instructions for making various kinds of curtains (203–6).

22. On the nineteenth-century seamstress, see Christina Walkley, *The Ghost in the Looking Glass: The Victorian Seamstress* (London: Peter Owen, 1981); Beth Harris, ed., *Famine and Fashion: Needlewomen in the Nineteenth Century* (Aldershot: Ashgate, 2005); and Christine Bayles Kortsch, *Dress Culture in Late Victorian Women's Fiction: Literacy, Textiles, and Activism* (Aldershot: Ashgate, 2009).

23. Elaine Freedgood, "'Fine Fingers': Victorian Handmade Lace and Utopian Consumption," *Victorian Studies* 45, no. 4 (2003): 634.

24. In *Hidden Hands: Working-Class Women and Victorian Social Problem Fiction* (Athens: Ohio University Press, 2001), Patricia E. Johnson examines the disturbing invisibility in *Mary Barton* and other midcentury industrial novels of female factory workers, this despite their actual predominance in Manchester's cotton industry and the growing trade union movement. As Johnson explains, this omission resonated with efforts by middle-class moralists and working-class men alike to return wage-earning women to the home, efforts that Gaskell's domestic emphasis may, indeed, ultimately serve to reinforce. Yet while sharing Johnson's concerns and admiring her project of recovering women's roles in manufacturing and activism, I note an occasional, accompanying bias against other forms of paid and unpaid female labor. When Johnson complains, for example, that in *Mary Barton*, "the working-class heroine is recast as a non-worker or in a more feminine occupation such as millinery" (12), she invokes a paradigm that fails to recognize "feminine" occupations such as millinery (or housework for one's own family) as work.

25. As Williams first noted, the removal of Gaskell's surviving characters to Canada further serves to evade or cancel the evils of British industrialism rather than to pursue "a solution within the actual situation" (*Culture and Society*, 91).

26. Compare Freedgood's reading of *Jane Eyre*, in which Jane's class/gender work of procuring and arranging furniture for Moor House—this by a character recently homeless, anticipating a household of three unmarried women—is viewed as an act of domination in tune with the "sadism" underwriting mahogany furniture production (*Ideas in Things*, 32). Freedgood further speculates that Jane, finding Ferndean unfurnished, may have "designs on this new residence" (33): like the "'blank' spaces on the map of empire, the idea of empty space invites the exercise of habitation as a demonstration of power" (33). Yet as Freedgood admits, Brontë's lengthy denouement makes no mention of redecorating. What's more, this argument neglects the fact that Mrs. Rochester, whatever her imperial designs, would have been powerless (in advance of the late-century Married Women's Property Acts) to purchase furniture in her own right.

27. On the working-class sense of privacy, see Martin Hewitt, "District Visiting and the Constitution of Domestic Space in the Mid-Nineteenth Century," in *Domestic Space: Reading the Nineteenth-Century Interior*, ed. Inga Bryden and Janet Floyd (Manchester: Manchester University Press, 1999), 121–41. While many have seen the routine intrusion into working-class homes by missionaries and other charitable visitors as precluding any concept of privacy, Hewitt's close examination of district visiting records gives ample evidence of resistance to these visits, bespeaking a robust sense of domestic boundaries.

3. DOMESTICITY BEYOND SENTIMENT

1. When it comes to ensuring or undermining women's domestic security, the author of *The House of Mirth* was well aware that the dynamics of class and gender are often intertwined, as they certainly are for Lily Bart.

2. Lauren Berlant, *The Female Complaint: The Unfinished Business of Sentimentality in American Culture* (Durham, N.C.: Duke University Press, 2008); Ann Douglas, *The Feminization of American Culture* (New York: Knopf, 1977); Jane P. Tompkins, "Sentimental Power: *Uncle Tom's Cabin* and the Politics of Literary History," *Glyph* 2 (1978): 79–101; Nina Baym, *Woman's Fiction: A Guide to Novels By and About Women in America, 1820–1870* (Ithaca, N.Y.: Cornell University Press, 1978); Gillian Brown, *Domestic Individualism: Imagining Self in Nineteenth-Century America* (Berkeley: University of California Press, 1990); Laura Wexler, "Tender Violence: Literary Eavesdropping, Domestic Fiction, and Educational Reform," in *The Culture of Sentiment: Race, Gender, and Sentimentality in Nineteenth-Century America*, ed. Shirley Samuels (New York: Oxford University Press, 1992), 9–38.

3. Lora Romero, *Home Fronts: Domesticity and Its Critics in the Antebellum United States* (Durham, N.C.: Duke University Press, 1997); Joanne Dobson, "Reclaiming Sentimental Literature," *American Literature* 69, no. 2 (1997): 263–88; Cathy N. Davidson, "Preface: No More Separate Spheres!" in "No More Separate Spheres!" ed. Cathy N. Davidson, special issue, *American Literature* 70, no. 3 (1998): 443–63; Amy Kaplan, "Manifest Domesticity," in "No More Separate Spheres!" ed. Davidson, 581–606; Lori Merish, *Sentimental Materialism: Gender, Commodity Culture, and Nineteenth-Century American Literature* (Durham, N.C.: Duke University Press, 2000); Berlant, *Female Complaint*, 2.

4. Davidson, "Preface," 451–52.

5. Kaplan, "Manifest Domesticity," 581. Contrast this pattern with discussions of British literature, in which nineteenth-century writers of domestic fiction (from Jane Austen to George Eliot) are seen as turning away, often quite self-consciously, from sentimental precursors as well as from contemporaneous works written in a more emotionally florid vein.

6. Amy Kaplan, *The Social Construction of American Realism* (Chicago: University of Chicago Press, 1988), 67. Kaplan stresses Wharton's professionalism both as an author and, in *The Decoration of Houses*, as a designer. I share this concern with her professionalism, and I second Kaplan's praise for Wharton's challenge to the gendered dichotomy between architecture and decorating, public exterior and private interior. My point here, however, is that Kaplan nevertheless continues to treat the "feminine," domestic side of this equation as largely negative.

7. Richard Guy Wilson, "Edith and Ogden: Writing, Decoration, and Architecture," in *Ogden Codman and "The Decoration of Houses,"* ed. Pauline C. Metcalf (Boston: Godine, 1988), 133–84; Judith Fryer, *Felicitous Space: The Imaginative Structures of Edith Wharton and Willa Cather* (Chapel Hill: University of North Carolina Press, 1986); Vanessa Chase, "Edith Wharton, *The Decoration of Houses*, and Gender in Turn-of-the-Century America," in *Architecture and Feminism*, ed. Debra Coleman, Elizabeth Danze, and Carol Henderson (New York: Princeton Architectural Press, 1996), 130–60. Betsy Currier Beacom highlights privacy as well in *"The Decoration of Houses* and the Role of Space in Edith Wharton's Construction of an Authorial

Self," *Edith Wharton Review* 28, no. 2 (2012): 9–16. For a contrasting view, see Lorna Brittan, "Edith Wharton's Alchemy of Publicity," *American Literature* 79, no. 4 (2007): 725–51, which argues that Wharton's notion of core identity (and not just professional persona) relied on publicity. For more on Wharton and space, see Kaplan, *Social Construction of American Realism*; Reneé Somers, *Edith Wharton as Spatial Activist and Analyst* (New York: Routledge, 2005); and Annette Benert, *The Architectural Imagination of Edith Wharton: Gender, Class, and Power in the Progressive Era* (Madison, N.J.: Fairleigh Dickinson University Press, 2007).

8. Edith Wharton, *A Backward Glance* (1934; New York: Scribner, 1964), 73. Subsequent references are cited in the text as *Backward Glance*.

9. D. A. Miller, *Narrative and Its Discontents: Problems of Closure in the Traditional Novel* (Princeton, N.J.: Princeton University Press, 1981).

10. Debra Ann MacComb, *Tales of Liberation, Strategies of Containment: Divorce and the Representation of Womanhood in American Fiction, 1880–1920* (New York: Routledge, 2000), 129. MacComb explores the canon of divorce novels originating in the Progressive Era. See also Kimberly A. Freeman, *Love American Style: Divorce and the American Novel, 1881–1976* (New York: Routledge, 2003). Both MacComb and Freeman devote a chapter to *The Custom of the Country*. On broader turn-of-the-century efforts, legal as well as literary, to rethink U.S. marriage practices, see Clare Virginia Eby, *Until Choice Do Us Part: Marriage Reform in the Progressive Era* (Chicago: University of Chicago Press, 2014).

11. Biographies of Wharton include R. W. B. Lewis, *Edith Wharton: A Biography* (New York: Harper & Row, 1975); Cynthia Griffin Wolff, *A Feast of Words: The Triumph of Edith Wharton* (New York: Oxford University Press, 1977); Shari Benstock, *No Gifts from Chance: A Biography of Edith Wharton* (New York: Scribner, 1994); and Hermione Lee, *Edith Wharton* (New York: Knopf, 2007).

12. Quoted in Wilson, "Edith and Ogden," 134. Subsequent references are cited in the text.

13. The timing of *The Custom of the Country* (1913; Oxford: Oxford University Press, 1995) may have functioned in part to provide some cover for Wharton by distancing her from the heartless Undine Spragg, with her multiple, self-serving divorces. Mac-Comb argues that Wharton's critique is directed less at Undine herself than at the profitable divorce industry and an economy based on insatiable consumerism, which combined to encourage "rotary marriage" (*Tales of Liberation*, 124–42). My own view is closer to that of Elizabeth Ammons, who argues that neither the ignoble heroine nor contemporary divorce practices but "the institution of marriage in the leisure class is the main target of Wharton's satire" (*Edith Wharton's Argument with America* [Athens: University of Georgia Press, 1980], 101–2).

14. Though Codman and Wharton began *The Decoration of Houses* as a joint venture, and his name appears (after Wharton's) on the title page, biographers concur in giving Wharton most, if not all, of the credit. Of course the actual writing was hers. In addition, according to Benstock, "records show that Edith formulated the book's ideas and organization, searched out many of the photographs and drawings that document its claims, prepared the bibliography, handled negotiations with editors, printers, and publicists, and lined up reviews in leading journals prior to publication" (*No Gifts from Chance*, 84). Wolff simply omits Codman altogether, describing *The Decoration of Houses* as "Wharton's first real book" (*Feast of Words*, 77).

15. This project is counterintuitive only because we are so accustomed to identify houses and, in particular, well-ordered houses with heterosexual compliance rather than alienation. For an analysis whose reverse logic agrees with mine, see Lee Wallace, "Dorothy Arzner's *Wife*: Heterosexual Sets, Homosexual Scenes," *Screen* 49, no. 4 (2008): 391–409. According to Wallace, Arzner's film *Craig's Wife* (1936) combines "lesbian director, gay designer, heterosexual mise-en-scene" (392) to queer normative domesticity. The Craigs' well-appointed home and Harriet Craig's meticulous housekeeping are made to signal marital dysfunction rather than harmony. Wallace credits designer William Haines with the "ability to imbue domestic interiors with a quality of heterosexual estrangement" (396). The eponymous wife's fervent identification with the house and its needs is actually mobilized *against* her marriage. As Wallace explains, "Harriet stonewalls her husband before the hearth that would ordinarily function as the heart of the home" (397).

16. On the home economics movement, see Sarah A. Leavitt, *From Catharine Beecher to Martha Stewart: A Cultural History of Domestic Advice* (Chapel Hill: University of North Carolina Press, 2002), 40–72; on experiments in feminist design by Gilman and others, see Dolores Hayden, *The Grand Domestic Revolution: A History of Feminist Designs for American Homes, Neighborhoods, and Cities* (Cambridge, Mass.: MIT Press, 1981); on the role of domestic architecture in shaping literary modernism, see Victoria Rosner, *Modernism and the Architecture of Private Life* (New York: Columbia University Press, 2005); and for a helpful discussion of Wharton's neoclassicism in the context of the American Renaissance, see Benert, *Architectural Imagination of Edith Wharton*, 38–54.

17. Quoted in Somers, *Edith Wharton as Spatial Activist and Analyst*, 113.

18. Benstock, *No Gifts from Chance*, 60.

19. Ibid., 61.

20. Quoted in ibid., 128.

21. Benstock departs from previous biographers in identifying Wharton's illnesses of the 1890s as primarily physical in origin. She debunks the long-standing theory that Wharton endured Weir Mitchell's infamous "rest cure" (he was actually abroad at the time of her alleged treatment) and downplays what the writer herself sometimes referred to as "neurasthenia." Instead, Benstock points to recurrent sinus, throat, and lung infections brought on by the sea air of Newport—thus the curative effect of moving to the Berkshires (*No Gifts from Chance*, 78–80, 93–96). See, by contrast, Wolff's insistently psychological account. I think Wolff places undue emphasis and blame on Wharton's mother, but my own reading follows her (and Lewis) in seeing Wharton's distress throughout the 1890s as significantly tied to her sexual, emotional, and intellectual dissatisfaction in marriage. Her spirits were thus improved, Wolff says, by the separate suite she built for herself at The Mount, the literary company she hosted, and, especially, her growing mastery as a writer (*Feast of Words*, 51–54).

22. Quoted in Fryer, *Felicitous Space*, 65 (italics in original).

23. Edith Wharton and Ogden Codman Jr., *The Decoration of Houses*, facsimile ed. (1897; New York: Rizzoli and the Mount, 2007), 22. Subsequent references are cited in the text.

24. Chase, "Edith Wharton, *The Decoration of Houses*," 146.

25. See also Fryer, *Felicitous Space*, 71; Chase, "Edith Wharton, *The Decoration of Houses*," 153–54; and Somers, *Edith Wharton as Spatial Activist and Analyst*, 124–26.

Somers identifies the bedroom, rather than the boudoir, as the room in which Wharton wrote, but she likewise stresses the sanctity of this space, its importance to Wharton's professional identity, and Teddy's strict exclusion from it (124–26).

26. Quoted in Chase, "Edith Wharton, *The Decoration of Houses*," 158.

27. Wolff, *Feast of Words*, 224.

28. Deborah Cohen notes that by the 1920s, "the photo had become the bedrock of the home decoration industry, a practice made possible by the refinement of half-tone printing at the turn of the century" (*Household Gods: The British and Their Possessions* [New Haven, Conn.: Yale University Press, 2006], 191). Deploying photographs as early as 1897, Wharton broke with the Victorian advice manual norm of sketches and etchings, opting for a medium well suited to her hard-edged domestic aesthetic.

29. Though de Wolfe was a protégé of Codman's and her book was essentially a popularization of *The Decoration of Houses*' tenets, Wilson describes it as "less rigorous and philosophical," "far more personal," and full of "gossipy chatter" about her own residences ("Edith and Ogden," 158). As Wilson further observes (154), *The Decoration of Houses* loosely followed the structure of, while also setting out to counter, both Clarence Cook, *The House Beautiful: An Unabridged Reprint of the Classic Victorian Stylebook* (1877; Mineola, N.Y.: Dover, 1995); and Charles Locke Eastlake, *Hints on Household Taste: The Classic Handbook of Victorian Interior Design* (1868; Mineola, N.Y.: Dover, 1986). Eastlake includes his own sketches of tables and beds as well as smaller objects from door knockers to tableware. While there are no human figures in *Hints*, the style and scale of Eastlake's line drawings, combined with his casual tone and title, nevertheless evoke the personal, as Wharton's book does not.

30. This tension runs throughout the tradition of home decoration and home maintenance texts and remains a feature as well of contemporary shelter and service magazines for women (more on which in chapter 4). Works in this genre typically advocate simplicity for reasons of good taste and frugality while also catering shamelessly to middle-class fantasies of lushly opulent, aristocratic surroundings. A twenty-first-century example is the magazine *Real Simple*, whose title is surely undercut by images of huge refrigerators overstuffed with arcane lettuces and beautifully bottled drinks (along with tips for decluttering). Cook's *House Beautiful*, while contrasting sharply with *The Decoration of Houses* in ways detailed later, resembles it in likewise counseling one thing while picturing another. Indeed, Cook's closing chapter includes a sheepish reply to those who noted (when the material first appeared in *Scribner's Monthly*) "the want of consistency shown by the writer in preaching economy and simplicity, while, at the same time, he at once tempted and teased the people with short purses by showing them Mr. Lathrop's charming drawings of the prettiest and costliest furniture to be found" (*House Beautiful*, 323).

31. It is true that Cook's well-populated pages are somewhat atypical, although see Lucy Orrinsmith's similarly illustrated work, *The Drawing-Room, Its Decorations and Furniture* (London: Macmillan, 1877). But while design books like Eastlake's *Hints on Household Taste* and Mary Eliza Haweis's *The Art of Decoration* (London: Chatto & Windus, 1881) may not have included human figures, they were imbued with a human presence. Their scale was intimate and their spaces replete with objects suggesting daily use. In Wharton's photos, by contrast, rooms appear not just empty but never lived in, people not just absent but wholly irrelevant.

32. See note 30.

33. Cook, *House Beautiful*, 56. Subsequent references are cited in the text.
34. On Wharton's war relief efforts, see Benert, *Architectural Imagination of Edith Wharton*, 166–85; and Lee, *Edith Wharton*, 472–508. On *The Book of the Homeless*, see Susan Goodman, "Bearing Witness: Edith Wharton's *The Book of the Homeless*," *Mosaic* 46, no. 2 (2013): 87–103.

4. BAD GIRLS OF GOOD HOUSEKEEPING

1. Circulation and ad revenues for shelter magazines increased dramatically during the postwar housing boom of the 1950s. Sales fell off, however, in the postfeminist 1980s, leading publishers to reinvent old standards and diversify the field with specialized publications aimed at a narrower but wealthier readership. The resulting array features homes Romantic or Victorian, natural or traditional, country or metropolitan, in the South or on the Coast, aging and well patinated or scarcely unwrapped. At one end of the spectrum are glossy European imports; at the other are those like *Country Living* and *Better Homes and Gardens*, sold at the checkout counter for less than $5.00. A large number of shelter magazines were casualties of the most recent recession, including *House & Garden*, which folded in 2007; *O at Home*, *Metropolitan Home*, and *Domino* were among those shuttered over the next two years. It took until 2011 for the surviving publications to see significant gains in ad pages and circulation rates. Yet throughout this entire period, new shelter mags continued to be launched in both traditional and digital formats.
2. *Better Homes and Gardens*, founded in 1922, was originally called *Fruit, Garden and Home*. Other examples of the service genre include *Family Circle*, *Woman's Day*, *Ladies' Home Journal*, and *Good Housekeeping*; the latter two date back, respectively, to 1883 and 1885.
3. Rosalind Coward, *Female Desire: Women's Sexuality Today* (London: Paladin, 1984), 69.
4. Ibid.
5. Ibid., 70–71.
6. For more on the increasingly symbiotic relationship between women's magazines and advertisers, see Ellen McCracken, *Decoding Women's Magazines: From Mademoiselle to Ms.* (New York: St. Martin's Press, 1993), 64–66; Jennifer Scanlon, *Inarticulate Longings: The Ladies' Home Journal, Gender, and the Promises of Consumer Culture* (New York: Routledge, 1995), 169–227; and Nancy A. Walker, *Shaping Our Mothers' World: American Women's Magazines* (Jackson: University Press of Mississippi, 2000), 102–10. See also Noliwe M. Rooks, *Ladies' Pages: African American Women's Magazines and the Culture That Made Them* (New Brunswick. N.J.: Rutgers University Press, 2004), 56–60, 131–32; and Mary Ellen Zuckerman, *A History of Popular Women's Magazines in the United States, 1792–1995* (Westport, Conn.: Greenwood Press, 1998), 59–77. As mentioned in chapter 3, early shelter writer Clarence Cook had to admit his critics were right that he preached simplicity but pictured luxury goods in *The House Beautiful: An Unabridged Reprint of the Classic Victorian Stylebook* (1877; Mineola, N.Y.: Dover, 1995), 323.
7. *House & Garden*, founded in 1901, was fading when Dominique Browning took over in 1996 but regained its luster under her much-admired editorship; nevertheless,

Condé Nast abruptly dropped this venerable publication at the end of 2007. Browning produced four books with *House & Garden* and is the author of three autobiographical works—most recently, *Slow Love: How I Lost My Job, Put on My Pajamas, and Found Happiness* (New York: Atlas, 2010). She publishes frequently in the *New York Times* and blogs about house, garden, and the environment at SlowLoveLife.com. Browning also writes a column for the Environmental Defense Fund, with which she partnered to found an activist group of parents against air pollution. The Martha Stewart empire currently includes two regularly published magazines, radio and television shows, websites and blogs, lines of housewares with Macy's and elsewhere, additional Martha Stewart-brand products from paint to coffee, and books (eighty-five to date) on everything from weddings to entrepreneurship.

8.   McCracken, *Decoding Women's Magazines*, 272.

9.   Scanlon, *Inarticulate Longings*, 4.

10.   Walker, *Shaping Our Mothers' World*, vii.

11.   Ibid., xvii.

12.   Scanlon, *Inarticulate Longings*, 168.

13.   Sarah A. Leavitt, *From Catharine Beecher to Martha Stewart: A Cultural History of Domestic Advice* (Chapel Hill: University of North Carolina Press, 2002), 205. Subsequent references are cited in the text.

14.   Harriet Spofford, "Nagging Women: A Reply to Dr. Edson," *North American Review*, March 1895, 312–15.

15.   Harriet Spofford, "Petticoat Government: A Reply to Max O'Rell," *North American Review*, July 1896, 112.

16.   Harriet Spofford, "Shall Our Daughters Have Dowries? A Reply to C. S. Messinger," *North American Review*, December 1890, 754.

17.   On ties between the professional aspirations of early female decorators and the British campaign for women's suffrage, see Deborah Cohen, *Household Gods: The British and Their Possessions* (New Haven, Conn.: Yale University Press, 2006). As Cohen observes, women such as Agnes Garrett and Emmeline Pankhurst were pioneers in the furnishing business as well as leaders in the suffrage movement (105–8).

18.   Terry Castle, "Home Alone," in *The Professor and Other Writings* (New York: Harper-Collins, 2010), 109. Subsequent references are cited in the text. "Home Alone" originally appeared as "Home Alone: The Dark Heart of Shelter-Lit Addiction," *Atlantic Monthly*, March 2006, 117–29.

19.   Nor do such remedial visions necessarily coincide with denial. Fittingly enough, Castle herself singles out Dominique Browning, praising her candid response to the attacks of September 11, which occurred midway through her editorship of *House & Garden*. Breaking ranks with shelter-mag peers, who by and large remained silent on this topic, Browning alone bravely attempted to address mass death and home renovation in the same breath. According to Castle, she did so "awkwardly yet movingly" in editorial columns over the course of several issues ("Home Alone," 121–22).

20.   Dominique Browning, *Around the House and in the Garden: A Memoir of Heartbreak, Healing, and Home Improvement* (New York: Scribner, 2002), 23. Subsequent references are cited in the text.

21.   Sara Ahmed, *Queer Phenomenology: Orientations, Objects, Others* (Durham, N.C.: Duke University Press, 2006), 3.

22.   Dominique Browning, "The Takeout Blues," *House & Garden*, May 2007, 6.

23. Dominique Browning, "A Chance Encounter," *House & Garden*, June 2007, 12.

24. Of course, the story doesn't end here. Browning's next memoir, *Paths of Desire: The Passions of a Suburban Gardener* (New York: Scribner, 2004), begins with a wall collapsing; six years later, *Slow Love* finds her unemployed and, self-sufficiency flown, tied to an emotionally unavailable man. As Browning herself is well aware, all three texts are lessons in the continual need to remake homes (and selves).

25. Biographies include Jerry Oppenheimer's relentlessly vicious *Martha Stewart—Just Desserts: The Unauthorized Biography* (New York: Morrow, 1997); Christopher Byron's grudgingly appreciative *Martha Inc.: The Incredible Story of Martha Stewart Living Omnimedia* (New York: Wiley, 2002); and Lloyd Allen's redemptive *Being Martha: The Inside Story of Martha Stewart and Her Amazing Life* (New York: Wiley, 2006), by Stewart's longtime friend. NBC's biopic *Martha Inc.* (2003) was followed by CBS's *Martha: Behind Bars* (2005), both starring Cybill Shepherd. Scholarly studies include Kyla Wazana and Zoe Newman, eds., *No Place Like Home: Making Sense of Martha Stewart* (Toronto: Anansi Press, 1999); Cynthia Duquette Smith, "Discipline—It's a 'Good Thing': Rhetorical Constitution and Martha Stewart Living Omnimedia," *Women's Studies in Communication* 23, no. 3 (2000): 337–66; Ann Mason and Marian Meyers, "Living with Martha Stewart Media: Chosen Domesticity in the Experience of Fans," *Journal of Communication* 51, no. 4 (2001): 801–23, an ethnographic study of fans; Carol A. Stabile, "Getting What She Deserved: The News Media, Martha Stewart, and Masculine Domination," *Feminist Media Studies* 4, no. 3 (2004): 315–32, on coverage of the insider trading case; and Emily Jane Cohen, "Kitschen Witches: Martha Stewart, Gothic Housewife, Corporate CEO," *Journal of Popular Culture* 38, no. 4 (2005): 650–77, on Martha as a "gothic housewife." See also the excellent "Martha Stewart Roundtable," in *American Studies* 42, no. 2 (2001); notable articles include Shirley Teresa Wajda, "Kmartha" (71–88); Amy Bentley, "Martha's Food: Whiteness of a Certain Kind" (89–110); and Sarah A. Leavitt, "It was Always a Good Thing: Historical Precedents for Martha Stewart" (125–31).

26. See, for example, Karen Finley, *Living It Up: Humorous Adventures in Hyperdomesticity* (New York: Doubleday, 1996); Tom Connor and Jim Downey, *Is Martha Stewart Living?* (New York: HarperCollins, 1995); and such common online satires as "The Top 10 Signs You're Being Stalked by Martha Stewart."

27. Oppenheimer, *Martha Stewart*, 3–5. Subsequent references are cited in the text.

28. Adding to this impression, Alexis went on to cohost the television show *Whatever, Martha* (premiering in 2008) devoted to satirizing her famous mother. She is rumored to be working on a book in a similar vein.

29. But see Wajda's contrary view of DIY as a nostalgic investment in "family-centered ritual and reverie" ("Kmartha," 79).

30. Mason and Meyers, "Living with Martha Stewart Media," 816–17. Subsequent references are cited in the text.

31. For comments on Stewart and class aspirations, see Smith, "Discipline," 362; Mason and Meyers, "Living with Martha Stewart Media," 814–16; and Bentley, "Martha's Food," 91–92; among others.

32. Smith argues for the disciplinary effects of Stewart's didacticism, in "Discipline," 346–52. Mason and Meyers, by contrast, stress the active way in which women consume Martha products, modifying her instructions to suit their own purposes, in "Living with Martha Stewart Media," 816–18.

33. An updated version of this feature now goes under the rubric "From Martha: Teach and Inspire."

34. Stewart's aestheticized domestic work ethic clearly invites comparison with Giard's "Doing-Cooking." Like Giard in her microstudy, Stewart would have us appreciate the beauty and know-how evoked by such humble objects as homemade pickles carefully shelved in hand-labeled jars. Yet as Bentley argues, Stewart's culinary aesthetic both dissents from modes of mass production and signifies the privileges of upper-middle-class whiteness ("Martha's Food," 93–95).

35. Quoted in Joann F. Price, *Martha Stewart: A Biography* (Westport, Conn.: Greenwood Press, 2007), 7.

36. As Stabile argues, "Powerful women who do not conform to subservient and heteronormative models . . . are simply not tolerated. . . . Stewart never conformed . . . she never exhibited the ethic of care enacted by [Rosie] O'Donnell and [Oprah] Winfrey" ("Getting What She Deserved," 317). Stabile goes on to show the disproportionate amount and far more punitive tone of media commentary on Stewart's insider trading case, as opposed to that concerning Enron criminal Kenneth Lay (318–19). Stewart's commercializing of "private" domestic matters drew particular wrath, the implicit comparison being, Stabile suggests, to prostitution (319).

37. Tom Connor and Jim Downey, *Martha Stewart's Better Than You at Entertaining* (New York: HarperCollins, 1996).

5. UNDOCUMENTED HOMES

1. Dominique Browning, *Around the House and in the Garden: A Memoir of Heartbreak, Healing, and Home Improvement* (New York: Scribner, 2002), 11.

2. Roz Chast, "Martha Stewart Takes Over the Universe," *New Yorker*, June 25, 1990.

3. In *Touching Liberty: Abolition, Feminism, and the Politics of the Body* (Berkeley: University of California Press, 1993), Karen Sánchez-Eppler's comments on Harriet Jacobs's *Incidents in the Life of a Slave Girl* point to the antebellum origins of this logic. Unlike her male counterparts, Linda Brent escapes from slavery by "burrowing into domestic spaces" (87). Although Linda has her own "Crusoe" moment (finding a tool with which to bore a peephole), Sánchez-Eppler memorably observes that Linda "never comes to inhabit the domestic; rather, as a slave and particularly as a female slave she *is* the domestic. In her effort to escape, her body literally lines the floors and ceilings of houses, just as in servitude her body and its labor sustains the Southern home" (87). This is true even on Jacobs's last page, which leaves Linda still longing for a "hearthstone" of her own. On *Incidents* as a work of political theory tying the home to both racial exclusion and resistance, see Mark Rifkin, "'A Home Made Sacred by Protecting Laws': Black Activist Homemaking and Geographies of Citizenship in *Incidents in the Life of a Slave Girl*," *differences* 18, no. 2 (2007): 72–102. As we will see, Kincaid's late-twentieth-century protagonist continues to be haunted by this history.

4. Despite her high-WASP appearance, Stewart herself was raised in a working-class, ethnic enclave, the daughter of immigrants from Poland. So hers is also an immigrant domesticity, shaped in this case by class mobility and distancing from her immigrant roots. See Jerry Oppenheimer, *Martha Stewart—Just Desserts: The Unauthorized Biography* (New York: Morrow, 1997), 11–21, 85–86, 157.

5.   My thoughts on this topic have been influenced by important feminist contributions
     to theories of migration, notably by Sara Ahmed and Irene Gedalof. Ahmed criticizes
     Iain Chambers and Rosi Braidotti for celebrating migrancy (often in a sense more
     metaphorical than literal) over against a notion of home reduced to "stasis, bound-
     aries, identity, and fixity" (*Strange Encounters: Embodied Others on Post-Coloniality*
     [New York: Routledge, 2000], 87). Within this paradigm, home is defined negatively
     as "that which must be overcome" (87). Building on Ahmed's recuperation of "home"
     as multiple and always under construction, I myself affirm the domestic not only as
     protean but also as a site of *wished-for* boundaries and fixity, however provisional.
     Ahmed's critique is elaborated in Sara Ahmed, Claudia Castañeda, Anne-Marie
     Fortier, and Mimi Sheller, eds., *Uprootings/Regroundings: Questions of Home and
     Migration* (New York: Berg, 2003), whose project is "to call into question the natu-
     ralization of homes as origins, and the romanticization of mobility as travel, tran-
     scendence and transformation" ("Introduction," 1). See especially Irene Gedalof's
     contribution to this volume, "Taking (a) Place: Female Embodiment and the Re-
     grounding of Community," which challenges women's confinement to the home
     while also wishing "to take into account and *value* the work that women do to repro-
     duce a sense of 'home' and community belonging" (92 [italics added]).
6.   Audre Lorde, *Zami: A New Spelling of My Name* (New York: Crossing Press, 1982), 71.
7.   Influential texts theorizing cultural hybridity, especially in the context of (post)
     colonial encounters, include Gloria Anzaldúa, *Borderlands*/La Frontera: *The New
     Mestiza* (San Francisco: Aunt Lute, 1987); Homi K. Bhabha, *The Location of Culture*
     (New York: Routledge, 1994); and Lisa Lowe, *Immigrant Acts: On Asian American
     Cultural Politics* (Durham, N.C.: Duke University Press, 1996). On the "past-present"
     nature of culinary techniques, see Luce Giard, "Doing-Cooking," in *The Practice of
     Everyday Life*, vol. 2, *Living and Cooking*, by Michel de Certeau, Luce Giard, and
     Pierre Mayol, trans. Timothy J. Tomasik (Minneapolis: University of Minnesota
     Press, 1998), 212–13.
8.   For incisive comments on heterogeneity and inequity in domestic spaces, stressing
     the way that children and women in particular might dissent from reigning notions
     of happy home life, see Karen Fog Olwig, "Contested Homes: Home-making and the
     Making of Anthropology," in *Migrants of Identity: Perceptions of Home in a World
     of Movement*, ed. Nigel Rapport and Andrew Dawson (Oxford: Berg, 1998), 225–35;
     Sara Ahmed, *The Promise of Happiness* (Durham, N.C.: Duke University Press, 2010),
     esp. 45–59, is also pertinent here.
9   Gish Jen, *Mona in the Promised Land* (New York: Knopf, 1996), 4.
10. Ibid., 7.
11. Ibid., 8.
12. Maxine Hong Kingston offers a notable statement to this effect: "Chinese-Americans,
     when you try to understand what things in you are Chinese, how do you separate
     what is peculiar to childhood, to poverty, insanities, one family, your mother who
     marked your growing with stories, from what is Chinese? What is Chinese tradition
     and what is the movies?" (*The Woman Warrior: Memoirs of a Girlhood Among Ghosts*
     [New York: Random House, 1975], 6).
13. Some foundational works revising Marx to include women's unpaid and often invis-
     ible domestic labor are Ellen Malos, ed., *The Politics of Housework* (New York: New
     Clarion Press, 1975); Bonnie Fox, ed., *Hidden in the Household: Women's Domestic*

Labour Under Capitalism (Toronto: Women Educational Press, 1980); Lise Vogel, *Marxism and the Oppression of Women: Toward a Unitary Theory* (New Brunswick, N.J.: Rutgers University Press, 1983); Heidi I. Hartmann, "The Family as the Locus of Gender, Class, and Political Struggle: The Example of Housework," in *Feminism and Methodology*, ed. Sandra Harding (Bloomington: Indiana University Press, 1987), 109–34; and the collection of essays from 1975 onward by Silvia Federici, *Revolution at Point Zero: Housework, Reproduction, and Feminist Struggle* (Oakland, Calif.: PM Press, 2012). We have seen that Giard recuperates this labor, stressing its creativity. While sympathizing with Giard, I would also acknowledge Simone de Beauvoir's vehement rejection of housework as repetitious, negative, and fundamental to women's oppression:

> Few tasks are more similar to the torment of Sisyphus than those of the housewife; day after day, one must wash dishes, dust furniture, mend clothes that will be dirty, dusty, and torn again. The housewife wears herself out running on the spot; she does nothing; she only perpetuates the present; she never gains the sense that she is conquering a positive Good, but struggles indefinitely against Evil. (*The Second Sex*, trans. Constance Borde and Sheila Malovany-Chevallier [New York: Vintage Books, 2011], 474)

14. Sandra Cisneros, *The House on Mango Street* (1984; New York: Random House, 1991), 3. Subsequent references are cited in the text.

15. Cisneros has said in interviews that *The House on Mango Street* was written as a counter to Gaston Bachelard's psychopoetic rendering of the house as cozy nest in *The Poetics of Space*. See Jacqueline Doyle, "More Room of Her Own: Sandra Cisneros's *The House on Mango Street*," *MELUS* 19, no. 4 (1994): 12.

16. Cisneros's chapter "Bums in the Attic" may even be an allusion to Sandra M. Gilbert and Susan Gubar's *The Madwoman in the Attic: The Woman Writer and the Nineteenth-Century Literary Imagination* (New Haven, Conn.: Yale University Press, 1979). The "Bums" chapter is a critically neglected and somewhat disconcerting moment in *The House on Mango Street*. Vowing never to forget her origins, Esperanza imagines one day owning a comfortable home and inviting "bums" to take refuge there. The gesture of inclusion is undercut, however, when she relegates her "bums" to the attic while "guests" enjoy dinner below. When the guests mistake rustling overhead for rats, Esperanza corrects them: "Bums, I'll say, and I'll be happy" (87). I myself am less happy with this nexus of bums, attic, and rats, which seems to me an instance (inadvertent on Cisneros's part) of domesticity for one person at the expense of others who remain on the margins. For more on "bums," see my next chapter on homemaking by the unsheltered.

17. Brontë's madwoman, Bertha Mason, is described as a white Creole, but as many have noted, she is insistently racialized and marginalized as nonwhite. Rhys's rewriting from this figure's point of view specifies her position as the daughter of a white Jamaican planter; at the same time, the setting, characters, and plot all are evocative of racial impurity and cultural hybridity.

18. June Dwyer, "Ethnic Home Improvement: Gentrifying the Ghetto, Spicing Up the Suburbs," *ISLE* 14, no. 2 (2007): 179 (italics in original).

19.   Amalia Mesa-Bains, "*Domesticana*: The Sensibility of Chicano *Rasquachismo*," in *Chicana Feminisms: A Critical Reader*, ed. Gabriela F. Arrendondo et al. (Durham, N.C.: Duke University Press, 2003), 160. Herself an artist as well as a critic, Mesa-Bains claims these quotidian practices as the formal and material basis for a visual arts mode she dubs *domesticana Chicana*. As with the repurposing of everyday materials by Chicano *rasquachismo*, works of *domesticana* play with the iconography of barrio homes. They do so to affirm the domestic sensibilities of Mexican American women while also interrogating the patriarchal constraints of their home lives. I am indebted to Marci McMahon for citing Mesa-Bains in relation to Cisneros and for broadening the concept of *domesticana* to describe a general strategy of mobilizing domesticity for subversive purposes (*Domestic Negotiations: Gender, Nation, and Self-Fashioning in US Mexicana and Chicana Literature and Art* [New Brunswick, N.J.: Rutgers University Press, 2013], 4–5, 114). While agreeing with McMahon that Cisneros offers a "postnationalist domesticity," I offer an alternative view of the way *The House on Mango Street* speaks back to white feminism as well as to Chicano nationalism.

20.   Refusing to take *The House on Mango Street* on its own terms, Alejandro Morales accuses the character of Esperanza of "deterritorialization" or estrangement from her world, in "The Deterritorialization of Esperanza Cordero: A Paraesthetic Inquiry," in *Gender, Self, and Society: Proceedings of the IV International Conference on the Hispanic Cultures of the United States*, ed. Renate von Bardeleben (Frankfurt: Peter Lang, 1993), 227–35: symptoms include lack of respect for her parents (228), failure to identify with her abducted great-grandmother (227–28), and preference for isolation over group affiliation (230–31). Without explicitly criticizing Cisneros, he describes her heroine's feminist discontent as pathological and tragically alienated from Chicano community and values. Geoffrey Sanborn, by contrast, champions the very isolationism that Morales condemns, in "Keeping Her Distance: Cisneros, Dickinson, and the Politics of Private Enjoyment," *PMLA* 116, no. 5 (2001): 1334–48. While noting Dickinson's limitations as a model for the working-class Cisneros (1341) and promising a "new" collectivity sprung from privacy (1335, 1343), its overall goal is to link these two women writers in terms of a shared, autoerotic pleasure in withdrawal from communal life. Though I appreciate Sanborn's defense of female privacy, it remains the case that he downplays the ethnic and class specificity of Cisneros's project.

21.   Additional feminist readings of Cisneros include Ellen McCracken, "Sandra Cisneros' *The House on Mango Street*: Community-Oriented Introspection and the Demystification of Patriarchal Violence," in *Breaking Boundaries: Latina Writing and Critical Readings*, ed. Asunción Homo-Delgado et al. (Amherst: University of Massachusetts Press, 1989), 62–71; and María Elena de Valdés, "The Critical Reception of Cisneros's *The House on Mango Street*," in *Gender, Self, and Society*, ed. Bardeleben, 287–300.

22.   Doyle, "More Room of Her Own," 7.

23.   McMahon, *Domestic Negotiations*, 114. Subsequent references are cited in the text.

24.   Although Doyle's recuperation of nonelite women is meant to affirm their diverse perspectives, she actually (as her title suggests) goes on to analyze Cisneros's feminism in terms largely consonant with Virginia Woolf's.

25.   Chicano nationalism arose in the 1970s alongside other radical social movements growing out of the U.S. civil rights movement. The 1980s and 1990s saw the emergence

of Chicana feminism, with landmark formulations by Cherríe Moraga, Gloria Anzaldúa, and Ana Castillo. For a collection of interdisciplinary essays by Chicana feminists, see Arrendondo et al., eds., *Chicana Feminisms*.

26. McMahon gives credit for this point to Monika Kaup, "The Architecture of Ethnicity in Chicano Literature," *American Literature* 69, no. 2 (1997): 361–97.

27. Ibid., 387.

28. Quoted in Amy S. Greenberg, *A Wicked War: Polk, Clay, Lincoln, and the 1846 U.S. Invasion of Mexico* (New York: Knopf, 2012), 249.

29. Ibid., 131. Greenberg examines not only the war but also what she calls "America's first national antiwar movement" (xvi). On southwestern ethnic relations in the war's long aftermath, see David Montejano, *Anglos and Mexicans in the Making of Texas, 1836–1986* (Austin: University of Texas Press, 1987).

30. Howard Zinn, *A People's History of the United States* (New York: HarperCollins, 2005), 169. Zinn closes his discussion with a final, wry observation: "The United States paid Mexico $15 million, which led the *Whig Intelligencer* to conclude that 'we take nothing by conquest. . . . Thank God'" (169).

31. Kim David Chanbonpin, "How the Border Crossed Us: Filling the Gap Between *Plume v. Seward* and the Dispossession of Mexican Landowners in California After 1848," *Cleveland State Law Review* 52, nos. 1–2 (2005): 304. Subsequent references are cited in the text.

32. For more on changes in the Treaty of Guadalupe Hidalgo facilitating Anglo land acquisition, see Jon Michael Haynes, "What Is It About Saying We're Sorry? New Federal Legislation and the Forgotten Promises of the Treaty of Guadalupe Hidalgo," *Scholar: St. Mary's Law Review* 3, no. 2 (2001): 248–55. Haynes's article also addresses the treaty's subsequent interpretation—its "forgotten promises" in both legislative and judicial contexts (256–63). It is only, he notes, since 1997 that congressional bills have been introduced addressing the issue of Mexican American dispossession (232–35). Both Haynes and Chanbonpin call for reparations on the model of those made to Japanese Americans "confined, relocated or dispossessed of property" during World War II (264). Haynes includes, too, a discussion of "violence and other extra-judicial means of dispossession" suffered by Mexican Americans (263). William D. Carrigan and Clive Webb report that "at least 597 Mexicans" were lynched during this eighty-year period, amounting to a per capita rate comparable to that for African Americans, in "The Lynching of Persons of Mexican Origin or Descent in the United States, 1848 to 1928," *Journal of Social History* 37, no. 2 (2003): 411–38.

33. Kevin R. Johnson, "The Forgotten 'Repatriation' of Persons of Mexican Ancestry and Lessons for the 'War on Terror,'" *Pace Law Review* 26, no. 1 (2005): 4, 9. Subsequent references are cited in the text.

34. Kaup, "Architecture of Ethnicity," 389, 390. While I appreciate Kaup's attention to the street in *The House on Mango Street*, I differ from her in stressing the built-in continuity (rather than opposition) between the categories of "house" and "street" (as well as between the categories of "house" and "land"). Here and throughout, I aim to complicate views of houses as simply static and cordoned off from the public sphere. And although Woolf's "room" is intended to situate writers in their social context, I believe Cisneros's "house" more vividly captures the worldly, located character of domesticity.

35. For more on the brouhaha around Cisneros's purple house, see Dwyer, "Ethnic Home Improvement: Gentrifying the Ghetto, Spicing Up The Suburbs." While this essay is great on the artifice and bias of "historic districts," I detect a tension between the two parts of its subtitle. Dwyer's critique of "ethnics" displaced by gentrification is framed—incongruously, I think—by a defense of ethnic *contributions* to gentrification. By implication, the displacement of working-class whites and ethnics is redeemed by a version of gentrification "spiced up" by a sprinkling of well-heeled people of color.

36. Jamaica Kincaid, *Lucy: A Novel* (New York: Farrar, Straus & Giroux, 1990), 3. Subsequent references are cited in the text.

37. Ahmed, *Strange Encounters*, 89–90.

38. As Ahmed explains, in the work of Iain Chambers migration "comes to represent the very nature of thinking itself, in which to think is to move, and to move away, from any fixed home or origin" (*Strange Encounters*, 80). Migrancy and its study become the basis for "authentically migrant theorising, a theorising that refuses to think in terms of fixed entities" (82). Ahmed comments similarly on Rosi Braidotti's celebration of "nomadism," in which "transgressive" theory is likened to "dislocation from any secure origin or place" (82). I strongly second Ahmed's objection to the fact that both these views idealize migrancy while equating "home" with conformist thinking—or with no thinking at all.

39. For more on the context of Lucy's specific departure from the West Indian "fringes" circa 1968, see Charmaine Crawford, "African-Caribbean Women, Diaspora and Transnationality," *Canadian Woman Studies / Les cahiers de la femme* 23, no. 2 (2004): 97–103. Glossing Stuart Hall on Caribbean people as "twice diasporized," Crawford describes, following their first migration from Africa, "secondary migratory movements in search of better economic opportunities to England in the post–World War II period and Canada and the United States in the 1960s and onward" (98). Crawford points as well to "the increased female out-migration from the Caribbean to Canada and the United States during the 1970s" (97). She attributes this to the latter's need for semiskilled labor along with World Bank and International Monetary Fund policies exacerbating poverty and unemployment in the Caribbean. As a group, female migrants from the Caribbean "experienced labour segregation and exploitation in the domestic work sector" (99). I will elaborate on this general pattern shortly.

40. Lucy is from "a very small island, twelve miles long and eight miles wide" (134). Though unnamed, its dimensions approximate those of Antigua, Kincaid's own birthplace. Her autobiographical volume, *A Small Place* (New York: Farrar, Straus & Giroux, 1988), gives that island's measurements as twelve miles long and nine miles wide (9). While *A Small Place* does not recount Kincaid's own migration to the United States, it does foreground the histories of slavery and colonialism in Antigua that I see as subtexts to *Lucy*'s story of migration. Since the novel is set around 1969 and independence isn't gained until 1981, Antigua is still a British colony when the novel takes place.

41. Eve Sedgwick, *Epistemology of the Closet* (Berkeley: University of California Press, 1990), 4–8.

42. Barbara Ehrenreich and Arlie Russell Hochschild, *Global Woman: Nannies, Maids, and Sex Workers in the New Economy* (New York: Holt, 2002), 5, 8.

43. Ibid., 2–7.

44. As the subtitle of *Global Woman* indicates, in countries like the United States, female immigrants perform a large share of "maid" as well as "nanny" work. In this case,

however, the "actual maid" (skeptical of Lucy's West Indian accent and dancing to a Supremes-like girl group) appears to be coded as African American. Brent Hayes Edwards concurs, remarking that "Lucy does not ever quite engage the other African diasporic others she encounters in the metropolis" ("Selvedge Salvage," *Cultural Studies* 17, no. 1 [2003]: 31).

45. Lucy's telling comment points to my project throughout *Extreme Domesticity*: unlike traditional historians (but like novelists from Gaskell to Kincaid), I am exceedingly interested in the dining-room table along with the dramas of everyday life to be found there.

46. Critics have generally stressed not Lucy's adventures in homemaking but, on the contrary, her relentless, oppositional mobility. See, for example, Gary E. Holcomb, "Travels of a Transnational Slut: Sexual Migration in Kincaid's *Lucy*," *Critique: Studies in Contemporary Fiction* 44, no. 3 (2003): 295–312; and Jennifer J. Nichols, "'Poor Visitor': Mobility as/of Voice in Jamaica Kincaid's *Lucy*," *MELUS* 34, no. 4 (2009): 187–207.

47. Gayatri Chakravorty Spivak offers a similar though not identical reading of Kincaid's ending. In *A Critique of Postcolonial Reason: Toward a History of the Vanishing Present* (Cambridge, Mass.: Harvard University Press, 1999), she argues that *Lucy* ultimately claims for its migrant protagonist "the right/responsibility of loving" (x). In "Thinking Cultural Questions in 'Pure' Literary Terms," in *Without Guarantees: In Honor of Stuart Hall*, ed. Paul Gilroy, Lawrence Grossberg, and Angela McRobbie (London: Verso, 2000), she specifies further that the end promises not "access to the self, but rather an access to others, through a self-annihilating love" (351). I myself am more willing to claim Lucy's interiority, a self blurred but not annihilated. For other critics responding to Spivak on *Lucy*, see Edwards, "Selvedge Salvage"; and Bruce Robbins, "Soul Making: Gayatri Spivak on Upward Mobility," *Cultural Studies* 17, no. 1 (2003): 16–26.

48. Ronald Takaki, *A Different Mirror: A History of Multicultural America*, rev. ed. (Boston: Little, Brown, 2008), 342. For more on Japanese internment and service in the U.S. military, see Takaki's helpful overview (342–50). More in-depth accounts of internment include Greg Robinson, *By Order of the President: FDR and the Internment of Japanese Americans* (Cambridge, Mass.: Harvard University Press, 2001), and *A Tragedy of Democracy: Japanese Confinement in North America* (New York: Columbia University Press, 2009).

49. Crystal Parikh does list internment along with "the recruitment, immigration, and later exclusion of Asian workers in Hawaii and the U.S. during the late nineteenth and early twentieth centuries" ("Blue Hawaii: Asian Hawaiian Cultural Production and Racial Melancholia," *Journal of Asian American Studies* 5, no. 3 [2002]: 205). In Parikh's analysis of racial melancholia in *Blu's Hanging*, the body scarred by leprosy incarnates a long history of racial and class wounding. Building on this general observation, my own analysis homes in on a passage identifying the race-space logic of quarantine for leprosy with the specific domestic dislocation and internment effected by World War II.

50. Lois-Ann Yamanaka, *Blu's Hanging* (New York: Avon, 1998), 141. Subsequent references are cited in the text.

51. On the problematic absence of Hawaiians from Yamanaka's work, see Candace Fujikane, "Sweeping Racism Under the Rug of 'Censorship': The Controversy over

Lois-Ann Yamanaka's *Blu's Hanging*," *Amerasia* 26, no. 2 (2000): 158–94. Accusing the novel of reproducing ethnic hierarchies, Fujikane represents one side of the debate sparked in 1998 when the Association for Asian American Studies awarded Yamanaka its fiction prize. A dissenting cohort objected, above all, to the character of Uncle Paulo as a stereotype of the sexually predatory Filipino, prompting the AAAS to rescind its award. The controversy reflected long-standing tensions in the Asian American community—in particular, the subordination of Filipino Americans relative to Japanese Americans and Chinese Americans, both culturally in the AAAS and socioeconomically in Hawaii. For more on the latter, see note 53.

52. On *Blu's Hanging* and the discourse of leprosy, see Emily Russell, "Locating Cure: Leprosy and Lois-Ann Yamanaka's *Blu's Hanging*," *MELUS* 31, no. 1 (2006): 53–80. According to Russell, "Writing leprosy as the hidden narrative of the novel and family repeats widespread policies of institutionalization and quarantine for people with disabilities" (66). Russell faults the novel for reinforcing myths that "attach the mutually constitutive registers of sexuality, race, and disability to the body. This burden," she continues, "rests so heavily upon representations of leprosy that it consistently excludes the imaginative possibility of cure" (65). Erin Suzuki views the elusiveness of cure in Yamanaka in more positive terms, in "Consuming Desires: Melancholia and Consumption in *Blu's Hanging*," *MELUS* 31, no. 1 (2006): 35–52. Echoing Parikh, Suzuki calls on Anne Cheng's notion of racial melancholia to recuperate the characters' chronic suffering: "*Blu's Hanging* disputes the idea of melancholia as pathology by presenting a nuanced portrait of the development of a melancholic agency in the Ogata family and their community" (37). I share this appreciation for Yamanaka's depiction of racialized loss, but at the same time, I am finally less interested in a romance of loss than in the strategies for redemption suggested by the characters of Ivah and Blu.

53. As Takaki explains, plantation-era labor practices were designed to "divide and conquer" the ethnically diverse labor force. Tactics for thwarting effective organizing across groups included differential wages and unequal living conditions, with Japanese favored over Filipinos (*Different Mirror*, 237–47). The demonization of Filipino men as predators reflects a further difference: the "marked discrepancy in gender ratios among ethnic groups, with Filipinos overall having the greatest percentage of men" (Cynthia Wu, "Revisiting *Blu's Hanging*: A Critique of Queer Transgression in the Lois-Ann Yamanaka Controversy," *Meridians* 10, no. 1 [2009]: 35). The anger evoked by Yamanaka's villain is a righteous reaction to this demonization (see note 51). Yet as others have noted, there's a fine line, but a difference nonetheless, between representing and endorsing racist dynamics. Overall, I agree with Suzuki's conclusion that "the book's unsparing portrait of these racial dynamics in fact call [sic] attention to the material and social divisions and inequalities that exist within a predominantly Asian American community" ("Consuming Desires," 48).

54. For more on the origins of pidgin, see Takaki's account of how a "language of command" became a "language of community," characterized by "luxuriant cadences, lyrical sounds, and expressive hand gestures" (*Different Mirror*, 249).

55. Wu, "Revisiting *Blu's Hanging*," 41–42.

56. For Kandice Chuh, *Imagine Otherwise: On Asian Americanist Critique* (Durham, N.C.: Duke University Press, 2003), Sandi Ito and Big Sis's queer household poses a challenge to hegemonic notions of nation as well as family. For Wu, by contrast,

though heavily coded as lesbian, the tie between these Japanese women "actually re-produces and maintains structures of both heterosexual and East Asian ethnic/class privilege" ("Revisiting *Blu's Hanging*," 40).

57.   Parikh, for example, disparages Ivah's development as the production of a "normative" and "nationalist" subject, whose "liberal, educated, autonomous ego" comes at the expense of identification with racial loss ("Blue Hawaii," 208). Rather than dismiss a subaltern's quest for education as selling out, I do not begrudge Ivah the appropria-tion of a bildungsroman usually reserved for white males. I would, however, underline the coexistence of Blu's alternative ending, and I agree with Parikh that critics err by identifying Ivah alone—and not the book's title character—with Yamanaka's own views (209).

58.   Blu is the site of other deconstructed binaries as well. Among the most disconcerting moments in this no-holds-barred text is when he owns feelings of pleasure as well as pain in the experience of being raped (253). As Suzuki puts it, his admission chal-lenges the "dynamics of victim and victimizer" ("Consuming Desires," 45). The book's very last sentence—Ivah's image of her brother crooning songs of "sweet, sweet, sorrow" (260)—recapitulates Blu's embrace of seeming incongruities.

6. DOMESTICITY IN EXTREMIS

1.   Sara Ahmed, *Queer Phenomenology: Orientations, Objects, Others* (Durham, N.C.: Duke University Press, 2006), 9. Subsequent references are cited in the text.

2.   On homeless people viewed as blights on the cityscape instead of rightful city residents, architectural strategies for excluding and corralling them, along with Victorian precedents for both, see Regenia Gagnier, "Homelessness as 'An Aesthetic Issue': Past and Present," in *Homes and Homelessness in the Victorian Imagination*, ed. Murray Baumgarten and H. M. Daleski (New York: AMS, 1998), 167–86. On the relevance of beauty to the lives of Victorian tenement dwellers, see Diana Maltz, "Beauty at Home or Not? Octavia Hill and the Aesthetics of Tenement Reform," in *Homes and Homelessness in the Victorian Imagination*, ed. Baumgarten and Daleski, 187–211. Maltz disparages what she sees as Hill's paternalistic emphasis on light, airiness, color, and natural beauty in housing for the poor—an attempt, in Maltz's view, to "refine" working-class tastes by imposing her own. Less confident than Maltz that such values as natural light are class specific, I am inclined to sympathize with Hill's concerns. As usual, I question the tendency to vilify domestic beautification as inherently "bourgeois."

3.   For first-person accounts and photos of families repeatedly displaced by alcoholic parents, violent partners, callous slumlords, and the unsafe conditions of shelter after shelter—this in combination with lost jobs, disability, and other impoverishing circumstances—see Mary Ellen Mark, *A Cry for Help: Stories of Homelessness and Hope* (New York: Touchstone, 1996). Affiliated with a 1986 New York State housing initiative (H.E.L.P.), this book's emphasis on the inadequacy of emergency shelters is clearly motivated, but its critique of the shelter system is echoed elsewhere. See, for example, Barry Jay Seltser and Donald E. Miller, *Homeless Families: The Struggle for Dignity* (Champaign: University of Illinois Press, 1993); and Jean Calterone Williams, *"A Roof Over My Head": Homeless Women and the Shelter Industry* (Boulder: University

of Colorado Press, 2003). On the abusive backgrounds of homeless teens, many of them gay, see Katherine Coleman Lundy, *Sidewalks Talk: A Naturalistic Study of Street Kids* (New York: Garland, 1995). On street people in flight from their families of origin, see David Wagner, "The Family: No Haven," in *Checkerboard Square: Culture and Resistance in a Homeless Community* (Boulder, Colo.: Westview Press, 1993), 45–66.

4. See the example of "Suzi," the lone woman living among the Los Angeles "Bridge People," in anthropologist Jackson Underwood's *The Bridge People: Daily Life in a Camp of the Homeless* (Lanham, Md.: University Press of America, 1993). Underwood describes her being "passed from man to man" (38), beaten up by Underwood's primary respondent (87), sent on errands and ordered around by all the men (130), and "so used to being interrupted by her companions that she sometimes didn't bother to finish her sentences" (201). Ironically, though noting her low status (130), Underwood himself pays little more attention to Suzi's perspective, or the specific experience of women, than they do. Reports of women raped and murdered are passed over with none of the editorializing that appears elsewhere. Only in his conclusion does Underwood offer the general observation that homeless women are continually the targets of violence (307).

5. Stephanie Golden, *The Woman Outside: Meanings and Myths of Homelessness* (Berkeley: University of California Press, 1992), 132.

6. Elliot Liebow, *Tell Them Who I Am: The Lives of Homeless Women* (New York: Free Press, 1993), 54.

7. Ibid., 61–64. For an astute discussion of the manifold factors, personal and socioeconomic, making it difficult for female shelter residents (much less those on the street) to get and keep jobs, see 51–79.

8. Kathleen Hirsch offers in-depth histories of two homeless women illustrating the pros and cons of shelter life as well as one woman's refusal of services, in *Songs from the Alley* (New York: Ticknor & Fields, 1989). In addition to studies focused on individual female subjects, works addressing the ideological and practical ways that gender informs homelessness include Golden, *Woman Outside*; Joanne Passaro, *The Unequal Homeless: Men on the Streets, Women in Their Place* (New York: Routledge, 1996); and Williams, "A Roof Over My Head." While Golden and Williams agree that women without shelter may elicit the greatest sympathy, contingent on being "well behaved," they also argue that homeless women are especially vulnerable both to violence and to bureaucratic interference with their lives and those of their children. Passaro, by contrast, arguing that homeless African American men have the fewest options for getting off the street, stresses (and, in my view, overstates) the relative advantages of being a homeless woman with children.

9. Along with Jack London's *The Road* (1907) and George Orwell's *Down and Out in Paris and London* (1933), Lars Eighner's work belongs to a small subset of full-length memoirs by professional writers. Among these are several rags-to-riches accounts of rising up from homeless childhoods: Lauralee Summer, *Learning Joy from Dogs Without Collars* (New York: Simon & Schuster, 2003); Jeannette Walls, *The Glass Castle* (New York: Scribner, 2005); and Liz Murray, *Breaking Night: A Memoir of Forgiveness, Survival, and My Journey from Homeless to Harvard* (New York: Hyperion, 2010). A variation on this genre is Nick Flynn's well-known memoir, *Another Bullshit Night in Suck City* (New York: Norton, 2004), about reconnecting as an adult with a

father who is homeless. Other autobiographical materials are more mediated and/or less polished. *Living at the Edge of the World: A Teenager's Survival in the Tunnels of Grand Central Station* (New York: St. Martin's Press, 2000) is a memoir by "Tina S." as told to Jamie Pastor Bolnick. The collections of materials by homeless men and women include Ann Marie Rousseau, ed., *Shopping Bag Ladies: Homeless Women Speak About Their Lives* (New York: Pilgrim Press, 1981); Tom Fowler and Malcolm Garcia, eds., *Out of the Rain: An Anthology of Drawings, Writings, and Photography by the Homeless of San Francisco* (San Francisco: St. Vincent de Paul Society, 1988); and Ray Gamache, ed., *Under the Bridge: Stories and Poems by Manchester's Homeless* (Manchester, N.H.: Notre Dame College, 2000). Ethnographies also typically embed a variety of first-person narratives.

10. Kenneth L. Kusmer, *Down and Out, on the Road: The Homeless in American History* (New York: Oxford University Press, 2002), 13–15. Subsequent references are cited in the text.

11. This view was not without a modicum of justification; the Wobblies, International Workers of the World, targeted tramps as part of their campaign to organize unskilled, migratory laborers, according to John Allen, *Homelessness in American Literature: Romanticism, Realism, and Testimony* (New York: Routledge, 2004), 97–98.

12. As Susan M. Schweik has shown, the late-nineteenth-century criminalization of homeless people in the United States further overlapped with the stigmatizing of non-normative bodies. See her powerful analysis of laws prohibiting "unsightly beggars," in *The Ugly Laws: Disability in Public* (New York: New York University Press, 2009).

13. National Coalition for the Homeless, "How Many People Experience Homelessness?" July 2009, http://www.nationalhomeless.org/factsheets/How_Many.html, which specifies the average length of stay at emergency shelters (two to three months), transitional housing (less than one year), and permanent supportive housing (less than two years). On the high rate of intermittent homelessness due to serial evictions—rising to epidemic levels since the 2008 recession—see Matthew Desmond, *Evicted: Poverty and Profit in the American City* (New York: Crown, 2016). According to Desmond, high rents, low wages, and inadequate federal aid currently leave millions devoting as much as 70 to 80 percent of their income to rent, thereby making repeated default, eviction, and stints of homelessness virtually inevitable.

14. Jonathan Kozol, *Rachel and Her Children: Homeless Families in America* (New York: Crown, 1988), 12. According to Kozol, "Federal support for low-income housing dropped from $28 billion to $9 billion between 1981 and 1986" (12). See also Peter Dreier's observation that "the most dramatic cut in domestic spending during the Reagan years was for low-income housing subsidies" ("Reagan's Real Legacy," *Nation*, February 4, 2011, http://www.thenation.com/article/158321/reagans-real-legacy).

15. Kozol, *Rachel and Her Children*, 4.

16. John M. Quigley and Steven Raphael "find that rather straightforward conditions in US housing markets—not complex social pathologies, drug usage, or deficiencies in mental health treatments—are largely responsible for variations in rates of homelessness" ("The Economics of Homelessness: The Evidence from North America," *European Journal of Housing Policy* 1, no. 3 [2001]: 324–25). Citing Brendan O'Flaherty, *Making Room: The Economics of Homelessness* (1996), Quigley and Raphael also observe that when forced to choose between paying a large portion of their income for unsafe, "abandonment-quality housing" and using that money for food and

other necessities, the very poor might quite rationally opt to take their chances out of doors: "Homelessness in this model results from decision-making under extreme income constraints and not from a preference for the 'homeless lifestyle'" (329). Underwood reaches a similar conclusion: "Although the Bridge People obviously have severe problems and self-destructive habits, these problems did NOT cause their homelessness. Homelessness is a housing problem, and a poverty problem" (*Bridge People*, 314). Among numerous other studies along these lines, see also Peter H. Rossi's influential work, *Down and Out in America: The Origins of Homelessness* (Chicago: University of Chicago Press, 1989), which examines the homeless as a "subset of the extremely poor" (13). Agreeing with Rossi and others, I would point out that addiction and mental illness are prevalent in the general population but rarely lead to homelessness for those with wealth, family, and quality medical care. When they do become contributing factors, it is typically within a larger context of deprivation. Moreover, as Lars Eighner shrewdly observes from personal experience, self-sedation and disorientation are not only causal factors but also the likely *effects* of homelessness (*Travels with Lizbeth: Three Years on the Road and on the Streets* [New York: St. Martin's Press, 1993], 161, 172).

17. Allen, *Homelessness in American Literature*, 115–36.

18. Ibid., 95–113.

19. Allen's analysis of American texts is the only book I know of on literary representations of homelessness. On journalistic images from the 1990s, see Eungjun Min, ed., *Reading the Homeless: The Media's Image of Homeless Culture* (Westport, Conn.: Praeger, 1999). On the challenges of putting poverty into words, see Gayle Salamon, "Here Are the Dogs: Poverty in Theory," *differences* 21, no. 1 (2010): 169–77. According to Salamon, the common assumption (for instance, by Orwell and William Vollmann) "that language describing the poor must be mimetically impoverished, as bare and minimal as the lives of the poor themselves, is both a misrecognition of the lives of the poor and inattentive to the complexities of languages of poverty" (171). Though my own focus is not on language, I likewise question the view that impoverished domesticity is necessarily "bare and minimal," stripped down to the utilitarian without room for extraneous or aesthetic elements. I point instead to domestic cultures that, however precarious, include such "extra" elements as cosmetics, recipes, mementoes, musical instruments, and pets.

20. Supporting his claim that texts about homelessness proliferated as the 1980s drew to a close, Allen notes that in 1983, *Books in Print* listed just four works under "homelessness"; in the 1990s, this number swelled to well over one hundred (*Homelessness in American Literature*, 172). A casual glance at the University of Virginia's library holdings seems to confirm this finding: under "Homelessness and the United States," there are just five works published in 1983, in contrast to more than thirty published in 1990. The latter includes transcripts of various congressional hearings, since legislators, too, began the new decade with growing concern about record levels of homelessness. The homeless were also widely represented during this period in magazines, movies, television shows, stage plays, and the like (139).

21. Wagner, *Checkerboard Square*, 1–3, 11–16.

22. Allen, *Homelessness in American Literature*, 3–4.

23. Homelessness may, of course, at times be "chosen" as the lesser of two evils—as preferable to institutionalization, for example, or as a matter of budgetary priorities (see

note 16). But cases of homelessness freely chosen as an alternative to safe, affordable housing are the exception.

24. See, for example, John Fiske, "For Cultural Interpretation: A Study of the Culture of Homelessness," in *Reading the Homeless*, ed. Min, 1–21. His analysis focuses exclusively on men resistant to shelter culture and its "norms of domesticity" (2). Likewise, in *Unequal Homeless*, Passaro sees women in shelters as more acquiescent than men on the street and therefore less sympathetic. Allen Carey-Webb is similarly inclined to disparage the use of shelter services as capitulation to a charity model and conformity to mainstream values, in his review essay "Representing the Homeless," *American Literary History* 4, no. 4 (1992): 702–5. Even Wagner's *Checkerboard Square*, whose critique of the "family ethic" I admire, champions the radical subcultures of single adults living outside (many of them parents with children housed elsewhere) at the expense of those in shelters (notably women caring for children), who are seen as complying with normative views of family.

25. As Barbara Smith puts it when speaking of African American women: "Home has always meant a lot to people who are ostracized as racial outsiders in the public sphere" (introduction to *Home Girls: A Black Feminist Anthology* [New York: Kitchen Table: Women of Color Press, 1983], li). Citing Smith, Rita Felski comments on "home" as figured by black women writers of the 1970s and 1980s: "Not, as a generation of white, middle-class feminists would have it, a space of female desolation and silent despair: rather, it is where black women gather together for welcome communion and respite from exhausting labor. It is a refuge and sanctuary rather than a prison" (*Literature After Feminism* [Chicago: University of Chicago Press, 2003], 81). bell hooks adds that "historically, African-American people believed that the construction of a homeplace, however fragile and tenuous (the slave hut, the wooden shack), had a radical political dimension" ("Homeplace: A Site of Resistance," in *Yearning: Race, Gender, and Cultural Politics* [Boston: South End Press, 1990], 42). Beyond the racism/sexism of their labor for white households and the sexism they may encounter at home, hooks celebrates black women for creating a domesticity more about solidarity than service: "private space where we do not directly encounter white racist aggression. . . . a crucial site for organizing" (47). Likewise, see Maurice Wallace, *Constructing the Black Masculine: Identity and Ideality in African American Men's Literature and Culture, 1775–1995* (Durham, N.C.: Duke University Press, 2002), on "the black masculinist fondness for the home, the shanty, the underground room, the crypt, and the closet . . . as opposed to the Oedipal dread of them as domesticating, even emasculating" (123). His chapter "A Man's Place" claims the closet or small house as a trope for black male consciousness safely hidden away, impervious to a tyrannizing racial gaze.

26. Equally valuable, shelters may provide a literal mailing address, enabling those without an address of their own to get Social Security checks, paychecks, legal and medical documents, and the like.

27. Underwood, *Bridge People*, 7.

28. Ibid.

29. This concept of kinship resembles that formulated by Kath Weston's study of queer households and affiliations in San Francisco, in *Families We Choose: Lesbians, Gays, Kinship* (New York: Columbia University Press, 1991).

30. Kozol, *Rachel and Her Children*, 39–48. Subsequent references are cited in the text.

31. Unfortunately, the nice landlady was indeed just a "dream" no less than the landlord she envisioned while asleep. In reality, her social worker refused to authorize the deal (Kozol, *Rachel and Her Children*, 42).

32. See note 9.

33. Eighner, *Travels with Lizbeth*, 2–3. Subsequent references are cited in the text.

34. Allen, *Homelessness in American Literature*, 141. As Eighner's account makes clear, his homelessness is based on poverty, not Thoreauvian principle. He does act according to an explicit ethical code, however: a "policy of not stealing and not begging on the streets" (*Travels with Lizbeth*, x). He makes an exception to the latter only once, to bail Lizbeth out of the pound before she is euthanized (213–14).

35. Allen, *Homelessness in American Literature*, 140.

36. Eighner makes several canny points about society's double standard where privacy is concerned, protecting it for some while disregarding the need for homeless women and men to sleep, shit, or shower without being observed or disturbed. An Austin ordinance against sleeping in public, for example, "is never enforced against picnickers or sunbathers, but only against those who have no better place to sleep" (*Travels with Lizbeth*, 128). A poor person dozing in a bedroll is routinely subject to ungentle intrusion by police, who also feel free to confiscate any property (197–98). In the chapter "Alcohol, Drugs, and Insanity," Eighner further observes, "The truth is that the vices of the homeless do not much differ from the vices of the housed, but the homeless, unless they become saints, must pursue their vices in public" (165). Finally, on the issue of homeless sanitation, Eighner proposes a modest investment in public restrooms with cold-water showers (139).

37. James Krasner, *Home Bodies: Tactile Experience in Domestic Space* (Columbus: Ohio State University Press, 2010). For another discussion of the way in which animals figure in producing alternative versions of home (albeit in relation to very different texts), see Juliana Schiesari, *Polymorphous Domesticities: Pets, Bodies, and Desire in Four Modern Writers* (Berkeley: University of California Press, 2012).

38. Krasner, *Home Bodies*, 5.

39. Ibid., 88.

40. Ibid., 100.

41. Ann Nietzke, *Natalie on the Street* (Corvalis, Ore.: Calyx Books, 1994). Subsequent references are cited in the text. Nietzke describes Natalie as schizophrenic and speculates that she may have been among those released from psychiatric wards in the late 1950s and early 1960s (xiii). As I have noted, deinstitutionalization appears to have been a contributing factor to, though not the primary cause of, increased homelessness in the 1980s. Mental illness is disproportionately present among the homeless but, at around 25 percent, less universal than commonly supposed. For an ethnography focused narrowly on this population, see Robert Desjarlais, *Shelter Blues: Sanity and Selfhood Among the Homeless* (Philadelphia: University of Pennsylvania Press, 1997).

42. For more on the problem of storage and its relation to "bag ladies," see Liebow, *Tell Them Who I Am*, 32–38. I agree with Liebow that material objects may have intense emotional meaning for women without homes: "Past and future, then, and even one's self, were embedded in one's belongings" (35). Steven Connor's wonderful remarks on humans as a *carrying* species (and therefore devoted to bags) are also pertinent here: "We don't seem to be able to transport ourselves without transporting things

with us. Bags mean this possibility. Bags mean ownership, identity, self-possession. They are memory, the weight of all we have been" ("Rough Magic: Bags," in *The Everyday Life Reader*, ed. Ben Highmore [New York: Routledge, 2002], 348).

43. A survey conducted in 2013 by the Allianz Life Insurance of Company of North America shows that comfortably housed women in the United States nevertheless invoke "bag ladies" to express their sense of economic insecurity. See Walter Hamilton, "Almost Half of American Women Fear Becoming Bag Ladies, Study Says," *Los Angeles Times*, March 27, 2013. Nietzke makes a similar observation, noting that unmarried and aging women may feel especially vulnerable, in *Natalie on the Street*, 15.

44. Nietzke's comments along these lines are as sad as they are cogent. Of Natalie being taunted, she remarks: "With two words, *old bag*, a boy had reduced Natalie to an object of no more value than the thin sheets of plastic she used to organize and convey her life. Old bags. Old, dried-up breasts. Women past childbearing age, even proper, clean, sane ones, simply ain't worth what they used to be" (*Natalie on the Street*, 15). Similarly, on our fear of women like Natalie: "In a society that disdains old women even in the best of circumstances, we are naturally overwhelmed by those who belong to no person or place, those who in the very state of their existence violate every conventional notion of 'femininity' and force us to remember death" (3). For more on the perspectives of such women, see the first-person accounts gathered by Rousseau in *Shopping Bag Ladies*; for more on gendered stereotypes of homeless women, see Alix Kates Shulman, preface to *Shopping Bag Ladies*, 9–12. Shulman also explores this topic in her novel *On the Stroll* (New York: Knopf, 1981).

45. Some of the other neighborhood women bring Natalie food, but most respond to her with an unself-conscious mix of revulsion, pity, and fear (*Natalie on the Street*, 167–69). May, for example, wants Natalie off the street as an "eyesore" and "public health hazard" (though later rephrasing this as concern for Natalie's health and safety [45–46, 69–70]).

46. Underwood himself is not a well-documented figure; as far as I can tell, *The Bridge People* is his only publication.

47. While noting the effects of alcohol abuse on this community, Underwood stresses that federal policies fostering an increase in poverty and decrease in cheap housing (not alcoholism) were responsible for the rise in homelessness throughout this decade (*Bridge People*, 314–16; see also note 16). Subsequent references are cited in the text.

48. As Underwood observes, in identifying a couple of newcomers not as residents but as "transients," the Bridge People indicated their self-image as members of a stable community (*Bridge People*, 51).

49. Underwood explains that in the absence of middle-class forms of recreation, "social drinking took the place of television, movies, theater, spectator sports, dining out, counseling, and other aspects of 'normal' American life, including the New England town meeting" (*Bridge People*, 80).

50. Even Underwood has never seen homeless people actually occupying their camp until he visits for the first time with Jerry (*Bridge People*, 20). Though only yards away, entering this largely invisible, parallel culture means stepping back in time to an era when water must be hauled, food is cooked over a fire, and basic survival is an ongoing concern.

51. Not all these friends are members of the homeless community. Underwood gives numerous examples of people with homes reaching out to befriend Bridge People. The

panhandlers had "regulars" who stopped to chat and could be counted on for a contribution (*Bridge People*, 100, 263); certain merchants and restaurant owners went out of their way to be friendly and generous (31, 262); especially at holidays, donations of money, food, clothing, and bedding would come in over the fence (126, 252); one regular even took Tom home for a Thanksgiving meal and cleanup (274).

52. Underwood's study includes additional reports of violence against women in neighboring camps: one woman was murdered by her boyfriend (*Bridge People*, 10), and another was gang-raped (65). Overall, however, his attention to the status of homeless women is cursory at best (see note 4).

53. Wagner, *Checkerboard Square*, 150–66. Subsequent references are cited in the text.

54. Wagner explores these backstories of family violence and dysfunction in the chapter "The Family: No Haven," 45–66. There is one omission, though: the specific trials of queer youth, who make up a disproportionate segment of homeless teens. For more on homeless teens, see Lundy, *Sidewalks Talk*. Lundy includes a section on the drag ball culture of 1980s Harlem (154–65), which offered queer black and Latino youth an alternative domesticity in the form of "Houses," fashion cliques headed by "Mothers" and "Fathers." For a first-person account of teen homelessness, see Bolnick and Tina S., *Living at the Edge of the World*.

55. In contrast to Natalie, the mentally ill homeless women who led this group were neither isolated nor unsupported. Wagner remarks that with access to a variety of traditional and alternative resources, "this group hardly fits the public 'bag lady' stereotype" (*Checkerboard Square*, 160).

56. Although based on extensive interviewing and observing in the field, Wagner's study involved less actual "participation" than Underwood's did. As he explains, "Neither I nor my assistants participated in the homeless life in the sense of living on the streets or sharing the hardships; we were always clearly identified experts who went back to a middle-class life" (*Checkerboard Square*, 38).

57. Liebow, *Tell Them Who I Am*, 14–15. Subsequent references are cited in the text.

58. At this time, Liebow was best known for *Tally's Corner: A Study of Negro Streetcorner Men* (Boston: Little, Brown, 1967), an influential sociological study conducted in Washington, D.C.

59. Though not directly mentioned in the film, Margaret Morton was also a key player in the campaign for permanent housing. In addition to *The Tunnel: The Underground Homeless of New York City* (New Haven, Conn.: Yale University Press, 1995), Morton is the author of two other photographic and oral histories documenting transitory houses and gardens. I am indebted to her for the powerful photo of Bernard and Bob, included here to illustrate culinary dedication and friendship in the tunnel.

60. Quoted in Peter Debruge, "How a Manhattan Homeless Community Helped Make the Year's Most Stirring Documentary," *Austin Chronicle*, November 10, 2000.

61. Quoted in ibid.

62. For more on the film's collaborative production, see the short documentary produced by Patrick Anding, *The Making of "Dark Days,"* on *Dark Days: Special Edition DVD* (Palm Pictures, 2001). For a reading that ties it to other types of documentary narrative, see Joseph Heumann and Robin L. Murray, "*Dark Days*: A Narrative of Environmental Adaptation," *Jump Cut: A Review of Contemporary Media* 48, no. 1 (2006).

63. Debruge, "Manhattan Homeless Community."

CONCLUSION

1. James Clifford, *Routes: Travel and Translation in the Late Twentieth Century* (Cambridge, Mass.: Harvard University Press, 1997), 22–23, 17, 18, 30 (italics added). Subsequent references are cited in the text.

2. Like Clifford, Sara Ahmed argues that "'homes' always involve encounters between those who stay, those who arrive, and those who leave" (*Strange Encounters: Embodied Others in Post-Coloniality* [New York: Routledge, 2000], 88). In keeping with my own emphasis, Ahmed therefore opposes the pejorative poststructuralist conflation of "home" with "stasis, boundaries, identity and fixity . . . too familiar, safe and comfortable to allow for critical thought" (87). She also agrees with Clifford that complicating the opposition between "home" and "away" does not make all of us into nomads, and she objects to theories that abstract migration away from literal travel in order to idealize it as a metaphor for transgression (80–84).

3. On airports as temporary shelter, see Kim Hopper, "The Airport as Home," in *Reckoning with Homelessness* (Ithaca, N.Y.: Cornell University Press, 2003), 117–30.

4. Four of Delany's novels won the Nebula Award for best science-fiction novel of the year; other honors include two Hugo Awards, the Lambda Award, induction into the Science Fiction and Fantasy Hall of Fame, and nomination as a Grand Master by the Science Fiction Writers of America. There is also growing recognition beyond sci-fi circles of Delany's importance; critics have been especially interested in his use of science fiction and other modalities to explore the complexities of race, class, and sexuality. Two journals have recently devoted special attention to his work: Robert F. Reid-Pharr, "A Symposium on Samuel Delany: Introduction," *American Literary History* 24, no. 4 (2012): 680–85; and Terry Rowden, ed., "Delany Lately," special issue, *African American Review* 48, no. 3 (2015). "Delany Lately" includes two pieces specifically on *Bread & Wine*: Ann Matsuuchi, "'Happily Ever After': The Tragic Queer and Delany's Comic Book Fairy Tale" (271–87); and Michael Bucher and Simon Dickel, "An Affinity for the Lumpen: Depictions of Homelessness in Delany's *Bread & Wine* and *The Mad Man*" (289–304). As the latter title indicates, Delany's novel *The Mad Man* (New York: Masquerade Books, 1994) anticipates *Bread & Wine* in its affirming view of homeless figures and cross-class relationships. Bucher and Dickel place both of these 1990s texts (as I do those discussed in chapter 6) in relation to the soaring rate of homelessness under President Reagan. Other critical works on Delany include Jeffrey Allen Tucker, *A Sense of Wonder: Samuel R. Delany, Race, Identity, and Difference* (Middletown, Conn.: Wesleyan University Press, 2004); and Scott Darieck, *Extravagant Abjection: Blackness, Power, and Sexuality in the African American Literary Imagination* (New York: New York University Press, 2010).

5. Samuel R. Delany, *Bread & Wine: An Erotic Tale of New York* (New York: Juno Books, 1999), 30 (italics in original). Subsequent references are cited in the text.

6. The series, *Domestic* (1995–1998), includes thirteen portraits and seven still lifes. Opie began it in 1995 and completed it on her cross-country road trip in 1998. For a dozen of these images and some framing remarks, see Jennifer Blessing and Nat Trotman, eds., *Catherine Opie: American Photographer* (New York: Guggenheim Museum, 2008), 120–31. This volume accompanied a stunning retrospective of Opie's work at the Solomon R. Guggenheim Museum from September 26, 2008, to January 7, 2009.

With its rich stock of images, introduction by Blessing, additional notes by Trotman, interviews with Opie by Russell Ferguson, and a short essay by Dorothy Allison, this catalog is the single most comprehensive critical resource on Opie's work. For comments addressing specific works, see Judith Halberstam, *Female Masculinity* (Durham, N.C.: Duke University Press, 1998), 32–40; Orna Guralnik, "Being and Having an Identity: Catherine Opie," *Studies in Gender and Sexuality* 14, no. 3 (2013): 239–44; and Avgi Saketopoulou, "Catherine Opie: American Photographer, American Pervert," *Studies in Gender and Sexuality* 14, no. 3 (2013): 245–52.

BIBLIOGRAPHY

Adichie, Chimamanda Ngozi. "The Arrangers of Marriage." In *The Thing Around Your Neck*, 167–86. New York: Knopf, 2009.

Ahmed, Sara. *The Promise of Happiness*. Durham, N.C.: Duke University Press, 2010.

——. *Queer Phenomenology: Orientations, Objects, Others*. Durham, N.C.: Duke University Press, 2006.

——. *Strange Encounters: Embodied Others in Post-Coloniality*. New York: Routledge, 2000.

Ahmed, Sara, Claudia Castañeda, Anne-Marie Fortier, and Mimi Sheller, eds. *Uprootings/Regroundings: Questions of Home and Migration*. New York: Berg, 2003.

Allen, John. *Homelessness in American Literature: Romanticism, Realism, and Testimony*. New York: Routledge, 2004.

Allen, Lloyd. *Being Martha: The Inside Story of Martha Stewart and Her Amazing Life*. New York: Wiley, 2006.

Ammons, Elizabeth. *Edith Wharton's Argument with America*. Athens: University of Georgia Press, 1980.

Anding, Patrick, prod. *The Making of "Dark Days."* On *Dark Days: Special Edition DVD*. Palm Pictures, 2001.

Anzaldúa, Gloria. *Borderlands/La Frontera: The New Mestiza*. San Francisco: Aunt Lute, 1987.

Armstrong, Nancy. *Desire and Domestic Fiction: A Political History*. Oxford: Oxford University Press, 1987.

Arrendondo, Gabriela F., Aída Hurtado, Norma Klahn, Olga Nájera-Ramirez, and Patricia Zavella, eds. *Chicana Feminisms: A Critical Reader*. Durham, N.C.: Duke University Press, 2003.

Bachelard, Gaston. *The Poetics of Space*. 1958. Translated by Maria Jolas. Boston: Beacon Press, 1994.

Baym, Nina. *Woman's Fiction: A Guide to Novels By and About Women in America, 1820–1870*. Ithaca, N.Y.: Cornell University Press, 1978.

Beacom, Betsy Currier. "*The Decoration of Houses* and the Role of Space in Edith Wharton's Construction of an Authorial Self." *Edith Wharton Review* 28, no. 2 (2012): 9–16.

Beaujour, Michel. "Some Paradoxes of Description." In "Towards a Theory of Description," edited by Jeffrey Kittay. Special issue, *Yale French Studies* 61 (1981): 27–59.

Beauvoir, Simone de. *The Second Sex*. Translated by Constance Borde and Sheila Malovany-Chevallier. New York: Vintage Books, 2011.

Beecher, Catharine, and Harriet Beecher Stowe. *The American Woman's Home; or, Principles of Domestic Science*. 1869. New Brunswick, N.J.: Rutgers University Press, 2002.

Benert, Annette. *The Architectural Imagination of Edith Wharton: Gender, Class, and Power in the Progressive Era*. Madison, N.J.: Fairleigh Dickinson University Press, 2007.

Benstock, Shari. *No Gifts from Chance: A Biography of Edith Wharton*. New York: Scribner, 1994.

Bentley, Amy. "Martha's Food: Whiteness of a Certain Kind." *American Studies* 42, no. 2 (2001): 89–110.

Berlant, Lauren. *The Female Complaint: The Unfinished Business of Sentimentality in American Culture*. Durham, N.C.: Duke University Press, 2008.

Bhabha, Homi K. *The Location of Culture*. New York: Routledge, 1994.

Bieger, Laura. "No Place Like Home; or Dwelling in Narrative." *New Literary History* 46, no. 1 (2015): 17–39.

Blessing, Jennifer, and Nat Trotman, eds. *Catherine Opie: American Photographer*. New York: Guggenheim Museum, 2008.

Bodenheimer, Rosemarie. "Private Grief and Public Acts in *Mary Barton*." *Dickens Studies Annual* 9 (1981): 195–216.

Bolnick, Jamie Pastor, and Tina S. *Living at the Edge of the World: A Teenager's Survival in the Tunnels of Grand Central Station*. New York: St. Martin's Press, 2000.

Breckinridge, Sophonisba Preston, and Marion Talbot. *The Modern Household*. Boston: Whitcomb & Barrows, 1912. https://archive.org/details/modernhousehold01brecgoog.

Brittan, Lorna. "Edith Wharton's Alchemy of Publicity." *American Literature* 79, no. 4 (2007): 725–51.

Brontë, Charlotte. *Villette*. 1853. New York: Penguin, 1979.

Brown, Bill. *A Sense of Things: The Object Matter of American Literature*. Chicago: University of Chicago Press, 2003.

——, ed. *Things*. Chicago: University of Chicago Press, 2004.

Brown, Gillian. *Domestic Individualism: Imagining Self in Nineteenth-Century America*. Berkeley: University of California Press, 1990.

Brown, Michael. *Performing Medicine: Medical Culture and Identity in Provincial England, c. 1760–1850*. Manchester: Manchester University Press, 2011.

Browning, Dominique. *Around the House and in the Garden: A Memoir of Heartbreak, Healing, and Home Improvement*. New York: Scribner, 2002.

——. "A Chance Encounter." *House & Garden*, June 2007, 12.

——. *Paths of Desire: The Passions of a Suburban Gardener*. New York: Scribner, 2004.

——. *Slow Love: How I Lost My Job, Put on My Pajamas, and Found Happiness*. New York: Atlas, 2010.

——. "The Takeout Blues." *House & Garden*, May 2007, 6.

Bucher, Michael, and Simon Dickel. "An Affinity for the Lumpen: Depictions of Homelessness in Delany's *Bread & Wine* and *The Mad Man*." In "Delany Lately," edited by Terry Rowden. Special issue, *African American Review* 48, no. 3 (2015): 289–304.

Butler, Judith. *Gender Trouble: Feminism and the Subversion of Identity*. New York: Routledge, 1990.

——. *Precarious Life: The Powers of Mourning and Violence*. New York: Verso, 2004.

Byron, Christopher. *Martha Inc.: The Incredible Story of Martha Stewart Living Omnimedia*. New York: Wiley, 2002.

Carey-Webb, Allen. "Representing the Homeless." *American Literary History* 4, no. 4 (1992): 697–708.

Carrigan, William D., and Clive Webb. "The Lynching of Persons of Mexican Origin or Descent in the United States, 1848 to 1928." *Journal of Social History* 37, no. 2 (2003): 411–38.

Castle, Terry. *The Apparitional Lesbian: Female Homosexuality and Modern Culture*. New York: Columbia University Press, 1993.

——. "Home Alone." In *The Professor and Other Writings*, 107–27. New York: HarperCollins, 2010.

Certeau, Michel de. *The Practice of Everyday Life*. 1974. Translated by Steven Rendall. Berkeley: University of California Press, 1984.

Certeau, Michel de, Luce Giard, and Pierre Mayol. *The Practice of Everyday Life*. Vol. 2, *Living and Cooking*. 1980. Translated by Timothy J. Tomasik. Minneapolis: University of Minnesota Press, 1998.

Chanbonpin, Kim David. "How the Border Crossed Us: Filling the Gap Between *Plume v. Seward* and the Dispossession of Mexican Landowners in California After 1848." *Cleveland State Law Review* 52, nos. 1–2 (2005): 297–319.

Chase, Vanessa. "Edith Wharton, *The Decoration of Houses*, and Gender in Turn-of-the-Century America." In *Architecture and Feminism*, edited by Debra Coleman, Elizabeth Danze, and Carol Henderson, 130–60. New York: Princeton Architectural Press, 1996.

Chast, Roz. "Martha Stewart Takes Over the Universe." *New Yorker*, June 25, 1990.

Child, Lydia Maria. *The Frugal Housewife, Dedicated to Those Who Are Not Ashamed of Economy*. Boston: Carter & Hendee, 1829.

Chuh, Kandice. *Imagine Otherwise: On Asian Americanist Critique*. Durham, N.C.: Duke University Press, 2003.

Cisneros, Sandra. *The House on Mango Street*. New York: Random House, 1991.

Clifford, James. *Routes: Travel and Translation in the Late Twentieth Century*. Cambridge, Mass.: Harvard University Press, 1997.

Cohen, Deborah. *Household Gods: The British and Their Possessions*. New Haven, Conn.: Yale University Press, 2006.

Cohen, Emily Jane. "Kitschen Witches: Martha Stewart, Gothic Housewife, Corporate CEO." *Journal of Popular Culture* 38, no. 4 (2005): 650–77.

Connor, Steven. "Rough Magic: Bags." In *The Everyday Life Reader*, edited by Ben Highmore, 346–51. New York: Routledge, 2002.

Connor, Tom, and Jim Downey. *Is Martha Stewart Living?* New York: HarperCollins, 1995.

——. *Martha Stewart's Better Than You at Entertaining*. New York: HarperCollins, 1996.

Cook, Clarence. *The House Beautiful: An Unabridged Reprint of the Classic Victorian Stylebook*. 1877. Mineola, N.Y.: Dover, 1995.

Coward, Rosalind. *Female Desire: Women's Sexuality Today*. London: Paladin, 1984.

Crawford, Charmaine. "African-Caribbean Women, Diaspora and Transnationality." *Canadian Woman Studies / Les cahiers de la femme* 23, no. 2 (2004): 97–103.

Darieck, Scott. *Extravagant Abjection: Blackness, Power, and Sexuality in the African American Imagination*. New York: New York University Press, 2010.

Davidoff, Leonore, and Catherine Hall. *Family Fortunes: Men and Women of the English Middle Class, 1780–1850*. Chicago: University of Chicago Press, 1987.

Davidson, Cathy N. "Preface: No More Separate Spheres!" In "No More Separate Spheres!" edited by Cathy N. Davidson. Special issue, *American Literature* 70, no. 3 (1998): 443–63.

Debruge, Peter. "How a Manhattan Homeless Community Helped Make the Year's Most Stirring Documentary." *Austin Chronicle*, November 10, 2000.

Defoe, Daniel. *The Life and Strange Surprising Adventures of Robinson Crusoe.* Edited by W. P. Trent. Boston: Athenaeum, 1916.

——. *Robinson Crusoe.* New York: Penguin, 1965.

Delany, Samuel R. *Bread & Wine: An Erotic Tale of New York.* New York: Juno Books, 1999.

——. *The Mad Man.* New York: Masquerade Books, 1994.

Deleuze, Gilles, and Félix Guattari. *A Thousand Plateaus: Capitalism and Schizophrenia.* Minneapolis: University of Minnesota Press, 1987.

Desjarlais, Robert. *Shelter Blues: Sanity and Selfhood Among the Homeless.* Philadelphia: University of Pennsylvania Press, 1997.

Desmond, Matthew. *Evicted: Poverty and Profit in the American City.* New York: Crown, 2016.

Doan, Laura. "'Woman's Place *Is* the Home': Conservative Sapphic Modernity." In *Sapphic Modernities: Sexuality, Women and National Culture,* edited by Laura Doan and Jane Garrity, 91–108. New York: Palgrave, 2006.

Dobson, Joanne. "Reclaiming Sentimental Literature." *American Literature* 69, no. 2 (1997): 263–88.

Douglas, Ann. *The Feminization of American Culture.* New York: Knopf, 1977.

Doyle, Jacqueline. "More Room of Her Own: Sandra Cisneros's *The House on Mango Street.*" *MELUS* 19, no. 4 (1994): 5–35.

Dreier, Peter. "Reagan's Real Legacy." *Nation,* February 4, 2011. http://www.thenation.com /article/158321/reagans-real-legacy.

Dwyer, June. "Ethnic Home Improvement: Gentrifying the Ghetto, Spicing Up the Suburbs." *ISLE* 14, no. 2 (2007): 165–82.

Eastlake, Charles L. *Hints on Household Taste: The Classic Handbook of Victorian Interior Design.* 1868. Mineola, N.Y.: Dover, 1986.

Eby, Clare Virginia. *Until Choice Do Us Part: Marriage Reform in the Progressive Era.* Chicago: University of Chicago Press, 2014.

Edelman, Lee. *No Future: Queer Theory and the Death Drive.* Durham, N.C.: Duke University Press, 2004.

Edwards, Brent Hayes. "Selvedge Salvage." *Cultural Studies* 17, no. 1 (2003): 27–41.

Ehrenreich, Barbara. *Nickel and Dimed: On (Not) Getting By in America.* New York: Metro-politan Books, 2001.

Ehrenreich, Barbara, and Arlie Russell Hochschild. *Global Woman: Nannies, Maids, and Sex Workers in the New Economy.* New York: Holt, 2002.

Eighner, Lars. *Travels with Lizbeth: Three Years on the Road and on the Streets.* New York: St. Martin's Press, 1993.

Ellet, Elizabeth F. *The Practical Housekeeper: Cyclopædia of Domestic Economy.* New York: Stringer and Townsend, 1857. Feeding America: The Historic American Cookbook Proj-ect. http://digital.lib.msu.edu/projects/cookbooks/html/books/book_21.cfm.

——. *The Women of the American Revolution.* 3 vols. New York: Baker and Scribner, 1849. https://archive.org/details/womenofamericano2ellegoog.

Ellis, Kate Ferguson. *The Contested Castle: Gothic Novels and the Subversion of Domestic Ideology.* Champaign: University of Illinois Press, 1989.

Engels, Friedrich. *The Condition of the Working Class in England*. Translated and edited by W. O. Henderson and W. H. Chaloner. Stanford, Calif.: Stanford University Press, 1968.

Federici, Silvia. *Revolution at Point Zero: Housework, Reproduction, and Feminist Struggle*. Oakland, Calif.: PM Press, 2012.

Feinberg, Leslie. *Stone Butch Blues*. New York: Firebrand, 1993.

Felski, Rita. "Introduction: The Everyday." In "Everyday Life." Special issue, *New Literary History* 33, no. 4 (2002): 607–22.

——."The Invention of Everyday Life." In *Doing Time: Feminist Theory and Postmodern Culture*, 77–98. New York: New York University Press, 2000.

——. *Literature After Feminism*. Chicago: University of Chicago Press, 2003.

Finley, Karen. *Living It Up: Humorous Adventures in Hyperdomesticity*. New York: Doubleday, 1996.

Fiske, John. "For Cultural Interpretation: A Study of the Culture of Homelessness." In *Reading the Homeless: The Media's Image of Homeless Culture*, edited by Eungjun Min, 1–21. Westport, Conn.: Praeger, 1991.

Flynn, Nick. *Another Bullshit Night in Suck City*. New York: Norton, 2004.

Foster, Thomas. *Transformations of Domesticity in Modern Women's Writing: Homelessness at Home*. New York: Palgrave, 2002.

Fowler, Tom, and Malcolm Garcia, eds. *Out of the Rain: An Anthology of Drawings, Writings, and Photography by the Homeless of San Francisco*. San Francisco: St. Vincent de Paul Society, 1988.

Fox, Bonnie, ed. *Hidden in the Household: Women's Domestic Labour Under Capitalism*. Toronto: Women Educational Press, 1980.

Fraiman, Susan. *Cool Men and the Second Sex*. New York: Columbia University Press, 2003.

——. "Pussy Panic Versus Liking Animals: Tracking Gender in Animal Studies." *Critical Inquiry* 39 (2012): 89–115.

Freedgood, Elaine. " 'Fine Fingers': Victorian Handmade Lace and Utopian Consumption." *Victorian Studies* 45, no. 4 (2003): 625–47.

——. *The Ideas in Things: Fugitive Meaning in the Victorian Novel*. Chicago: University of Chicago Press, 2006.

——. "The Novelist and Her Poor." *Novel* 47, no. 2 (2014): 210–23.

Freeman, Kimberly A. *Love American Style: Divorce and the American Novel, 1881–1976*. New York: Routledge, 2003.

Friedan, Betty. "The Happy Housewife Heroine." In *The Feminine Mystique*, 28–61. New York: Dell, 1964.

Fryer, Judith. *Felicitous Space: The Imaginative Structures of Edith Wharton and Willa Cather*. Chapel Hill: University of North Carolina Press, 1986.

Fujikane, Candace. "Sweeping Racism Under the Rug of 'Censorship': The Controversy over Lois-Ann Yamanaka's *Blu's Hanging*." *Amerasia* 26, no. 2 (2000): 158–94.

Fyfe, Paul. "Accidents of a Novel Trade: Industrial Catastrophe, Fire Insurance, and *Mary Barton*." *Nineteenth-Century Literature* 65, no. 3 (2010): 315–47.

Gagnier, Regina. "Homelessness as 'An Aesthetic Issue': Past and Present." In *Homes and Homelessness in the Victorian Imagination*, edited by Murray Baumgarten and H. M. Daleski, 167–86. New York: AMS, 1998.

Gallagher, Catherine. *The Industrial Reformation of English Fiction: Social Discourse and Narrative Form, 1832–1867*. Chicago: University of Chicago Press, 1985.

Gamache, Ray, ed. *Under the Bridge: Stories and Poems by Manchester's Homeless*. Manchester, N.H.: Notre Dame College, 2000.

Gaskell, Elizabeth. *Mary Barton: A Tale of Manchester Life*. 1848. New York: Penguin, 1970.

Gedalof, Irene. "Taking (a) Place: Female Embodiment and the Re-grounding of Community." In *Uprootings/Regroundings: Questions of Home and Migration*, edited by Sara Ahmed, Claudia Castañeda, Anne-Marie Fortier, and Mimi Sheller, 91–112. New York: Berg, 2003.

Giard, Luce. "Doing-Cooking." In *The Practice of Everyday Life*. Vol. 2, *Living and Cooking*, by Michel de Certeau, Luce Giard, and Pierre Mayol, 149–247. Translated by Timothy J. Tomasik. Minneapolis: University of Minnesota Press, 1998.

——. "Introduction to Volume 1: History of a Research Project." In *The Practice of Everyday Life*. Vol. 2, *Living and Cooking*, by Michel de Certeau, Luce Giard, and Pierre Mayol, xiii–xxxiv. Translated by Timothy J. Tomasik. Minneapolis: University of Minnesota Press, 1998.

Gilbert, Sandra M., and Susan Gubar. *The Madwoman in the Attic: The Woman Writer and the Nineteenth-Century Literary Imagination*. New Haven, Conn.: Yale University Press, 1979.

Giles, Judy. *The Parlour and the Suburb: Domestic Identities, Class, Femininity and Modernity*. Oxford: Berg, 2004.

Gilman, Charlotte Perkins. *The Home: Its Work and Influence*. New York: McClure, Phillips, 1903.

——. "The Yellow Wallpaper." 1892. In *The Charlotte Perkins Gilman Reader*, edited by Ann J. Lane, 3–19. New York: Pantheon, 1980.

Ginsburg, Michal Peled, and Lorri G. Nandrea. "The Prose of the World." In *The Novel*. Vol. 2, *Forms and Themes*, edited by Franco Moretti, 244–73. Princeton, N.J.: Princeton University Press, 2007.

Goff, Lisa. *Shantytown U.S.A.: Forgotten Landscapes of the American Working Classes*. Cambridge, Mass.: Harvard University Press, 2016.

Golden, Catherine, ed. *The Captive Imagination: A Casebook on "The Yellow Wallpaper."* New York: Feminist Press, 1992.

Golden, Stephanie. *The Woman Outside: Meanings and Myths of Homelessness*. Berkeley: University of California Press, 1992.

Goodman, Susan. "Bearing Witness: Edith Wharton's *The Book of the Homeless*." *Mosaic* 46, no. 2 (2013): 87–103.

Gorman-Murray, Andrew. "Queering Home or Domesticating Deviance? Interrogating Gay Domesticity Through Lifestyle Television." *International Journal of Cultural Studies* 9, no. 2 (2006): 227–47.

Greenburg, Amy S. *A Wicked War: Polk, Clay, Lincoln, and the 1846 U.S. Invasion of Mexico*. New York: Knopf, 2012.

Guralnik, Orna. "Being and Having an Identity: Catherine Opie." *Studies in Gender and Sexuality* 14, no. 3 (2013): 239–44.

Halberstam, Judith. *Female Masculinity*. Durham, N.C.: Duke University Press, 1998.

Hale, Sarah Josepha Buell [A Lady, pseud.]. *The Workwoman's Guide, Containing Instructions to the Inexperienced in Cutting Out and Completing Those Articles of Wearing Apparel . . . ; Also, Explanations on Upholstery . . .* London: Simpkin, Marshall, 1838. https://books.google.com/books?id=spIQAQAAMAAJ&printsec=frontcover&source =gbs_ge_summary_r&cad=0#v=onepage&q&f=false.

Hall, Radclyffe. *The Well of Loneliness*. 1928. New York: Avon, 1981.

Hamilton, Walter. "Almost Half of American Women Fear Becoming Bag Ladies, Study Says." *Los Angeles Times*, March 27, 2013.

Hamon, Philippe. "Rhetorical Status of the Descriptive." In "Towards a Theory of Description," edited by Jeffrey Kittay. Special issue, *Yale French Studies* 61 (1981): 1–26.

Harris, Beth, ed. *Famine and Fashion: Needlewomen in the Nineteenth Century*. Aldershot: Ashgate, 2005.

Hartmann, Heidi I. "The Family as the Locus of Gender, Class, and Political Struggle: The Example of Housework." In *Feminism and Methodology*, edited by Sandra Harding, 109–34. Bloomington: Indiana University Press, 1987.

Haweis, Mary Eliza. *The Art of Decoration*. London: Chatto & Windus, 1881.

Hayden, Dolores. *The Grand Domestic Revolution: A History of Feminist Designs for American Homes, Neighborhoods, and Cities*. Cambridge, Mass.: MIT Press, 1981.

Haynes, Jon Michael. "What Is It About Saying We're Sorry? New Federal Legislation and the Forgotten Promises of the Treaty of Guadalupe Hidalgo." *Scholar: St. Mary's Law Review* 3, no. 2 (2001): 231–65.

Heidegger, Martin. "Building Dwelling Thinking." In *Poetry, Language, Thought*, 143–61. Translated by Albert Hofstadter. New York: Harper Colophon, 1971.

Heller, Dana. "Housebreaking History: Feminism's Troubled Romance with the Domestic Sphere." In *Feminism Beside Itself*, edited by Diane Elam and Robyn Wiegman, 217–33. New York: Routledge, 1995.

Heumann, Joseph, and Robin L. Murray. "*Dark Days*: A Narrative of Environmental Adaptation." *Jump Cut: A Review of Contemporary Media* 48, no. 1 (2006).

Hewitt, Martin. "District Visiting and the Constitution of Domestic Space in the Mid-Nineteenth Century." In *Domestic Space: Reading the Nineteenth-Century Interior*, edited by Inga Bryden and Janet Floyd, 121–41. Manchester: Manchester University Press, 1999.

Highmore, Ben, ed. *The Everyday Life Reader*. New York: Routledge, 2002.

——. "Homework: Routine, Social Aesthetics and the Ambiguity of Everyday Life." *Cultural Studies* 18, nos. 2–3 (2004): 306–27.

Hirsch, Kathleen. *Songs from the Alley*. New York: Ticknor & Fields, 1989.

Hochschild, Arlie. *The Second Shift: Working Parents and the Revolution at Home*. New York: Viking, 1989.

Holcomb, Gary E. "Travels of a Transnational Slut: Sexual Migration in Kincaid's *Lucy*." *Critique: Studies in Contemporary Fiction* 44, no. 3 (2003): 295–312.

hooks, bell. *Yearning: Race, Gender, and Cultural Politics*. Boston: South End Press, 1990.

Hopper, Kim. *Reckoning with Homelessness*. Ithaca, N.Y.: Cornell University Press, 2003.

Jacobs, Harriet A. *Incidents in the Life of a Slave Girl: Written by Herself*. 1861. Edited by Jean Fagan Yellin. Cambridge, Mass.: Harvard University Press, 1987.

Jen, Gish. *Mona in the Promised Land*. New York: Knopf, 1996.

Johnson, Kevin R. "The Forgotten 'Repatriation' of Persons of Mexican Ancestry and Lessons for the 'War on Terror.'" *Pace Law Review* 26, no. 1 (2005): 1–26.

Johnson, Leslie, and Justine Lloyd. *Sentenced to Everyday Life: Feminism and the Housewife*. Oxford: Berg, 2004.

Johnson, Patricia E. *Hidden Hands: Working-Class Women and Victorian Social Problem Fiction*. Athens: Ohio University Press, 2001.

Kaplan, Amy. "Manifest Domesticity." In "No More Separate Spheres!" edited by Cathy N. Davidson. Special issue, *American Literature* 70, no. 3 (1998): 581–606.

——. *The Social Construction of American Realism*. Chicago: University of Chicago Press, 1988.

Kaufman, Eleanor. "Living Virtually in a Cluttered House." *Angelaki: Journal of Theoretical Humanities* 7, no. 3 (2002): 159–69.

Kaup, Monika. "The Architecture of Ethnicity in Chicano Literature." *American Literature* 69, no. 2 (1997): 361–97.

Kelley, Victoria. *Soap and Water: Cleanliness, Dirt and the Working Classes in Victorian and Edwardian Britain*. London: Tauris, 2010.

Kincaid, Jamaica. *Lucy: A Novel*. New York: Farrar, Straus & Giroux, 1990.

——. *A Small Place*. New York: Farrar, Straus & Giroux, 1988.

Kingston, Maxine Hong. *The Woman Warrior: Memoirs of a Girlhood Among Ghosts*. New York: Random House, 1975.

Kittay, Jeffrey. "Introduction: Towards a Theory of Description." In "Towards a Theory of Description," edited by Jeffrey Kittay. Special issue, *Yale French Studies* 61 (1981): i–v.

Kortsch, Christine Bayles. *Dress Culture in Late Victorian Women's Fiction: Literacy, Textiles, and Activism*. Aldershot: Ashgate, 2009.

Kozol, Jonathan. *Rachel and Her Children: Homeless Families in America*. New York: Crown, 1988.

Kramp, Michael. "The Woman, the Gypsies, and England: Harriet Smith's National Role." *College Literature* 31, no. 1 (2004): 147–68.

Krasner, James. *Home Bodies: Tactile Experience in Domestic Space*. Columbus: Ohio State University Press, 2010.

Kusmer, Kenneth L. *Down and Out, on the Road: The Homeless in American History*. New York: Oxford University Press, 2002.

Langbauer, Laurie. "Cultural Studies and the Politics of the Everyday." *diacritics* 22, no. 1 (1992): 47–65.

Langland, Elizabeth. *Nobody's Angels: Middle-Class Women and Domestic Ideology in Victorian Culture*. Ithaca, N.Y.: Cornell University Press, 1995.

Leavitt, Sarah A. *From Catharine Beecher to Martha Stewart: A Cultural History of Domestic Advice*. Chapel Hill: University of North Carolina Press, 2002.

——. "It Was Always a Good Thing: Historical Precedents for Martha Stewart." *American Studies* 42, no. 2 (2001): 125–31.

Lee, Hermione. *Edith Wharton*. New York: Knopf, 2007.

Lefebvre, Henri. *Critique of Everyday Life*. 1958. Translated by John Moore. London: Verso, 1991.

Levine, Caroline. "Strategic Formalism: Toward a New Method in Cultural Studies," *Victorian Studies* 48, no. 4 (2006): 625–57.

Lewis, R. W. B. *Edith Wharton: A Biography*. New York: Harper & Row, 1975.

Liebow, Elliot. *Tally's Corner: A Study of Negro Streetcorner Men*. Boston: Little, Brown, 1967.

——. *Tell Them Who I Am: The Lives of Homeless Women*. New York: Free Press, 1993.

Liu, Lydia. "Robinson Crusoe's Earthenware Pot." *Critical Inquiry* 25, no. 4 (1999): 728–57.

London, Jack. *The Road*. New York: Macmillan, 1907.

Lorde, Audre. *Zami: A New Spelling of My Name*. New York: Crossing Press, 1982.

Lowe, Lisa. *Immigrant Acts: On Asian American Cultural Politics*. Durham, N.C.: Duke University Press, 1996.

Lundy, Katherine Coleman. *Sidewalks Talk: A Naturalistic Study of Street Kids*. New York: Garland, 1995.

Lyman, J. L. "The Metropolitan Police Act of 1829." *Journal of Criminal Law and Criminology* 55, no. 1 (1964): 141–54.

MacComb, Debra Ann. *Tales of Liberation, Strategies of Containment: Divorce and the Representation of Womanhood in American Fiction, 1880–1920*. New York: Routledge, 2000.

Malos, Ellen, ed. *The Politics of Housework*. New York: New Clarion Press, 1975.

Maltz, Diana. "Beauty at Home or Not? Octavia Hill and the Aesthetics of Tenement Reform." In *Homes and Homelessness in the Victorian Imagination*, edited by Murray Baumgarten and H. M. Daleski, 187–211. New York: AMS, 1998.

Mao, Douglas. *Fateful Beauty: Aesthetic Environments, Juvenile Development, and Literature, 1860–1960*. Princeton, N.J.: Princeton University Press, 2008.

Mark, Mary Ellen. *A Cry for Help: Stories of Homelessness and Hope*. New York: Touchstone, 1996.

Mason, Ann, and Marian Meyers. "Living with Martha Stewart Media: Chosen Domesticity in the Experience of Fans." *Journal of Communication* 51, no. 4 (2001): 801–23.

Matsuuchi, Ann. "'Happily Ever After': The Tragic Queer and Delany's Comic Book Fairy Tale." In "Delany Lately," edited by Terry Rowden. Special issue, *African American Review* 48, no. 3 (2015): 271–87.

May, Leila Silvana. "The Strong-Arming of Desire: A Reconsideration of Nancy Armstrong's *Desire and Domestic Fiction*." *ELH* 68, no. 1 (2001): 267–85.

McCleod, Mary. "Everyday and 'Other' Spaces." In *Architecture and Feminism*, edited by Debra Colman, Elizabeth Danze, and Carol Henderson, 1–37. Princeton, N.J.: Princeton Architectural Press, 1996.

McClintock, Anne. *Imperial Leather: Race, Gender and Sexuality in the Colonial Contest*. New York: Routledge, 1995.

McCracken, Ellen. *Decoding Women's Magazines: From Mademoiselle to Ms.* New York: St. Martin's Press, 1993.

——. "Sandra Cisneros' *The House on Mango Street*: Community-Oriented Introspection and the Demystification of Patriarchal Violence." In *Breaking Boundaries: Latina Writing and Critical Readings*, edited by Asunción Homo-Delgado, Eliana Ortega, Nina M. Scott, and Nancy Saporta Sternbach, 62–71. Amherst: University of Massachusetts Press, 1989.

McMahon, Marci. *Domestic Negotiations: Gender, Nation, and Self-Fashioning in US Mexicana and Chicana Literature and Art*. New Brunswick, N.J.: Rutgers University Press, 2013.

Merish, Lori. *Sentimental Materialism: Gender, Commodity Culture, and Nineteenth-Century American Literature*. Durham, N.C.: Duke University Press, 2000.

Mesa-Bains, Amalia. "*Domesticana*: The Sensibility of Chicano *Rasquachismo*." In *Chicana Feminisms: A Critical Reader*, edited by Gabriela F. Arrendondo, Aída Hurtado, Norma Klahn, Olga Nájera-Ramirez, and Patricia Zavella, 298–315. Durham, N.C.: Duke University Press, 2003.

Miller, D. A. *Narrative and Its Discontents: Problems of Closure in the Traditional Novel*. Princeton, N.J.: Princeton University Press, 1981.

Miller, Daniel. *The Comfort of Things*. Malden: Polity, 2008.

——. "Making Love in Supermarkets." In *The Everyday Life Reader*, edited by Ben Highmore, 339–45. New York: Routledge, 2002.

Min, Eungjun, ed. *Reading the Homeless: The Media's Image of Homeless Culture*. Westport, Conn.: Praeger, 1999.

Modleski, Tania. *Loving with a Vengeance: Mass-Produced Fantasies for Women*. New York: Methuen, 1984.

Montejano, David. *Anglos and Mexicans in the Making of Texas, 1836–1986*. Austin: University of Texas Press, 1987.

Morales, Alejandro. "The Deterritorialization of Esperanza Cordero: A Paraesthetic Inquiry." In *Gender, Self, and Society: Proceedings of the IV International Conference on the Hispanic Cultures of the United States*, edited by Renate von Bardeleben, 227–35. Frankfurt: Peter Lang, 1993.

Morrison, Toni. *The Bluest Eye*. New York: Holt, Rinehart and Winston, 1970.

Morton, Margaret. *The Tunnel: The Underground Homeless of New York City*. New Haven, Conn.: Yale University Press, 1995.

Moses, Cat. "Queering Class: Leslie Feinberg's *Stone Butch Blues*." *Studies in the Novel* 31, no. 1 (1999): 74–97.

Murray, Liz. *Breaking Night: A Memoir of Forgiveness, Survival, and My Journey from Homeless to Harvard*. New York: Hyperion, 2010.

Nandrea, Lorri. *Misfit Forms: Paths Not Taken by the British Novel*. New York: Fordham University Press, 2014.

National Coalition for the Homeless. "How Many People Experience Homelessness?" July 2009. http://www.nationalhomeless.org/factsheets/How_Many.html.

Nichols, Jennifer J. "'Poor Visitor': Mobility as/of Voice in Jamaica Kincaid's *Lucy*." *MELUS* 34, no. 4 (2009): 187–207.

Nietzke, Ann. *Natalie on the Street*. Corvalis, Ore.: Calyx Books, 1994.

Olwig, Karen Fog. "Contested Homes: Home-making and the Making of Anthropology." In *Migrants of Identity: Perceptions of Home in a World of Movement*, edited by Nigel Rapport and Andrew Dawson, 225–35. Oxford: Berg, 1998.

Oppenheimer, Jerry. *Martha Stewart—Just Desserts: The Unauthorized Biography*. New York: Morrow, 1997.

Orrinsmith, Lucy. *The Drawing-Room, Its Decorations and Furniture*. London: Macmillan, 1877.

Orwell, George. *Down and Out in Paris and London*. 1933. New York: Penguin, 2013.

Parikh, Crystal. "Blue Hawaii: Asian Hawaiian Cultural Production and Racial Melancholia." *Journal of Asian American Studies* 5, no. 3 (2002): 199–216.

Passaro, Joanne. *The Unequal Homeless: Men on the Streets, Women in Their Place*. New York: Routledge, 1996.

Pearson, Robin. *Insuring the Industrial Revolution: Fire Insurance in Great Britain, 1700–1850*. Aldershot: Ashgate, 2004.

Poovey, Mary. *Uneven Developments: The Ideological Work of Gender in Mid-Victorian England*. Chicago: University of Chicago Press, 1988.

Price, Joann F. *Martha Stewart: A Biography*. Westport, Conn.: Greenwood Press, 2007.

Prosser, Jay. *Second Skins: The Body Narratives of Transsexuality*. New York: Columbia University Press, 1998.

Quigley, John M., and Steven Raphael. "The Economics of Homelessness: The Evidence from North America." *European Journal of Housing Policy* 1, no. 3 (2001): 323–36.

Reid-Pharr, Robert F. "A Symposium on Samuel Delany: Introduction." *American Literary History* 24, no. 4 (2012): 680–85.

Richards, Ellen, and Marion Talbot. *Home Sanitation: A Manual for Housekeepers.* 1898. Boston: Whitcomb & Barrows, 1904. https://archive.org/details/homesanitationa 01alumgoog.

Rifkin, Mark. "'A Home Made Sacred by Protecting Laws': Black Activist Homemaking and Geographies of Citizenship in *Incidents in the Life of a Slave Girl.*" *differences* 18, no. 2 (2007): 72–102.

Robbins, Bruce. "Soul Making: Gayatri Spivak on Upward Mobility." *Cultural Studies* 17, no. 1 (2003): 16–26.

Robinson, Greg. *By Order of the President: FDR and the Internment of Japanese Americans.* Cambridge, Mass.: Harvard University Press, 2001.

——. *A Tragedy of Democracy: Japanese Confinement in North America.* New York: Columbia University Press, 2009.

Robinson, Marilynne. *Housekeeping: A Novel.* New York: Farrar, Straus & Giroux, 1980.

Rogers, Pat. "Crusoe's Home." *Essays in Criticism* 24, no. 4 (1974): 375–90.

Romero, Lora. *Home Fronts: Domesticity and Its Critics in the Antebellum United States.* Durham, N.C.: Duke University Press, 1997.

Rooks, Noliwe M. *Ladies' Pages: African American Women's Magazines and the Culture That Made Them.* New Brunswick. N.J.: Rutgers University Press, 2004.

Rosner, Victoria. *Modernism and the Architecture of Private Life.* New York: Columbia University Press, 2005.

——. "Once More into the Breach: *The Well of Loneliness* and the Spaces of Inversion." In *Palatable Poison: Critical Perspectives on "The Well of Loneliness,"* edited by Laura Doan and Jay Prosser, 316–35. New York: Columbia University Press, 2001.

Ross, Andrew. Introduction to *Microphone Fiends: Youth Music and Youth Culture*, edited by Andrew Ross and Tricia Rose, 1–16. New York: Routledge, 1994.

——. "No Question of Silence." In *Men in Feminism*, edited by Alice Jardine and Paul Smith, 85–92. New York: Methuen, 1987.

Ross, Ellen. *Love and Toil: Motherhood in Outcast London, 1870–1918.* New York: Oxford University Press, 1993.

Rossi, Peter H. *Down and Out in America: The Origins of Homelessness.* Chicago: University of Chicago Press, 1989.

Rousseau, Ann Marie. *Shopping Bag Ladies: Homeless Women Speak About Their Lives.* New York: Pilgrim Press, 1981.

Rowden, Terry, ed. "Delany Lately." Special issue, *African American Review* 48, no. 3 (2015).

Russell, Emily. "Locating Cure: Leprosy and Lois-Ann Yamanaka's *Blu's Hanging.*" *MELUS* 31, no. 1 (2006): 53–80.

Said, Edward. *Culture and Imperialism.* New York: Knopf, 1993.

Saketopoulou, Avgi. "Catherine Opie: American Photographer, American Pervert." *Studies in Gender and Sexuality* 14, no. 3 (2013): 245–52.

Salamon, Gayle. "Here Are the Dogs: Poverty in Theory." *differences* 21, no. 1 (2010): 169–77.

Sanborn, Geoffrey. "Keeping Her Distance: Cisneros, Dickinson, and the Politics of Private Enjoyment." *PMLA* 116, no. 5 (2001): 1334–48.

Sánchez-Eppler, Karen. *Touching Liberty: Abolition, Feminism, and the Politics of the Body.* Berkeley: University of California Press, 1993.

Scanlon, Jennifer. *Inarticulate Longings: The Ladies' Home Journal, Gender, and the Promises of Consumer Culture.* New York: Routledge, 1995.

Schiesari, Juliana. *Polymorphous Domesticities: Pets, Bodies, and Desire in Four Modern Writers*. Berkeley: University of California Press, 2012.

Schor, Naomi. *Reading in Detail: Aesthetics and the Feminine*. New York: Methuen, 1987.

Schweik, Susan M. *The Ugly Laws: Disability in Public*. New York: New York University Press, 2009.

Scott, Darieck. *Extravagant Abjection: Blackness, Power, and Sexuality in the African-American Literary Imagination*. New York: New York University Press, 2010.

Sedgwick, Eve. *Epistemology of the Closet*. Berkeley: University of California Press, 1990.

Seltser, Barry Jay, and Donald E. Miller. *Homeless Families: The Struggle for Dignity*. Champaign: University of Illinois Press, 1993.

Shulman, Alix Kates. *On the Stroll*. New York: Knopf, 1981.

——. Preface to *Shopping Bag Ladies: Homeless Women Speak About Their Lives*, edited by Ann Marie Rousseau, 9–12. New York: Pilgrim Press, 1981.

Sim, Lorraine. "Theorising the Everyday." *Australian Feminist Studies* 30, no. 84 (2015): 109–27.

Singer, Marc, dir. and prod. *Dark Days*. Palm Pictures, 2000.

Smith, Barbara. *Home Girls: A Black Feminist Anthology*. New York: Kitchen Table: Women of Color Press, 1983.

Smith, Cynthia Duquette. "Discipline—It's a 'Good Thing': Rhetorical Constitution and Martha Stewart Living Omnimedia." *Women's Studies in Communication* 23, no. 3 (2000): 337–66.

Smith, Valerie. " 'Loopholes of Retreat': Architecture and Ideology in Harriet Jacobs's *Incidents in the Life of a Slave Girl*." In *Reading Black, Reading Feminist: A Critical Anthology*, edited by Henry Louis Gates Jr., 212–26. New York: Penguin, 1990.

Smith-Rosenberg, Carroll. "The Female World of Love and Ritual: Relations Between Women in Nineteenth-Century America." *Signs* 1, no. 1 (1975): 1–29.

Somers, Reneé. *Edith Wharton as Spatial Activist and Analyst*. New York: Routledge, 2005.

Spivak, Gayatri Chakravorty. *A Critique of Postcolonial Reason: Toward a History of the Vanishing Present*. Cambridge, Mass.: Harvard University Press, 1999.

——. "Thinking Cultural Questions in 'Pure' Literary Terms." In *Without Guarantees: In Honor of Stuart Hall*, edited by Paul Gilroy, Lawrence Grossberg, and Angela McRobbie, 335–57. London: Verso, 2000.

Spofford, Harriet. *Art Decoration Applied to Furniture*. New York: Harper, 1878. https://archive.org/details/artdecorationappoospof.

——. "Nagging Women: A Reply to Dr. Edson." *North American Review*, March 1895, 312–15. http://ebooks.library.cornell.edu/cgi/t/text/pageviewer-idx?c=nora;cc=nora;rgn=full%20text;idno=nora0160-3;didno=nora0160-3;view=image;seq=0323;node=nora0160-3%3A9.

——. "Petticoat Government: A Reply to Max O'Rell." *North American Review*, July 1896, 109–12. http://ebooks.library.cornell.edu/cgi/t/text/pageviewer-idx?c=nora;cc=nora;rgn=full%20text;idno=nora0163-1;didno=nora0163-1;view=image;seq=0115;node=nora0163-1%3A13.

——. "Shall Our Daughters Have Dowries? A Reply to C. S. Messinger." *North American Review*, December 1890, 752–55. http://ebooks.library.cornell.edu/cgi/t/text/pageviewer-idx?c=nora;cc=nora;rgn=full%20text;idno=nora0151-6;didno=nora0151-6;view=image;seq=0756;node=nora0151-6%3A12.

Stabile, Carol A. "Getting What She Deserved: The News Media, Martha Stewart, and Masculine Domination." *Feminist Media Studies* 4, no. 3 (2004): 315–32.

Stockton, Kathryn Bond. "Cloth Wounds: Queer Aesthetics of Debasement." In *Aesthetic Subjects*, edited by David McWhirter and Pamela R. Matthews, 268–84. Minneapolis: University of Minnesota Press, 2003.

Stoneman, Patsy. *Elizabeth Gaskell.* Bloomington: Indiana University Press, 1987.

Straayer, Chris, and Tom Waugh, eds. "Queer TV Style." *GLQ* 11, no. 1 (2005): 95–117.

Summer, Lauralee. *Learning Joy from Dogs Without Collars.* New York: Simon & Schuster, 2003.

Surridge, Lisa. "Working-Class Masculinities in *Mary Barton*." *Victorian Literature and Culture* 28, no. 2 (2000): 331–43.

Suzuki, Erin. "Consuming Desires: Melancholia and Consumption in *Blu's Hanging*." *MELUS* 31, no. 1 (2006): 35–52.

Takaki, Ronald T. *A Different Mirror: A History of Multicultural America.* Rev. ed. Boston: Little, Brown, 2008.

Tilly, Louise A., and Joan W. Scott. *Women, Work, and Family.* New York: Holt, Rinehart and Winston, 1978.

Tomasik, Timothy J. "Certeau à la Carte: Translating Discursive *Terroir* in *The Practice of Everyday Life: Living and Cooking*." *South Atlantic Quarterly* 100, no. 2 (2001): 519–42.

Tompkins, Jane P. *Sensational Designs: The Cultural Work of American Fiction, 1790–1860.* New York: Oxford University Press, 1985.

——. "Sentimental Power: *Uncle Tom's Cabin* and the Politics of Literary History." *Glyph* 2 (1978): 79–101.

Trotter, David. *Cooking with Mud: The Idea of Mess in Nineteenth-Century Art and Fiction.* New York: Oxford University Press, 2000.

Tucker, Jeffrey Allen. *A Sense of Wonder: Samuel R. Delany, Race, Identity, and Difference.* Middletown, Conn.: Wesleyan University Press, 2004.

Underwood, Jackson. *The Bridge People: Daily Life in a Camp of the Homeless.* Lanham, Md.: University Press of America, 1993.

Valdés, María Elena de. "The Critical Reception of Cisneros's *The House on Mango Street*." In *Gender, Self, and Society: Proceedings of the IV International Conference on the Hispanic Cultures of the United States*, edited by Renate von Bardeleben, 287–300. Frankfurt: Peter Lang, 1993.

Van de Water, Virginia Terhune. *From Kitchen to Garret.* New York: Sturgis & Walton, 1910. https://archive.org/details/fromkitchentogao1wateggog.

——. *Why I Left My Husband, and Other Human Documents of Married Life.* New York: Moffat, Yard, 1912. https://archive.org/details/whyileftmyhusbaoocompgoog.

Vogel, Lise. *Marxism and the Oppression of Women: Toward a Unitary Theory.* New Brunswick, N.J.: Rutgers University Press, 1983.

Wagner, David. *Checkerboard Square: Culture and Resistance in a Homeless Community.* Boulder, Colo.: Westview Press, 1993.

Wajda, Shirley Teresa. "Kmartha." *American Studies* 42, no. 2 (2001): 71–88.

Walker, Nancy A. *Shaping Our Mothers' World: American Women's Magazines.* Jackson: University Press of Mississippi, 2000.

Walkley, Christina. *The Ghost in the Looking Glass: The Victorian Seamstress.* London: Peter Owen, 1981.

Walkowitz, Judith. *Prostitution and Victorian Society: Women, Class, and the State*. Cambridge: Cambridge University Press, 1980.

Wall, Cynthia. "Details of Space: Narrative Description in Early Eighteenth-Century Novels." *Eighteenth-Century Fiction* 10, no. 4 (1998): 387–405.

——. *The Prose of Things: Transformations of Description in the Eighteenth Century*. Chicago: University of Chicago Press, 2006.

——. "The Rhetoric of Description and the Spaces of Things." In *Eighteenth-Century Genre and Culture*, edited by Dennis Todd and Cynthia Wall, 261–79. Newark: University of Delaware Press, 2001.

Wallace, Lee. "Dorothy Arzner's *Wife*: Heterosexual Sets, Homosexual Scenes." *Screen* 49, no. 4 (2008): 391–409.

Wallace, Maurice. *Constructing the Black Masculine: Identity and Ideality in African American Men's Literature and Culture, 1775-1995*. Durham, N.C.: Duke University Press, 2002.

Walls, Jeanette. *The Glass Castle*. New York: Scribner, 2005.

Wazana, Kyla, and Zoe Newman, eds. *No Place Like Home: Making Sense of Martha Stewart*. Toronto: Anansi Press, 1999.

Weston, Kath. *Families We Choose: Lesbians, Gays, Kinship*. New York: Columbia University Press, 1991.

Wexler, Laura. "Tender Violence: Literary Eavesdropping, Domestic Fiction, and Educational Reform." In *The Culture of Sentiment: Race, Gender, and Sentimentality in Nineteenth-Century America*, edited by Shirley Samuels, 9–38. New York: Oxford University Press, 1992.

Wharton, Edith. *A Backward Glance*. 1934. New York: Scribner, 1964.

——. *The Book of the Homeless*. 1916. New York: Cosimo Classics, 2005.

——. *The Custom of the Country*. 1913. Oxford: Oxford University Press, 1995.

Wharton, Edith, and Ogden Codman Jr. *The Decoration of Houses*. Facsimile ed. 1897. New York: Rizzoli and The Mount, 2007.

Williams, Jean Calterone. *"A Roof Over My Head": Homeless Women and the Shelter Industry*. Boulder: University of Colorado Press, 2003.

Williams, Raymond. *Culture and Society: 1780–1950*. New York: Columbia University Press, 1983.

Wilson, Richard Guy. "Edith and Ogden: Writing, Decoration, and Architecture." In *Ogden Codman and "The Decoration of Houses,"* edited by Pauline C. Metcalf, 133–84. Boston: Godine, 1988.

Wolfe, Elsie de. *The House in Good Taste*. 1913. New York: Rizzoli, 2004.

Wolff, Cynthia Griffin. *A Feast of Words: The Triumph of Edith Wharton*. New York: Oxford University Press, 1977.

Woolf, Virginia. *The Death of the Moth and Other Essays*. New York: Harcourt Brace, 1942.

——. *To the Lighthouse*. New York: Harcourt Brace, 1927.

——. *A Room of One's Own*. New York: Harcourt Brace, 1929.

Wu, Cynthia. "Revisiting *Blu's Hanging*: A Critique of Queer Transgression in the Lois-Ann Yamanaka Controversy." *Meridians* 10, no. 1 (2009): 32–53.

Yaeger, Patricia. "Review: Beyond the Fragments." *Novel* 23, no. 2 (1990): 203–8.

Yamanaka, Lois-Ann. *Blu's Hanging*. New York: Avon, 1998.

——. *Saturday Night at the Pahala Theater*. Honolulu: Bamboo Ridge, 1993.

Zimmerman, Bonnie. *The Safe Sea of Women: Lesbian Fiction, 1969–1989.* Boston: Beacon Press, 1990.

Zinn, Howard. *A People's History of the United States.* New York: HarperCollins, 2005.

Zuckerman, Mary Ellen. *A History of Popular Women's Magazines in the United States, 1792–1995.* Westport, Conn.: Greenwood Press, 1998.

INDEX

Numbers in italics refer to pages on which illustrations appear.

GENDER AND CULTURE

A SERIES OF COLUMBIA UNIVERSITY PRESS

Nancy K. Miller and Victoria Rosner, Series Editors
Carolyn G. Heilbrun (1926–2003) and Nancy K. Miller, Founding Editors

GENDER AND CULTURE READERS

Modern Feminisms: Political, Literary, Cultural
Edited by Maggie Humm

Feminism and Sexuality: A Reader
Edited by Stevi Jackson and Sue Scott

Writing on the Body: Female Embodiment and Feminist Theory
Edited by Katie Conboy, Nadia Medina, and Sarah Stanbury